MEXICO
UNCONQUERED

MEXICO UNCONQUERED

CHRONICLES OF POWER AND REVOLT

JOHN GIBLER

with a foreword by Gloria Muñoz Ramírez

City Lights Books

SAN FRANCISCO

Text design: Gambrinus

Cover design: Pollen

Cover photograph: Street graffiti by Dr. Hofmann, San Cristóbal de Las Casas, Mexico, 2005.

Library of Congress Cataloging-in-Publication Data

Gibler, John.
    Mexico unconquered: chronicles of power and revolt / John Gibler.
        p. cm.
Includes bibliographical references.
    ISBN-13: 978-0-87286-493-1
    ISBN-10: 0-87286-493-6
1. Power (Social sciences)—Mexico. 2. Social conflict—Mexico. 3. Government, Resistance to—Mexico. 4. Political stability—Mexico. 5. Mexico—Social conditions. 6. Mexico—Politics and government. I. Title.
HN120.Z9P635 2008
306.20972—dc22   2008020490

City Lights Books are published at the City Lights Bookstore,
261 Columbus Avenue, San Francisco, CA 94133.
www.citylights.com

Para los de abajo

People are evidently inclined to grant legitimacy to anything that is or seems inevitable no matter how painful it may be. Otherwise the pain might be intolerable. The conquest of this sense of inevitability is essential to the development of politically effective moral outrage. For this to happen, people must perceive and define their situation as the consequence of human injustice: a situation that they need not, cannot, and ought not to endure.

—Barrington Moore Jr., *Injustice: The Social Bases of Obedience and Revolt*

Decolonization is always a violent event.

—Frantz Fanon, *The Wretched of the Earth*

CONTENTS

Foreword by Gloria Muñoz Ramírez xi

Prologue: A Nation Divided 1

1. The Historical Continuity of Conquest and Revolt 21

2. The Rule of Law 51

3. The Gulf 85

4. The Heist 105

5. The Oaxaca Uprising 139

6. Reclaiming Indigenous Autonomy 189

7. The Guerrilla 231

8. Empire and Revolt 267

Acknowledgments 299

Notes 303

Bibliography 327

Index 339

About the Authors 356

FOREWORD

JOHN GIBLER IS OMNIPRESENT. We run into him in the fervent streets of Oaxaca, along a muddy trail toward a Zapatista community besieged by paramilitary groups, in the midst of repression in the town of San Salvador Atenco, in a march against institutional violence in Mexico City, around the corner of any street in any state of an oppressed Mexico.

John Gibler cannot but remind us of two other Johns who, before him and in no less turbulent times, marked Mexico's history with a committed journalism, a conscious journalism that is aware that the world can only be understood if we begin by looking from below: John Kenneth Turner and John Reed. Like them, John Gibler knows that journalism is a commitment to justice, humanity, and life. And, like those two other Johns, he does not distance himself from what he sees, lives, and writes.

Mexico Unconquered is the result of years of intimate contact with the Mexico de abajo, the Mexico "below": with poverty and inequality, with political prisoners and victims of state violence and torture, with the people's movement of Oaxaca, with the struggle for land of the campesinos from Atenco, with families of migrants in communities impoverished by policies that those from "above" understand as "progress," with the Zapatista communities in rebellion and many other experiences in indigenous autonomy, with members of revolutionary movements.

That is the basis of this book—the author's multiple experiences in the other Mexico and the innumerable testimonies of the invisible protagonists of history. But the book goes even further. The concrete foundation of experiences and testimonies is enriched through ample historical, sociological, and theoretical research and sagacious analysis—a constant movement between personal histories and a global perspective that allows the reader to come closer to that Mexico which, despite its five centuries of oppression, remains unconquered.

—Gloria Muñoz Ramírez
October 2008
Mexico City

Translated from the Spanish by Alejandro Reyes

A NATION DIVIDED

HE CARRIED A GUN into the fields to face a federal army for the first time when he was 14 years old.[1] By the age of 18 he was a captain of Emiliano Zapata's Liberation Army of the South with thirty-three men in his troop. A rice farmer from the small town of Tlaquiltenango, in Zapata's home state of Morelos, Rubén Jaramillo, like so many of his companions in arms, only wanted to farm the land where he was born.

After the Mexican Revolution he worked to secure village titles to the land so many had spilled their blood to defend. He fought for the farmers and then worked to distribute loans for tools, fertilizers, and irrigation systems to help them recover from the devastation of war. He dared to think that the campesinos, or country people who work the land, should not only possess that land but should also possess the tools to turn their crops into useful products. He also believed that the people in the fields and the people in the factories should form unions and cooperatives together, and thus sever their dependence on distant cities and foreign-owned factories. He read Ricardo Flores Magón and Karl Marx. In 1933, he took a letter to presidential candidate Lázaro Cárdenas in which he proposed building a collectively owned and operated sugar mill in Morelos. Once elected, Cárdenas gave the nod and Jaramillo set about convincing the farmers of the region to join. He was successful. By February 5, 1938, when Cárdenas inaugurated the Emiliano Zapata Central Sugar Mill of Zacatepec, having invested fourteen million pesos in its construction (almost 8 percent of the entire federal budget for social works that year), 9,000 farmers organized into thirty-six agricultural companies took part in the cooperative. In March of that same year, the members of the cooperative elected Jaramillo president of its administrative council. Cárdenas asked Jaramillo to support the campaign of his chosen successor, Manuel Ávila Camacho; Jaramillo agreed. Cárdenas gave Jaramillo a horse to express his gratitude; Jaramillo named the horse El Agrarista ("The Agrarian").

But the new president appointed a new manager to the sugar mill, and the new manager expelled Jaramillo from the administrative council. The president and the governor of Morelos had decided that a cooperative might be less useful to them than a *cacicazgo*, a domineering, hierarchical rule exercised over the farmers: the powers to decide who would get loans and how much, who would get paid for their sugarcane and how much, would be wielded by a manager appointed directly by the president. The campesinos were not pleased with this turn of events. They sought out Cárdenas for help and advice but were not received; their letters went unanswered. Ávila Camacho sent in the army to enforce the new manager's decisions. Jaramillo helped organize a strike for April 9, 1942, to demand better prices for the farmers' sugar cane, but the army broke the strike and occupied the mill. In a special assembly, the new management expelled twenty-six partners in the co-op, all of them Jaramillo's supporters. A hit order went out on Jaramillo, so he saddled up his horse, kissed his wife, Epifania, goodbye, and took to the mountains. Within two days some thirty men were by his side; within weeks over 100 men rode with him through the countryside. Two months later, about 6,000 men and women had pledged to join his fight; they set out to take over the municipal seats of Jojutla, Zacatepec, and Tlaquiltenango.

Jaramillo and about 125 followers took control of Tlaquiltenango without encountering resistance, but the signals did
not come from the rebels in other towns and so they left three
hours after they arrived. The governor of Morelos was irate.
Former president Cárdenas called on Jaramillo to lay down his
arms and negotiate. Jaramillo agreed, and Cárdenas, also a former general, ordered the army to refrain from any aggression
against him. But the governor, Jesús Castillo López, ignoring
the pact, had his men kill one of Jaramillo's close allies,
Teodomiro Ortiz, and reinstated the orders to assassinate
Jaramillo—who again took to the mountains, visiting small villages to explain why he and his followers had risen up in arms
and asking villagers to defy the government's orders to detain
him. Soon the president called him to Mexico City for talks.
Ávila Camacho offered him complete amnesty and the rights
to unoccupied lands over a thousand miles away in Baja California. Jaramillo called an assembly to discuss the proposals,
but the campesinos preferred not to move. Jaramillo was
arrested and taken to jail in Morelos, then released about a
year later, in July 1945.

In the years that followed, Jaramillo tried time and time
again to put armed rebellion behind him and return to participation in local politics. He created the Morelos Agrarian
Workers Party (PAOM) in late 1945 and campaigned across
the state. He organized at a local market but was forced from
his job when he refused to support the Institutional Revolutionary Party (PRI) presidential candidate, Miguel Alemán. In
1946, the PAOM received broad support in local elections, but
fraud and bloody repression forced Jaramillo and his followers underground once more, with hired guns on their trail.
They tried again in 1952 and again met with fraud: gunmen
burned PAOM votes, and the army and state police repressed
the ensuing protests. Again they took to the mountains. In

1958, the PRI candidate, Adolfo López Mateos, sent Jaramillo an offer of amnesty and his promise to resolve the problems of the countryside in exchange for Jaramillo's support of his presidential campaign. Jaramillo agreed, and the two men posed for a picture together locked in an odd embrace, Jaramillo drawing in and López Mateos pushing away, two men smiling two very different smiles.

Jaramillo, protected by the amnesty, went back to the same sugar mill he had organized in 1938 and helped mount protests that eventually led to the ouster of the corrupt manager. This angered López Mateos. Jaramillo and allies then began to organize for abandoned lands to be granted to more than 6,000 landless families. Having laid down his guns, Jaramillo returned to his old thoughts of joining farmers and factory workers in a cooperative society. He sought the abandoned lands to set about building an internally sustainable community. Jaramillo and Manuel Leguízano formally petitioned the Agrarian Department. Little by little the agrarian officials in Mexico City signed and stamped all the papers necessary, including the final approval complete with the signature and seal of Roberto Barrios, head of the Agrarian Department. Then Barrios abruptly ceased communication. He would not accept visits or answer letters, until finally he notified Jaramillo and Leguízano that the lands appeared to have owners after all. The landless families called the owners to public talks twice, but no one ever came to claim the lands as theirs. The families decided that they would occupy the lands. As a concession, Barrios offered Jaramillo lands over 1,000 miles away in Yucatán. But despite threats from the army, the families rejected the Yucatán offer and on February 5, 1961, moved onto the lands. The army surrounded them. Jaramillo went to Mexico City to talk with López Mateos, but the president refused to see him and the army raided the families' camp. The families occupied the lands again a year later; the army again raided their camps and forced them off. On May 23, 1962, Jaramillo and his family were cleaning up after lunch. Jaramillo was still protected by a federal amnesty and trying to organize politically, without recourse to arms. At two in the afternoon more than sixty state police and federal troops surrounded his house in Tlaquiltenango. They shouted for the family to come out of the house. Epifania grabbed a machine gun and loaded it, saying, "We'll die, but with dignity."[2] Jaramillo stopped her, saying, "No! I promised no more guns! Remember, the kids are here!"[3] The soldiers broke into the house and pulled Jaramillo, Epifania—pregnant with her first child with Jaramillo—and Epifania's teenage children Ricardo, Filemón, and Enrique out into the street and threw them into army jeeps that were waiting outside. Epifania's daughter, Raquel, escaped out the back and ran for help. The army caravan drove the family to the Xichicalco archaeological site and gunned them down with Thompson submachine guns. The soldiers opened Filemón's mouth and stuffed it full of dirt while he was still alive. The soldiers waited for the moaning to stop, but apparently it took too long. They drew their pistols and finished off Jaramillo and each member of his family with a final shot to the forehead.[4] Journalists from Mexico City, including Carlos Fuentes and Fernando Benítez, traveled to Xichicalco the next day and found blood, torn clothes, and army issue bullets still on the rocks.[5]

MEXICO IS A NATION divided, not conquered. "If we take a long-term view of things," writes Mexican philosopher Bolívar Echeverría, "then we should keep in mind that the process begun in 1492, or in 1523, depending on where one wants to locate it, that is, the process of the Conquest, is an enterprise that has *not* finished. I think it is important to start from this idea: that the Conquest of America is still ongoing."[6] If the conquest is still ongoing, then there are people and places that remain unconquered.

The violence of the Spanish conquest had as its ultimate goal the submission of the land's original inhabitants rather than their elimination, but this submission was never wholly granted. While violence, disease, and forced labor killed more than 90 percent of the indigenous population of Mexico by 1650, sixty-two distinct indigenous groups survived. The period of conquest and the establishment of New Spain (1519–1821) created a strict order of social classes: men born in Spain ruled, men born in the Americas of Spanish parents could engage in the social world of commerce and local governance, men born of mixed parents could serve in the lower strata of the social world, and men born of indigenous parents were enslaved or forced to be serfs. As in many parts of the world, to be born a woman implied twice the curse of social and political domination. Through the 1810 War of Independence and the Mexican Revolution of 1910–1920, the racial and sex-based divisions of power were slowly cracked and recast as class divisions (although race and sex still haunt). The modern Mexican state was born of this reconfiguration of class divisions; the mask of inclusion and unity has never quite fit over the land or its people. Mexico is a country of divisions—violent, embedded divisions.

Class conflict in Mexico is unrelenting: present in even the most mundane social contact, at times subdued, at times hidden, yet at times explosive. Where you live, what you wear, how you travel, what you eat, and how you speak are all signs of your affiliation to one or another stratum of *indio*, *banda*, or *fresa* (roughly, "Indian," "cool," or "preppy," but carrying a great deal more weight than their English equivalents). Yet it is not so much class-based discrimination as a pervasive, low-intensity class war that permeates daily life in Mexico.

The hostility is mutual. The privileged use categories of class and race to insult. When, during the predawn hours of July 3, 2006, the supporters of the right-wing presidential candidate Felipe Calderón began to celebrate their candidate's declaration of victory they did not shout positive slogans of triumph but rather, "We did in that low-class scum!"— "*¡Acabamos con los pinches nacos!*"[7] However, it is just as cutting an insult to call a group of students clad in designer clothes "*pinches fresas*" ("damn strawberries"; *fresa*, literally strawberry, combines flavors of English words like preppy, prissy, and yuppie) as it is to shout from the rolled-down window of a BMW "*¡Vete, pinche naco!*" ("Get lost, you damn lowlife!") at the street kids who aggressively clean windshields at busy intersections for tips.

How wide is the wedge between social classes in Mexico? Consider the extremes. In 2007, Mexican businessman Carlos Slim Helú was the richest man in the world, with an estimated worth, according to *Fortune*, of $59 billion.[8] Much of Slim's wealth came from the privatization of Mexico's national telephone company under President Carlos Salinas (1988–1994), when Mr. Slim purchased it at far below the market price and received a guaranteed seven-year monopoly on all phone service in the country. According to *Forbes*, Slim's fortune grew by $19 billion in 2006; according to *Fortune*, it grew by another $12 billion in 2007.[9] In Metlatónoc, Guerrero, children die of diarrhea and dehydration because their parents do not have seven dollars to pay for the five-hour dirt-road drive to Tlapa, not to mention the forty dollars for medicine once they get there. The annual budget for the entire municipality of Metlatónoc, with a population of over 17,000 people, is $2.7 million, which averages out to $159 per person per year. Metlatónoc was long the poorest municipality in Mexico, before it was divided in two so that the federal government could point to its advancement up to sixth poorest. The section that was separated, Cochoapa el Grande, now holds the distinction of being the poorest. Before its recent "progress," Metlatónoc received steady visits from presidents, governors, and candidates flown in from Acapulco or Mexico City by helicopter to use the community as a backdrop for press events showing their commitment to the poor. Men in suits, surrounded by armed bodyguards and standing on a freshly assembled stage trucked in for the occasion, declared before the national television cameras their commitment to lifting up the poor with the power of transnational markets—promises pronounced in Spanish in a region where more than 95 percent of the people do not speak it. In Metlatónoc, dozens of light posts line the dirt roads, yet no light shines from them at night. Metlatónoc has never been connected to any electrical grid; it was only an opportunity for politicians to pose with indigenous people hoisting posts in the afternoon dust.

The disparity between Carlos Slim and the 12.7 million indigenous inhabitants of contemporary Mexico is much greater than that between Hernán Cortés, Viceroy Juan Vicente Güemea Pacheco y Padilla, or the thirty-year dictator Porfirio Díaz and the indigenous people of their respective times. And while Carlos Slim is the extreme, he is far from the exception. There are over 85,000 millionaires (in U.S. dollars) in Mexico, while fifty million people live in economic destitution on less than a few dollars a day. According to the Mexican national daily, *El Universal*, the thirty-nine richest families in Mexico own 13.5 percent of the nation's wealth, about $135 billion.[10]

It is misleading to present inequality in numbers like these: the numbers can tell you how vast the distance, but they do not tell you who created it and how; they do not tell you what machinations one side conducts to defend the inequality, nor what preparations the other side makes to dismantle it; they point to but do not describe the full and complex class structure in society. Statistics hint at the extent of a social wound but say nothing of the instrument used to make that wound, or the surgery required to close it. Poverty in Mexico, as elsewhere in this hemisphere, is a social creation largely of the nineteenth and twentieth centuries, though with deep roots in Spanish colonialism; it is a project as purposefully created and finely wrought as the national highway system, the telecommunications network, or the armed forces. Poverty is no accident, no unexpected outcome of bad choices, bad weather, or bad habits. Poverty is a product, and the wealthy hold the patent.

As noted by the sociologist Erik Olin Wright, when different groups of people in a given society have unequal rights and powers with respect to the productive resources available in that society, the relations between these groups can be described as class relations.[11] In the Viceroyalty of New Spain, for example, the Spanish-born could own property, build mines, and harvest fruit and grain for the transatlantic market; the indigenous, by decree, could not. When the Spanish-born would arrive in a new area and expel its original inhabitants, take over their fields, or force them into slave labor, they established class divisions that were clearly delineated by race. Of course, class divisions were not the unique invention of the Spanish—though they would become true masters of technique—and as will be discussed later, class divisions on a much smaller territorial scale were present in several indigenous societies. But the main features of the class divisions that pervade contemporary Mexico are inherited from Spanish rule.

A deep understanding of class structure in Mexico requires

consideration not only of the resources needed for material production, but also of those needed for cultural and political production, what we might call political capital, those things that enable sectors of society to possess and wield various forms of power.[12] Political office in Mexico has long been a station reserved for the ruling elite and a position from which class control over productive resources is administered. People amongst the marginalized classes in Mexico often talk of "*la clase política*"—"the political class"—to describe the fusion of political participation and economic exclusion and exploitation. The mechanics of class division can be explicit and overt: indigenous peoples and women of all races were barred from owning property under Spanish rule. Class divisions may also be opaque and covert: indigenous people were later granted the ability to own land, but the armed guards of local political bosses, known as caciques, prevented them from exercising their rights and women were later allowed to vote and run for office, but their husbands, male coworkers, and male relatives pressured them or threatened them with abuse to keep them from getting politically involved.

Though the language of class analysis may seem dated, the term "exploitation" still has its validity. It is more nuanced than "oppression," for it involves the exploiter's need for the labor of the people exploited. Massacring people is not exploitation, enslaving them is. Genocide is not exploitation, but the maquiladora is. Oppression and domination—the use of violence to control the actions of a person or class—are tactics used to perpetuate exploitative relations. Exploitation, borrowing again from Wright, is a form of interdependence between different classes in which the material interests of the exploiting class depend upon the deprivations of the exploited, and thus is predicated on the control of the labor efforts of the lower classes and their exclusion from access to certain resources.[13] Again Mexico's colonial history provides a text-book example: the wealth of the Spaniards required the misery of the indigenous, who were denied equal property and political rights and forced to work for the Spaniards in the mines and haciendas. Let us not forget, so much of the comforts and marvels of Western Europe and the elite societies of the Americas were built with slave labor and the materials wrested from invaded lands.

IT IS ONE of the saddest stories ever told: a "new" world "discovered," and so many worlds laid to waste—this rich field of human diversity eviscerated and burned by men possessed by the logic of possession, men who believed in the divine right of hierarchy, in the principle of an inviolable order, from God to pope to king and queen, through the ornate array of royalty and their armies to the serfs, the servants, the slaves, the savages. This order, they believed, was itself the word of God, sacred and just; any offense against this order was something to be crushed.

I learned about the conquest of the indigenous civilizations in Mexico in elementary school. In class we learned the Spanish alphabet, we memorized the names of the colors, and we learned that the Aztecs were gone. I saw photographs of their calendar and their pyramids. It gave me nightmares—to think, a people no more, entire worlds gone: the Aztec, the Maya. That is what I was taught, the story of conquest, terrifying for its violence, but even more so for its finality. Worlds gone. Worlds no more. I did not yet know that the story of conquest is its own continuation, that the teaching of lost worlds is part of the sorcery that tries to make these worlds disappear. I did not know that the story is the justification—horror and all—of the history; Bartolomé de las Casas—who advocated against some of the brutalities of the Spanish invaders—may now be praised for decrying colonial violence and racism, because the deeds are done.

That history would be different now, the story says, for the surviving world, the world of the "discoverers," the "conquerors," is no longer a world of imperial design, a world of slaves and a divine hierarchy of humanity, brutally enforced, from God to savage. The surviving world is one of law, a world where hierarchy has been leveled by individual freedom, where the inviolable order has been pulled down, broken apart, and replaced with the vast plateau of democracy. Where once stood kings, now citizens form a line to vote, the former aristocratic monopoly of culture is now available to anyone able to pay. The "New World" has learned from the bloodshed of the past. This world, our world, is at last free. And this freedom absolves the present from the past.

In many parts of this "New World" it is easy to believe that the past is buried and the debris cleared away. But in Mexico, one has only to walk out into the street, take the subway, or open a newspaper to find the past very much alive, vital, hungry and far from forgetful, far from forgiving. History, here, still has much to say. Time is the collage of divided worlds, the continued collision of conquest and revolt. There is no one time, flat, steady, and measurable by clocks and calendars: time is an open battlefield. Aztec ruins lie next to the seat of the federal government, a man with a mule pulling a two-wheeled wooden carriage forges his way against a fierce current of automobile traffic, past and present are tangled throughout the same terrain.

The conquest is not buried, not contained in the chapters of history texts, not relegated to a distinct and final past; it continues. The pulse of conquest animates the government institutions, mafia-like power brokers, military and police forces, media, and private enterprises that rule the country. In

Mexico, the concepts of history, the rule of law, poverty, and migration are ideologically loaded with myths cultivated over hundreds of years to mask the violence and solidify the legitimacy of plunder, invasion, and exploitation. And thus the pulse of revolt against ongoing conquest animates resistance and uprisings across Mexico, from the everyday resistance of street vendors in Mexico City to the barricades in Oaxaca to the autonomous municipalities in Zapatista rebel territory. Edward Said wrote: "'Imperialism' means the practice, the theory, and the attitudes of a dominating metropolitan center ruling a distant territory; 'colonialism,' which is almost always a consequence of imperialism, is the implanting of settlements on a distant territory."[14] Mexico's independence from Spain only shifted the dominating metropolitan center from Madrid to Mexico City. During the 200 years since independence, Mexico's ruling class has continued the practice of imperialism, forcing its rule over distant territories and the incredibly diverse cultures of people who live there. But Mexico's ruling class has also largely cooperated with the dictates of the larger imperial designs of the United States.

It is now fashionable for pundits on both sides of the U.S.-Mexico border to acknowledge the long list of crimes, tricks, ingenuities, and horrors used by the PRI to monopolize the state for seventy-one years. This agreement is made possible by another myth: the myth that everything changed in 2000 when Vicente Fox of the conservative National Action Party (PAN) defeated the PRI and won the presidential election. Fox was not the first opposition candidate to win, but he was the first allowed to win *and* take office, and the very institutions of state and capital that were most threatened by the PRI's irrevocably corroded legitimacy raised the loudest voices celebrating his victory. While the quasi-official sanctioning of criticism of the PRI has provided a wealth of new information on the daily mechanics of building and running a stratified society, the elite strip this information of political relevance by pointing to the "triumph of democracy" in the 2000 elections.

The events of the past six years of "democratic transition," however, debunk the myth. Between 2000 and 2005, more than four million Mexicans left their homes to cross into the United States in search of work, making Mexico the top migrant "exporting" country in the world. Since Fox took power, the violence of warring drug cartels has exploded, reaching extremes that make the maneuvers of Al Capone seem quaint. During Fox's last year in office, assassins working for the drug-trafficking cartels began decapitating their victims—police, members of competing cartels, and citizens who dared to complain—and impaling their heads on poles outside government buildings, or rolling them out like bowling balls across the dance floors of packed night clubs. During Felipe Calderón's first eighteen months in office, drug gang assassins executed over 4,400 people.[15]

Also during Fox's final year in office, while drug lords killed with impunity, state and federal police raided protesters barricaded in the small town of San Salvador Atenco, brutally beating hundreds of people and raping more than thirty women in a bus while transporting them to jail. At dawn on June 14, Oaxaca state governor Ulises Ruiz Ortiz sent 1,000 of his state police to repeat the Atenco operation against striking teachers camped out in Oaxaca City's town square, or Zócalo. Ortiz's plan backfired: the teachers and outraged Oaxaca City residents took to the streets, counterattacked, and drove the police out of town. This ill-fated police operation sparked a six-month protester takeover of Oaxaca City, during which state and local police formed death squads that killed more than twenty people with total impunity.

But perhaps the most ironic exposure of the myth of "democratic transition" came in the 2006 presidential elections.[16] Fox and his coterie had unleashed a series of made-for-TV scandal pieces meant to block Andrés Manuel López Obrador, then mayor of Mexico City, from running for president as the candidate of the Democratic Revolutionary Party (PRD). The media hit pieces flopped, widely and correctly perceived as a conspiracy of the right-wing elite. Rather than block his candidacy, the affair increased popular support for López Obrador more than a year out from the elections, making him the clear front-runner. Once the campaigns began in earnest in January 2006, Fox illegally used the presidency to campaign on behalf of PAN candidate Felipe Calderón and to attack López Obrador. (The Federal Electoral Tribunal would declare after the elections that Fox's actions were indeed illegal though not "decisive.") Business and conservative Catholic groups supporting Calderón flooded the television and radio airwaves with sinister attack ads associating López Obrador with Hitler, Mussolini, and Hugo Chávez. "López Obrador: a danger for Mexico," declared the voice-over. After months of airtime, the Federal Electoral Tribunal declared these ads to be illegal and ordered them off the air.

Then, a little after eleven on election night, July 2, 2006, the president of the Federal Electoral Institute, the agency in charge of conducting the elections, Luis Ugalde, appeared on television in a prerecorded video message praising the institutions of democracy, voter participation, and the scientific rigor of the vote count, before saying that the election was too close to call and urging both candidates to wait for official results. Just seconds after the message ended, President Fox appeared in another prerecorded video message equally baroque and didactic in its praise of institutions, voters, and science, also urging Mexicans to wait patiently for the official results. Few waited. Both candidates declared victory that night.

Over the following days serious irregularities in the vote counts came to light—everything from statistical impossibilities to millions of "missing" votes to urns used to collect ballots found in trash dumps and floating in dirty rivers outside Mexico City. As the evidence increased and popular suspicion swelled, the situation was hauntingly reminiscent of the last time an opposition candidate seemed poised to win, in 1988, when "the computer crashed," or so they said. The PAN and the IFE began a massive ad campaign portraying those who alleged fraud as anti-Mexican, insulting to the volunteer poll staff and the millions of Mexicans who voted on July 2. López Obrador took his protests to the streets, calling between one and two million people to Mexico City's Zócalo in marches before finally organizing a protest encampment in the Zócalo and along major avenues downtown. But the IFE called the election for Calderón and the Federal Electoral Tribunal refused to authorize a complete recount. López Obrador lifted his protest and Calderón's inauguration took place in the midst of an ostentatious military and police siege meant to keep protesters away from Congress.

The 2006 elections were a referendum of sorts on class divisions in Mexico. López Obrador's massive crowds reflected the everyday people in the streets, on the subway, working in the fields, hammering away at construction sites across the country (and across the United States as well). Felipe Calderón's die-hard supporters, dressed in designer clothes and arriving at political events in SUVs, represented the business owners and foreign-trained technocrats now running the country. (On election day, however, a significant number of the down and out voted for Calderón, terrified by the prospect that a López Obrador victory would devalue the peso and lead to an economic crisis.) The content of the Right's political advertisements associated class consciousness with fascist dictatorships, while López Obrador's stump speech called for taking the country back from the extreme rich. The election's outcome was a message to the underdogs of Mexico: you cannot win, even if you follow all the rules and participate in the game of electoral democracy; we will take power, just as we have for centuries, by tricks, chicanery, and, if necessary, imposition of violence. In 2006, the short-lived myth of the Great Transition came to an end.

The Mexican state is a creature of the legacy of conquest and imperialism. In Mexico, the façade of legitimacy constructed over the state is chipped and broken. This is largely the result of the authoritarianism of the ruling class—which is too flamboyant to conceal itself—and the intensity and perseverance of local rebellions for basic rights, for land, for autonomy, and against contemporary state colonialism. And the nation, the "imagined community" that in Mexico is fused with authoritarian political power, is cracking apart as those who have always been excluded, who have always been subjected to the violence of "national stability," continue to imagine and fight for something else, something different.[17]

Mexico Unconquered chronicles the hidden crevices of Mexico's class war. It makes two arguments. First, the conquest never finished, but evolved and transformed from Spanish imperialism into an internal colonialism combined with forms of economic domination imposed by the United States. Mexico's political class uses various nationalist, economic, rule-of-law, and poverty ideologies as catechisms for converting and dominating the still uncolonized sectors of the population, both indigenous and nonindigenous, from the Zapatista rebels in Chiapas to the Raramuri in Chiuahua, from the Mexico City street vendors to the teachers of Oaxaca. Second, precisely due to the neocolonial character of internal processes of exploitation, exclusion, and repression in Mexico, compounded by a deep and continuing history of United States military, political, and economic interventions in Mexico, resistance movements take on an anticolonial dimension that challenges and threatens the legitimacy of the fundamental tenets of the state and leads to bold, creative, massive, and energetic social participation. Mexico's class war is a fight against the ongoing conquest, a social struggle for dignity and autonomy.

Philosopher Slavoj Žižek writes: "The fundamental level of ideology . . . is not of an illusion masking the real state of things, but that of an (unconscious) fantasy structuring our social reality itself."[18] Ideology serves to normalize remarkable and horrid social relations. With the magic of a well-placed word or two, duly impregnated with ideology, the most absurd and unacceptable of situations are made to seem natural. Ideology tells us that when the Mexican police routinely kill and torture, well, it is part of the rule of law; if twenty million Mexicans live in hunger, their children dying of diarrhea, well, that is the sad reality of poverty; as nearly half a million Mexicans cross the border into the United States every year seeking their own labor exploitation just to keep their families alive, well, they are looking for a better life, hence they migrate; if Mexico's twelve million indigenous people live on the margin of the state, constantly subject to massacres, everyday racism, and the ravage of hunger, well, the indigenous were always like that, even before the Spaniards came, that's the indigenous past. This book seeks to examine the broken fantasies of contemporary ideology, fantasies that have been rejected by Mexico's territories in revolt.

Mexico Unconquered draws from a wide array of academic, theoretical, and journalistic sources, provides references, and uses material from over two years of reporting in Mexico. I intend it to be an invitation to reflection and a call to act. It does not aim to have the last word; it does not believe in last words. It is an attempt to arouse curiosity, convoke critical thinking, open spaces of reflection and political imagination. The language of the book moves through argumentative, lyrical, and narrative forms. While this is a reflection on empire and revolt in Mexico, I hope that the thoughts and stories presented herein will be of use to others reflecting on similar social conditions in other lands. Finally, although this book is divided into chapters, each chapter could be embedded in all of the others, or put another way, each chapter bleeds into all the others: they all share the same blood.

THE HISTORICAL CONTINUITY OF CONQUEST AND REVOLT

Appeals to the past are among the commonest of strategies in interpretations of the present. What animates such appeals is not only disagreement about what happened in the past and what the past was, but uncertainty about whether the past really is past, over and concluded, or whether it continues, albeit in different forms, perhaps.

—Edward Said, *Culture and Imperialism*

In two senses the histories of the indigenous peoples of Mexico are not yet history. In the first place, they are not history because they have yet to be written; that which has been written up to now about these histories is above all else a discourse of power from the vision of the colonizer to justify their domination, to rationalize it. They are not yet histories, in the second sense, because they are not concluded histories, completed cycles of peoples who have fulfilled their destiny and "moved on into history," but rather open histories, in process, that demand their own future.

—Guillermo Bonfil Batalla, "Historias que no son todavía historia"

SOMEWHERE BETWEEN 20,000 and 35,000 years ago, migrating hunters may have crossed an Ice Age land bridge from Asia into the American continent. By the time Columbus stumbled upon the Caribbean while looking for the Indies, millions of people, gathered in hundreds of distinct cultures and language groups, inhabited the Americas from Alaska to Patagonia. When Hernán Cortés marched on the city of Tenochtitlán, most of the millions of indigenous people across the land that would become Mexico had never seen the Great Temple, or even heard of it: the Raramuri, the Ñu Savi, the Seri, the Chol, the Yaqui, the Pápago, the Tojolabal, the Kiliwa. The amazing diversity of indigenous peoples across the territory now known as Mexico at the time of the Spanish incursion is typically reduced to the Aztec and Mayan empires, with brief mention of the disappeared Olmec or architecturally sophisticated societies like the Zapotecs. This reduction is part of the conquest itself, of talking about the indigenous as subjects of the past, not existing societies—the Mayan Empire collapsed on its own and the Aztec Empire fell to Hernán Cortés. They are gone. But over twelve million indigenous people remain, many denied both their history and their present.

This Aztec-reductionism also serves to justify Spanish plunder. Alan Riding, former *New York Times* correspondent in Mexico and author of the aptly titled book *Distant Neighbors*, wrote this of the Spanish invasion: "After the Conquest, it was just another god who arrived, in whose name the Indians were subjected to new exploitation."[1] The Aztecs—or, more accurately, the Triple Alliance—were a brutal imperial force in central and southern Mexico for over ninety years (1428–1519).[2] By melding all of Mexico's indigenous cultures into the Aztec Empire, commentators like Riding can then draw a smooth line of exploitation from the pre-Columbian era to the Viceroyalty of New Spain to the present, and in so doing make exploitation itself seem as old and natural as weaving baskets or growing corn. "The Indians were just as despotic and murderous as the Spaniards, they even cut people's hearts out while they were still alive," their logic says, "the poor have always suffered, always fallen to violent oppressors, that's just the way it is, nothing can change this." Pre-Columbian cultures were not violence-free utopias. Many toiled under imperial rule, but their diversity and differences are erased under Aztec-reductionism, and their oppression becomes naturalized and vaguely justified.

The Valley of Mexico, site of present-day Mexico City, the most populated urban area in the Western Hemisphere, once held vast lakes with fertile agricultural shore lands and islands. The first regional hegemonic societies, sometimes called early states, developed in the Valley of Mexico. Around the first century A.D., the city of Teotihuacan emerged as the multi-ethnic capital city of the first Mesoamerican empire, reaching a population of around 150,000 by 500 A.D.[3] Teotihuacan's control over regional trade in obsidian (used to make cutting tools and weapons) fueled its expansion in the valley until competition amongst local elites led to the political fragmentation of the region. The next hegemonic society did not develop until some 500 years later when the Toltecs gained control of obsidian production and built a mercantile empire on a foundation of military innovations including a curved twenty-inch sword with obsidian blades on each side.[4] The Toltec capital Tollan fell in 1179 and warring city-states filled the power vacuum, with the Tepanecs controlling the west side of the Valley of Mexico and developing military-imperial tactics that foreshadowed the 100-year Aztec reign.[5]

The Aztecs migrated southeast to the Valley of Mexico in the twelfth century and settled in Tenochtitlán—an island city near the western shore of Lake Texcoco—perhaps because they had left a lake region in what is now southern Guanajuato or Lake Mexcaltitlán in Nayarit.[6] Originally outsiders and tributaries within the Tepanec area of control, the Aztecs sought to consolidate local power through strategic intermarriages and participation in Tepanec military conquests.[7] In 1409, a battle broke out between potential heirs to the Tepanec Empire. The Aztec king Itzcóatl built an alliance with the kings of Texcoco and Tlacopan to overthrow the Tepanecs. This Triple Alliance defeated the Tepanec ruler Maxtla and consolidated control over the Valley of Mexico through a series of campaigns to subdue or conquer surrounding city-states.[8]

The Aztec kings, supported by the Triple Alliance, in less than 100 years built an imperial power unrivaled in Mesoamerica. Their power was largely based on the control of trade routes and the imposition of tributes on conquered areas, both backed up by the threat (and often demonstration) of brutal repression. While the Aztecs did not create an empire in the sense of strict control over an extended territory exercised from a centralized authority and maintained through military occupation, they did develop a region of domination in which the failure of local authorities to comply with Aztec demands brought targeted, vicious military campaigns.[9] The Aztecs sought to induce people—mainly major towns in agricultural valleys—to submit to their rule through overwhelming threats of destruction, forcing them without battle to surrender tribute and allow Aztec merchants (also doubling as spies) to operate.[10] Except for these two impositions, the Aztecs left the local power structures intact, and "conquest typically caused few other overt changes in local society."[11] Those who refused or rebelled would face war and often be crushed. Many small societies in what is now Guerrero and Oaxaca fell to the obsidian blade of the Aztec. The also hegemonic regimes of the Tarascans to the west and the Tlaxcalans to the east resisted Aztec dominion for decades—

and provided through continual warfare many of the prisoners executed on Aztec temples—up until the Spanish invasion. The Aztecs developed several oppressive institutions such as slavery, draconian laws (death by strangling for theft or public drunkenness), ideological control through religious education, and rewriting their own history to serve political ambitions.[12] But no tactic of the Aztecs is so demonized—justly, if anachronistically—though little understood, as their practice of human "sacrifice." Human sacrifice did occur throughout the Aztec realm (as it did throughout the realms of their Tarascan and Tlaxcalan enemies) and was related to cannibalism.[13] Public executions also took place during the same time period across Europe.[14] While in Europe human sacrifice—the public spectacle of state killings—was largely a punitive affair, theatrical punishment for transgressions against religious or political order, in the Aztec Empire human sacrifice was more of a naked exposition of imperial power: prisoners and volunteers alike were sacrificed not for punishment, but as a show of military power and economic wealth meant both to impress the conquered and to intimidate or terrorize those resisting Aztec expansion.[15] Such imperial displays were deeply embedded in spiritual beliefs as well; human sacrifice was thought to maintain the sun in its course, the rainfall from the sky, and the continual resurgence of spring.[16] Neither the Aztec practice of pulling the still beating heart from the chest of a prisoner nor the European practice of burning at the stake or drawing and quartering heretics is more or less brutal: both sought to symbolize state power before awestruck subjects, both were tools of oppression and empire building. The Aztec Empire should not be defended nor airbrushed to seem like a utopia of collective land ownership (though the vast bulk of the land within the Aztec realm was owned collectively by the people who worked it);[17] its empire was devastating, and thousands fell to or were enslaved by its violence.

Aztec imperial ambition reached its geographical limits at what is now the Mexican border with Guatemala by the time of the Spaniards' arrival.[18] Moctezuma II (1503–1520) sought to shift Aztec policy from expansion to stabilization in the southern reaches of the empire, while building a fierce concentration of power in his person.[19] Moctezuma's retrenchment led to a fracture in the Triple Alliance and a loss of both military momentum and ideological cohesion that weakened the Aztecs on the eve of Hernán Cortés's arrival in Tenochtitlán.[20]

While Christopher Columbus's immediate intent was to chart a direct route to East Asia, his voyage was part of a greater design of conquest: he sought to accumulate the wealth necessary for a Catholic crusade to take Jerusalem. In his own words: "I declare to Your Highness that all gain of this my enterprise should be spent in the conquest of Jerusalem." And later: "At the moment when I undertook to discover the Indies, it was with the intention of beseeching the King and the Queen, our Sovereigns, that they might determine to spend the revenues possibly accruing to them from the Indies for the conquest of Jerusalem; and it is indeed this thing which I have asked of them."[21] This religion-driven imperial impulse remained and prevailed when Columbus stumbled upon a very different place than the one he had sought.

In the first 100 years of Spanish invasion, slaughter, forced labor, and disease combined to kill, as mentioned above, over 90 percent of Mexico's First Peoples. Eighty million people inhabited the Americas in 1491; the indigenous population was 10 million in 1550. In Mexico, the native population fell from 25 million to 1 million by 1600.[22] In the Valley of Mexico, the seat of the Triple Alliance and later of Spanish power, indigenous civilizations dropped from an estimated population of 1.5 million to 70,000 between 1520 and 1650 (and rose again to 200,000 by 1800).²³ The Spanish formed alliances with regional power brokers, whom they called caciques, to administer their dominion. A few priests participating in the imposition of Catholicism decried the brutality with which their fellow Spaniards treated the indigenous peoples. They did not question the right to impose Christianity and even subject the indigenous to forced labor, they only thought it should be done with less gore. The urgings of Fray Bartolomé de las Casas persuaded the pope to issue a papal bull in 1537 declaring the liberty of the indigenous peoples, and in 1542 the Spanish Crown forced the New Laws upon the colonies, forbidding further massacres and land grabs. With the New Laws the first seeds of impunity in the modern sense were planted in Mexico: the colonists brazenly refused to follow the law, saying, "*Obedezco pero no cumplo*" (I will obey you, but I will not comply). The New Laws were repealed three years later, opening the door for continued colonial invasions of indigenous land. Then, in 1573, the Crown developed the Standard Law, in which the word "conquest" was replaced by the word "pacification," thus satisfying the moral sensitivities of the Spanish Crown.²⁴

From the first point of contact, the Spaniards viewed the indigenous people as objects, like exotic species of birds and lizards, things to be collected, taken back to Europe and exhibited (Columbus), or at best, as producers of objects, nameless creatures like worms that spin silk, to be taken back to Europe (Cortés).²⁵ Enslaving the people and taking their lands was an economic affair for the Spaniards, not in any way a moral one.²⁶ The indigenous people's status as object was literally burned into their skin. Slaves had the royal brand as well as their successive owners' initials seared into their faces. One Spanish chronicler of the conquest wrote: "They produced so many marks on their faces, in addition to the royal brand, that they had their faces covered with letters, for they bore the marks of all who had bought and sold them."[27] The violence of this initial contact—the Spaniards' refusal to acknowledge the people of Mexico as fellow humans—forever marked social divisions in Mexico, and it has yet to be forgotten.

Consider this eyewitness account—and its blasé narration—of events in the Carib islands in 1519:

> Some Christians encountered an Indian woman, who was carrying in her arms a child at suck; and since the dog they had with them was hungry, they tore the child from the mother's arms and flung it still living to the dog, who proceeded to devour it before the mother's eyes . . . When there were among the prisoners some women who had recently given birth, if the new-born babes happened to cry they seized them by the legs and hurled them against the rocks, or flung them into the jungle so that they would be certain to die there.[28]

Mexico's original inhabitants did not simply bow their heads to foreign authority and violence; they rejected attempts to be dominated. The indigenous revolted all across the country, continuously and steadily, throughout the entire colonial period. The Yaquis fiercely repelled Spanish land invasions for over 100 years. The Yopes rose up in 1531. The Mixtón Rebellion of 1541 and the Chichimeca wars of 1576–1606 challenged Spanish imperial expansion. The Tarahumara rebelled against the Spaniards throughout the seventeenth century (1616, 1646, 1650, 1652, 1689, 1696–97). Indigenous societies fought to retain autonomy in Oaxaca, rising up in

1660. Today there are more than 400 autonomous indigenous municipalities in Oaxaca. The Pueblo of contemporary New Mexico revolted in 1680. The Tzeltal, in Chiapas, revolted in 1712. In the north, the Seris rose up in 1725–26 and the Yaquis and Mayos rebelled in 1740–42. Another Seri revolt in alliance with the Pima and Pápago in 1748 stretched throughout the 1750s. The Maya revolted in 1761. Small farmers and indigenous in the Sierra Gorda, where Querétaro, Guanajuato, and San Luis Potosí all join, rose up in arms in 1847. That same year, in the Yucatán, Maya communities went to war against the European-descended upper classes; the so-called Caste War took decades to suppress. The Huasteca indigenous people held off the Spanish for hundreds of years and then unleashed a series of rebellions in the late nineteenth century that helped launch the Mexican Revolution of 1910–1920. Throughout the nineteenth century there were more than forty rebellions in seventeen states.[29] Mexico's history of revolt is as deep as its history of exploitation, though that history remains largely untold, a silence that itself reinforces the ideology of the finality of conquest.

Colonial authority in New Spain laid the foundations for several pillars of contemporary Mexican politics: centralized power, monopoly capitalism, corruption and cronyism, *caciquismo*, racism, class stratification, and labor exploitation. The Crown was the ultimate arbiter in New Spain's political affairs, but as Spain's power in Europe was waning, the Spanish-born colonial authorities assumed considerable power over everyday affairs. Silver mining became one of New Spain's main economic pursuits, with Mexico soon surpassing Peru as the chief supplier of silver on the world market, particularly for use in trade with East Asia. Corruption grew rampant early on, with mine owners and merchant-financiers buying off colonial bureaucrats to bypass the Crown's taxes. By 1660, colonial authorities themselves estimated that trading in untaxed silver surpassed by more than 30 percent the duly regulated trade.[30] In this process, the Spanish-born merchant-financiers with built-up capital from their monopoly control over Atlantic trading emerged as the main power brokers in New Spain, even more so than hacienda landowners, who were virtual feudal lords in the countryside.

The Spanish brought Africans to Mexico as slaves for over a century, though never in numbers as large as those taken to the United States and Brazil. While the Crown felt the need to use euphemisms like "pacification" to window-dress the land invasions and forced labor of the indigenous, African peoples were the only ones openly called slaves in the colonial period. This introduced a color scale of racism that persists to this day, with African Mexicans together with indigenous at the bottom of the brutal pit of contemporary racism. The social strata of race in New Spain became known as the *castas*, with various names for people of mixed racial heritage, and while most of the *castas* were excluded from autonomous participation in social and economic life, the lighter one's skin, the less virulent was one's rejection. The *castas* participated vigorously in the urban uprisings of the seventeenth century. The Spanish called these uprisings *tumultos*—rabble-rousing riots—to strip them of political content, a technique still employed by the elite today. In one uprising led by women to protest the rising price of food in 1692, the *castas* burned down the palace of the viceroyalty, the city hall, and the royal court.[31]

Sor Juana Inés de la Cruz (1648–1695) provides a glimpse into the subjugation of women during the colonial era through her poems and letters, which inveigh against the sexual double standard and advocate for equal education opportunities for women.[32] At the age of 42, Sor Juana Inés was forbidden to read or write, though legend has it that she continued to write with her own blood.[33] Colonial patriarchy weighed women down in political, economic, and religious life, but they constantly challenged and subverted patriarchal practices through forms of everyday resistance in the home and community.[34]

The economy of indigenous civilization up to 1491 was largely based on sedentary agriculture and collective land ownership, though many areas were subjected to brutal serfdom by imperial powers like the Triple Alliance.[35] During the first two centuries of colonial New Spain, the economy consisted of a heterogeneous system of "despotic tributes," feudalism, and embryonic capitalism, all acting as an organic whole. Two structures made up the system: the despotic tributes of the indigenous and the feudal-capitalism of the Spaniards. The despotic-tribute structure (built on the existing economy of the Triple Alliance Empire) held the indigenous communities on one side and the Spanish Crown and the Church on the other. The agrarian community was the basic unit of production. The basic units of the Spanish economy were estates, plantations, artisan workshops, *obrajes*, and mines.[36] Historian Enrique Semo writes: "The income of the dominant classes came from the work of indigenous laborers indentured or sent off to the Spaniards' properties, slaves, salaried workers, peons, and the commercial exploitation of communities and small producers."[37]

The Spanish Crown tightly controlled the economy, seeking to prevent the indigenous or criollo (Mexican-born Spanish) classes from developing economic competition or any other form of threat to colonial power. New Spain was tied to the emergence of capitalism in Europe during the sixteenth and seventeenth centuries, but it did not convert the hybrid colonial economy predicated on land invasion and forced labor into a similar form of nascent capitalism. In the first half of the eighteenth century, Mexico remained largely precapitalist, especially in the countryside, where debt peonage and semi-free labor prevailed: indigenous people forced from their lands could hardly avoid some form of labor relation with the Spanish hacienda.[38]

The revolutionary fervor that led to Mexico's Wars of Independence (1810–1822) had two currents. One, embodied in the mixed-race priest José María Morelos, sought a social as well as an anticolonial revolution. Morelos organized a guerrilla group that fast developed into the most disciplined of the early independence armies. The Morelos platform, articulated in the 1813 Congress of Chilpancingo, called for the redistribution of wealth, the abolition of slavery and all forms of caste distinctions, the nullification of state monopolies, higher wage laws, an end to the sales tax and tributes, and the creation of an income tax.[39] Morelos was captured and executed in 1815.

The second current, embodied in the criollo hacienda owner Augustín de Iturbide, sought to save the elite criollo class from liberal reforms implemented in Spain and the rise of social revolution in the countryside. Iturbide defended New Spain against the first wave of independence struggles, fighting against Morelos's army. After the 1820 coup in Spain led to laws protecting indigenous rights and land in the American colonies, Iturbide capitalized on the criollo desire to be freed of the Crown's restrictions on trade and commerce and convinced them of the need to separate from Spain to keep their lock on rural power and indigenous labor. Even the Spanish Viceroy supported Iturbide, who also tricked the more socially radical army under Vicente Guerrero into joining forces to overthrow the Spanish. (Conservatives assassinated Guerrero in 1831.) Iturbide exhibited his true class colors by appointing himself Emperor Augustín I of Mexico upon securing independence. A few months later he was chased out of the country. He returned a year later only to be executed by elite republican forces led by Antonio López de Santa Anna.[40] The socially conservative—though republican rather than monarchical—forces triumphed in the Wars of Independence, but this opened the doors to four decades of utter chaos. In forty years, Mexico suffered through fifty distinct governments and lost half of its territory in war with the United States (a war initiated under the false pretext of a bloody confrontation with Mexican forces on U.S. soil—the battle actually took place in Mexico—and justified under the racist doctrine of "manifest destiny").[41] During the post-Independence period landowners led more invasions of communal indigenous lands than at any previous time and their political importance grew.[42] In 1861, when Benito Juárez, Mexico's first and only indigenous president, suspended foreign debt payments for two years to strengthen the national economy, Britain, France, and Spain decided to intervene and take over the Mexican ports. A year later, France launched an imperial invasion, and Britain and Spain pulled back. Mexico's Conservative Party sided with the French and welcomed the witless Hapsburg Archduke Ferdinand Maximilian as the Emperor of Mexico. Juárez never left Mexico, rallying support amongst the liberal elite, the indigenous, and campesinos to wage a continued guerrilla war, eventually overthrowing Maximilian, executing him—and the Conservative generals who supported him—by firing squad in 1867.[43]

Benito Juárez, a Zapotec indigenous man from Oaxaca, born in 1806, worked his way through school to become a lawyer, a liberal delegate to the National Congress in 1847, governor of Oaxaca, vice president, and finally president of Mexico. Juárez is now a celebrated figure in the Mexican canon of national heroes, with a huge marble statue in his honor in Mexico City's historic center. He was a pivotal figure in founding Mexican nationalism and the institutional power of the Mexican president, and his indigenous identity became essential to his success and posthumous canonization as a hero of the nation.[44] As president of Mexico, however, he was not dedicated to indigenous liberation and autonomy. He believed that the indigenous must show their ability to "rise" to the heights of European culture by mastering law and science. His land reform policies, aimed at stripping power from the Church, had the side effect of exposing indigenous communal lands to expropriation.

Juárez twice defeated the Oaxaca cacique Porfirio Díaz in the presidential elections. And after Juárez died of a heart attack in 1872 and Vice President Sebastián Lerdo de Tejada succeeded him, Díaz lost again when Lerdo was reelected in 1876. In an unintended ironic twist, Díaz then kicked off the era of his personal rule, known in Spanish as the Porfiriato, by revolting against Lerdo and winning the subsequent election under the campaign slogan "No reelection!" After stepping down at the end of his term in 1880, Díaz then ran for reelection in 1884. Believing it his own private "manifest destiny" to rule Mexico, Díaz rigged seven reelections for himself between 1884 and 1910.

Commentators often describe Díaz's thirty-year dictatorship as the young nation's first period of stability.[45] Extrapolation from this observation became a twentieth-century motif in Mexico, amounting to something like this: "Violent authoritarian rule that suppresses class dissent— though it may be a bit dirty, perhaps ungentlemanly—keeps the rabble in line, the economy running, and foreign investment flowing into the country." This idea of "stability" washes the grime of racism, murder, and hoarding from the palace steps of legitimacy. While the "anti-democratic" tilt of the dictatorship may be lamented in the national consciousness—the regime's gross violation of liberal values was its inability to produce convincing electoral theater—its coercive economics and continued policies of rural conquest and forced labor are forgiven in the name of "stability." The same that was said of Díaz was later said of the PRI.[46]

Díaz wanted to "modernize" Mexico, a code word of sorts for "Europeanize," which really meant to continue to colonize.[47] For Díaz and his clan—known as the *científicos* or the scientists, for their flair for industrialization and social Darwinism—modernization required racial homogenization, code for the elimination of indigenous societies.[48] The *científicos*, "saw the future of Mexico in the reduction and obliteration of the Indian element, which they regarded as inferior and hence incapable of development."[49] Díaz's racism was both official policy and covertly buried in his development model: using railway expansion as a means to dispossess indigenous communities and force the conversion of subsistence farmers to wage laborers.[50] Díaz said that Mexico should have little to do with politics and much to do with administration, which again, translated from rhetoric into action, meant that Díaz should be the only politician and that he would closely administer the fate of the nation.[51]

Díaz built over 10,000 miles of railway, which, as was the case in the U.S. westward expansion fifty years earlier, opened new indigenous lands to colonization and enabled the mine and hacienda owners to expand their operations and capitalize on increased access to ports and markets.[52] Díaz pulled in ever increasing amounts of foreign investment to complete most of the railway, highway, and other major construction projects. By the time Díaz was forced into exile in 1910, foreign investors from the United States, Britain, France, and Germany controlled 130 of the 170 largest firms in Mexico, and over 60 percent of the country's private capital.[53]

During the Porfiriato, business owners and their investors used bogus legalism and newly created rural police forces (*los rurales*) to break up communal lands and expand their own holdings, leading to the highest concentration of land ownership in Mexican history. By 1906 the government-associated oligarchy had taken possession of nearly 49 million hectares—a quarter of the arable land in the country. By 1910, the Díaz government had expropriated 95 percent of village communal lands in the country.[54] During this time the social and economic divisions between north and south increased, as mining, textile, and early industrial agricultural operations concentrated their land grabs in the north. In Chihuahua state alone, one individual owned seven million hectares.[55]

In Morelos state, about fifty miles south of downtown Mexico City, the politics of land grabs ignited the rural unrest that would build into a revolutionary army led by Emiliano Zapata. Here, one man, Manuel Araoz, already possessed 31,000 acres of the most fertile land in Morelos.[56] Araoz, a sugar baron eager to take advantage of the railroad lines to export sugar, wanted more land. But rural villagers did not want to sell, even when offered good prices. Thus, to get the land from under them, planters like Araoz "had to resort to political and judicial maneuvers—condemnations, court orders, foreclosures, and defective-title rulings."[57] Two years before the Mexican Revolution, seventeen planters owned most of the good land in the state, 25 percent of the total surface of Morelos.[58] And still, they wanted more.

Throughout the Porfiriato the indigenous, campesinos, and industrial workers led revolts, protests, and strikes against the regime, all meeting the same fate: brutal repression. Between 1906 and 1908 the Mexican Liberal Party (PLM) led the nation in organized resistance, launching strikes and several armed uprisings, seriously challenging the legitimacy of the regime and helping to foment both revolutionary disquiet and the foundation of an opposition program. Through its nationally distributed clandestine newspaper, *Regeneración*, and the intellectual leadership of the Flores Magón brothers, Ricardo and Enrique, the PLM spread the calls for labor, electoral and land reforms. The brothers were critical of Francisco I. Madero—who would emerge as a revolutionary leader—for reducing his opposition to purely electoral reform, writing that "the malady that afflicts the Mexican people cannot be cured by removing Díaz from office and putting in his place another man. . . . Our electoral ballots will be bullets from our guns."[59]

Emiliano Zapata, just turned 30, was elected to lead the village council of Anenecuilco, in Morelos state, during a clandestine meeting on Sunday, September 12, 1909. A small farmer, mule driver, and horse trader, Zapata first organized armed resistance in the early summer of 1910 to guard village farmers as they went out to plant where the Hospital hacienda had moved to usurp village land.[60] Once Madero made his call for a national uprising to overthrow Porfirio Díaz on November 20, the very local and mundane rebellion of the Anenecuilco farmers would not only join but far surpass the limited electoral goals of the Maderistas.

The meaning of the Mexican Revolution is itself highly contested territory. The Revolution forms the symbolic foundation of Mexican nationalism, the shape-shifting ideology claimed in various forms by every national political party and social movement in the country. There is no subversive subculture of flag burning in Mexico, where even the most committed on the Left stand in attention beneath the flag to sing the national anthem. Mexico is fiercely nationalist, and national identity is the field on which the major battles of social legitimacy are fought. Political organizations from the PRI and PAN to the guerrilla Zapatista Army of National Liberation (EZLN) accuse their enemies of being unfaithful to the nation, of sullying the flag, of not being real Mexicans. This ubiquitous love of the nation on all sides of Mexico's political spectrum has its roots in the people's rejection of repeated foreign invasions, though it has been repeatedly co-opted by the architects of the PRI and later the PAN to justify repression of dissent.[61] Some of the forces that vied for control of the nation-state during the Mexican Revolution had no intention of challenging, much less undoing, forms of oppression set in motion and continually evolving since Spanish incursion. Those who pursued a social revolution—resisting land grabs and racist legalism to stay put and live as they wished on their land—were betrayed time and time again, leading to their assassination and later post-mortem incorporation into the official nationalist ideology of the PRI. The Mexican Revolution did not uproot the nation's race and class divisions; rather, it more firmly implanted them and served to ingeniously create a new aura of legitimacy around the dominant classes.

Francisco I. Madero, "a spiritualist scion of a great landed family in the north" and a former student at the University of California at Berkeley, wanted to get Díaz out of office but not to change much else.[62] After Díaz gave an interview in 1908 to a U.S. reporter, saying that he would retire when his term ended in 1910 and that he would respect an opposition victory in the elections, Madero published a popular book on the presidential succession and launched his campaign under the slogan "a real vote, and no reelection."[63] Madero's campaign drew large crowds, so Díaz—who changed his mind and decided to run for his seventh reelection—had him arrested. Díaz then fixed his electoral victory while Madero was in jail in San Luis Potosí.[64] After a month in prison, Madero escaped to Texas and issued his Plan of San Luis Potosí, a revolutionary manifesto that outlined his program and called for a national uprising against Díaz to take place on November 20, 1910.[65]

The farmers in Anenecuilco took note of a clause in the third article of Madero's manifesto that promised to restore lands that had been unjustly snatched from villages and small farmers. Zapata and the other village leaders dispatched an envoy to find Madero and gauge his commitment to restoring land to the people who had been dispossessed. After three months, during which time tensions rose with the planters as well as with other armed bands answering Madero's call, Zapata's envoy returned and the villagers planned to make their move on Cuautla, the regional seat of power. Zapata's command over his forces drew on his reputation as a straightforward and hard-working local who knew the countryside and the respect he commanded for having stayed close to home to defend the village land from encroaching haciendas. Zapata emerged through cunning and caution as the top revolutionary leader in Morelos, having pulled together one of the largest armies in the revolution, composed mostly of local farmers like himself.[66]

As armies surged and moved on Mexico City, Porfirio Díaz negotiated his exile with Madero in Ciudad Juárez. Soon after Madero arrived in Mexico City as the revolutionary hero, he and his party called on the insurgent armies to cease all hostilities, especially against haciendas, and lay down their weapons. Madero, while waiting for new elections to be organized, quickly moved to keep the Porfirian order intact; he offered only vague promises to Zapata's specific requests to begin studying the land conflicts in Morelos, but insisted that the Zapatistas turn in their weapons.[67] Zapata disarmed in good faith, only to take up weapons again as part of a rural revolutionary police force. The planters and the Maderistas conspired to portray Zapata and his army as bandits on the loose, while Zapata proclaimed his loyalty to Madero, insisting however on the new government's compliance with the land policy outlined in the Plan of San Luis Potosí.

Madero won the elections, and within days of taking office on November 6, 1911, ordered Zapata's immediate and unconditional surrender, authorizing federal troops to attack him. In response, the Zapatistas declared revolution against Madero, calling him "inept at realizing the promises of the revolution of which he was the author, because he [had] betrayed the principles with which he tricked the will of the people and was able to get into power."[68] Madero's betrayal of his commitment to land reform, combined with his exclusion of rank-and-file revolutionaries from political participation and appointment of former Díaz officials to state office, exacerbated his isolation.[69] Francisco "Pancho" Villa reactivated his army, the Northern Division, and peasant movements similar to the Zapatistas rose up across the south. The more conservative forces of General Victoriano Huerta rushed into the breach, assassinated Madero in February 1913, and claimed control over the national government. Huerta held on for little more than a year when his government, and with it any semblance of a national state, collapsed.[70]

The Zapatistas and Villa's Northern Division were then the most radical in their social demands, and for a time they controlled the country and briefly occupied Mexico City. However, the two forces came to distrust one another; the Zapatistas' singular focus on land reform was not shared by many of the small ranch owners and land-owning elite pooled together in the Northern Division. They drifted apart, abandoning Mexico City for their regional spheres of influence.[71] Venustiano Carranza's "Constitutionalist" forces had retreated to the coasts, where they received protection and arms from the U.S. government through the Marines' occupation of Veracruz. U.S. landowners and business proprietors had become particularly worried that a rural social revolution might triumph in Mexico and result in the expropriation of their properties, thus they lobbied hard for the United States to intervene.[72]

In April, 1914, U.S. warships attacked and occupied Mexico's port of Veracruz. The U.S. intervention would enable a retreating Carranza to rearm and train before counterattacking the Zapatistas and Villistas.[73] Indeed, Carranza's armies, led by Álvaro Obregón, defeated the Northern Division and pushed back the Zapatistas in 1915. Obregón was already considered a "benefactor" of U.S. companies in Sonora during the first years of the Revolution, when he fought against indigenous and workers' rebellions.[74] Carranza began to issue decrees supporting the right to village lands, a concession to the widespread legitimacy of the rural uprisings across the country. Against Carranza's wishes, a majority of the delegates to the 1916 constitutional convention in Querétaro voted to include village land rights in the new constitution, creating Article 27.[75] The Constitution of 1917 also granted the right to form unions and strike, and severely limited the power of the Catholic Church, but it concentrated immense power in the executive, opening the door for a mafia-style, centralized state that could bend the words of the Constitution to its will.[76] When Carranza was elected in 1917, neither Villa nor Zapata put down their arms and accepted his government; instead they continued their guerrilla warfare pursuing social revolution. Though isolated and reduced in numbers, neither movement could be destroyed by military force. Thus Carranza's forces organized an ambush, using a false defector to assassinate Zapata on April 10, 1919.[77] An Obregón supporter assassinated Carranza a year later, and Villa was assassinated in 1923 during Obregón's presidency, possibly at the behest of the United States.[78]

In the words of historian Adolfo Gilly, the Mexican Revolution was "interrupted." The elite were able to claim national control over the masses—with the help of the U.S. Marines—but they could not hold power without making concessions. Gilly writes that the social revolutionary forces behind Generals Zapata and Villa did not triumph, but neither were they entirely defeated—or perhaps, their hunger was not defeated.[79]

During the ten years following Obregón's ascension to power political chaos prevailed: over 1,000 strikes at factories across the country; an unsuccessful rebellion in December 1923 against Obregón's chosen successor, Plutarco Elías Calles; an intense three-year rebellion led by the Catholic Church and supported by devout rural farmers, known as the Cristero Rebellion; and Obregón's assassination in 1928 after being "elected" to a second though nonconsecutive term.[80] To halt the unraveling of the precarious infant regime, Calles and his supporters formed the National Revolutionary Party (PNR), pulling military officers, regional political bosses, and rival parties into the fold.[81] The PNR finally solved the reelection conundrum: no single individual could be reelected for federal, state, or municipal office, but the party would be forever and everywhere reelected. The genius of the PNR—which would change its name twice, eventually settling on the Institutional Revolutionary Party, or PRI, and rule the nation for seven decades—was to claim to be the only legitimate party born of the Mexican Revolution. It consolidated ruling-class control using the aura of the blood sacrifices made by those who sought to do away with the tyranny and centralized authoritarianism of the ruling class under Porfirio Díaz. The man who made this possible—and who ironically is celebrated more by the Left whose growth he stunted, than by the Right whose flourishing he secured—was General Lázaro Cárdenas, true father of Mexican revolutionary nationalism, true genius behind the PRI's monopoly capitalism.

Cárdenas built, depended upon, and remained largely faithful to his alliances with organized labor and rural farmers. The support of these mass organizations protected his reform project from foreign, conservative, and cacique opposition and enabled him to displace Calles as the national cacique.[82] Cárdenas—who fought against Pancho Villa with the Constitutionalist forces—first courted the military, raising salaries and making promotions, and reached out to the conservative Catholics, appointing a pro-Catholic general to his cabinet as minister of agriculture. With the military and the Catholics appeased, it was his alliances with and co-opting of mass organizations that would cement his power. During the first year of Cárdenas's presidency strikes broke out against foreign companies across the country, and the General Confederation of Workers and Peasants of Mexico (CGOCM) coordinated a national general strike. Cárdenas, eager to assert his power over Calles, approved the CGOCM strike and set out to incorporate the labor movement into his own sphere of influence. Cárdenas officially recognized the CGOCM, which was renamed the Confederation of Mexican Workers (CTM), strategically excluding the "peasants" or rural farmers and the indigenous from the organization. Controlled by Lombardo Toledano, the CTM pulled together about 3,000 unions and 600,000 workers into its folds. The CTM would become the most powerful and brutally anti-worker labor union in the country, controlling labor contracts and the right to strike like political fiefdoms. The CTM would become the PRI's mechanism for exercising monopoly control over the labor movement, keeping it leashed to the needs and the will of the state.[83]

Cárdenas did not simply buy off movement leaders; he first convinced them with very real political actions, thus pulling them deeply into the arms of the state. He nationalized the railroads, created the Federal Electricity Commission, redistributed 17.9 million hectares of land to village *ejidos* (local agricultural land collectives) and other small holders, created the National Peasant Confederation (CNC)—and famously, brilliantly, on March 18, 1938, after two years of mounting strikes by oil workers that had been ignored by foreign companies, he nationalized oil, expropriating all non-Mexican-controlled oil fields.[84] After centuries of destruction and exploitation, Cárdenas's land, labor, and oil reforms made him the most popular president in Mexican history, a figure of popular reverence up there with Pancho Villa—whom he battled in the northern deserts of Chihuahua. Few seemed to notice and few seem to recall that his reforms cemented the subordination of popular movements to the state, which was itself controlled for seven decades by one party. Cárdenas's reforms sought to strengthen capitalism in Mexico and even the involvement of U.S. capitalism, but shrouded its development in "revolutionary" nationalist institutions.

While Cárdenas was a master at statecraft that made subordination look and feel like freedom, he did make a few enemies. On September 16, 1939, Manuel Gómez Morín and Efraín González Luna founded the National Action Party (PAN), pulling disgruntled Catholics, landowners, and businessmen into its embrace. Ten years later the PRI would recognize the PAN as a "legal" national party, and little by little, over the course of decades, the PRI would allow the PAN select electoral victories. Ever true to its highly conservative ideology and business-class makeup, the PAN would be the longest-running and loudest critic of the PRI's electoral machine—even denouncing occasional excessive acts of repression against protesters the PAN would have nothing to do with politically or socially—continually hammering away at the PRI's thick coat of revolutionary legitimacy.[85]

Between the end of Cárdenas's term in 1940 and the mid-1960s, when social protests once again erupted across the country, the PRI consolidated its unique power system and its ideology of revolutionary nationalism. And while serious strikes and uprisings challenged the state during this time, they were pale in comparison to the upheavals of the revolutionary era and would be outdone in number and scope by the armed and unarmed movements of the 1960s to the present day.[86] The PRI survived through creating dependence, buying off leaders, giving in just enough to avoid social explosions, and beating, jailing, and killing its opponents when necessary.

On October 2, 1968, the Mexican army planned and carried out a massacre of hundreds of high school and university students in Mexico City's Tlatelolco Plaza. The PRI steamrolled through public criticism and outcry for investigations. Controlling all three branches of government, they had no trouble remaining unaccountable to public scrutiny. But survivors' and reporters' accounts would seriously undermine their claim to legitimacy.[87] Perhaps because the victims of this massacre were urban and in many cases middle class, perhaps because they were all so young, perhaps because the bloodshed took place in the heart of the national capital in the presence of reporters, the Tlatelolco massacre has scarred Mexican history in a way that so many massacres of rural farmers, union workers, and indigenous people do not: Yet Tlatelolco was not then, and is not now, an isolated nor entirely unique act of repression.[88]

Only a year before, on August 20, 1967, police killed more than eighty copra* workers, injuring hundreds more, who had come together for a national labor union meeting in Acapulco.

* Copra is the dried meat of the coconut.

Few remember the date. That same year, state police opened fire on teachers and parents at a protest in the town square of Atoyac de Álvarez, northeast of Acapulco, killing five people. The leader of the teachers' movement, Lucio Cabañas, escaped and formed an armed self-defense force that evolved into the Party of the Poor (Partido de los Pobres), a guerrilla army that ambushed military and police convoys in the mountains and earned broad support in the region. The federal and state governments colluded to destroy Cabañas's army by unleashing an unprecedented counterinsurgency war in nearby rural villages. Thousands of people were rounded up, interrogated, beaten, raped, and tortured. The large numbers of non-Spanish-speaking indigenous people frustrated the army's intelligence gathering and often led to brutal torture sessions with interrogators demanding answers to questions that the torture victim could not even understand. Over 400 people were "disappeared" between 1967 and 1974, when the army finally deployed tens of thousands of soldiers to slowly encircle and kill Cabañas and his rag-and-bone army.[89]

Throughout the 1970s as the Mexican economy staggered, the state rode blind to the early warning signs of a mounting crisis, and the underdogs continued organizing. Rural and urban guerrilla movements formed, though the army sought them out and assassinated most participants.[90] Squatters in Mexico's cities formed neighborhood fronts to demand legalization of their settlements and government provision of services.[91] Workers organized independent labor unions to challenge the state collusion and boss rule that dominated the PRI-sanctioned unions.[92] Feminist movements surged, organizing protests, forging coalitions, and directly challenging the government.[93] But it was neither a strike nor a sit-in nor an armed guerrilla attack that would deliver the next devastating blow to the heart of the PRI: it was the working-class folk taking to the streets in an attempt to save lives and recover dead bodies after the 1985 Mexico City earthquake. Measuring 8.1 on the Richter scale, the force of the temblor that hammered Mexico City at 7:19 a.m. on September 19, 1985, caused buildings, houses, and hospitals to crumble to the ground. With thousands of people trapped in the rubble, a second quake hit at 7:38 p.m., measuring 6.5 on the Richter scale.[94]

The PRI froze. City and federal officials either could not or would not act to organize emergency rescue and relief operations. "All of a sudden we were in a city without a government," said one resident who had sought government help and then quickly moved to mount rescue and relief actions with other residents.[95] One of the first government measures was to order the army into the streets to begin the almost immediate bulldozing of ruined buildings. But the residents refused. Students from the National Autonomous University of Mexico (UNAM) and other volunteer rescuers blocked government bulldozers with their bodies to carry out their rescue efforts. Two days *after* the government had ordered the fallen pavilion of Juárez Hospital to be leveled, students and volunteers pulled one 23-year-old medical student and eight infants—all still alive—from the wreckage.[96] The spontaneous cohesion of earthquake survivors into neighborhood groups to seek and aid other survivors trapped in the fallen buildings evolved into citywide organizations that would fight the government for years to come over the need for housing projects to accommodate the thousands left homeless. It also gave the participants in urban movements an extra edge of courage in confronting the state, for they had seen that in a moment of disaster, when the strength of the PRI had vanished, the people's unity and organization enabled them to pull survivors from the debris and save lives.[97] Riding this wave of independent strength, coupled with disdain for the ruling party, a dissident faction that split off from the PRI accomplished the seemingly impossible: it won a presidential election by actually having more people vote for its candidate. But although the dissidents did win more votes, in the end, that did not matter.

Cuauhtémoc Cárdenas, son of the beloved ex-president General Lazaro Cárdenas, had become involved in the PRI through the party's rural arm, the CNC, in 1966 and worked his way up to an appointment to the Mexican Senate in 1976 and election as governor of Michoacán in 1980. During his career in the PRI, Cárdenas did not protest government massacres of workers, farmers, or students, but President Miguel de la Madrid's wave of privatizations and corresponding technocratic turn stimulated him to voice opposition. His father's son, Cárdenas sensed, it seems, that the economic policies of the technocrats—following the call by the International Monetary Fund and U.S. big business call to strip away public institutions and replace them bit by bit with private, corporate activity—would upset the delicate balance that enabled the PRI's state monopoly. In 1986, Cárdenas and a few other PRI operatives formed a "democratic current" within the party, though the PRI's president would not officially recognize the faction. The CNC expressed solidarity, while the PRI-controlled union, CTM, attacked Cárdenas for fomenting divisions in the party. Cárdenas fought with the party leadership but at the same time campaigned to be nominated on the PRI ticket as presidential candidate for the 1988 elections. De la Madrid instead chose a devoted technocrat follower, Carlos Salinas de Gortari, and Cárdenas quickly registered his candidacy with the tiny, centrist Party of the Authentic Mexican Revolution (PARM) and created an umbrella organization—the National Democratic Front—to draw Left parties and political organizations into his campaign.[98]

Cárdenas's campaign—authentic or ruse—pulled in hundreds of thousands of people, especially rural farmers who had received village lands from his father's recognition of the *ejido* communal land system and Mexico City underdogs who had mobilized and formed organizations after the earthquake. Cárdenas's campaign provided a way to express discontent and rage toward the PRI. And Cárdenas won on July 6, 1988. But, of course, he could not win. Through electoral fraud, the PRI secured Carlos Salinas's "victory."[99] Protesters by the hundreds of thousands took to the streets, many willing to come to blows to defend their votes, but Cárdenas urged restraint and perseverance. Salinas took office amid exuberant military pomp and ceremony. Cárdenas formed a new party, the Party of the Democratic Revolution (PRD), was elected mayor of Mexico City, then went on to get legitimately defeated in two more presidential elections (1994 and 2000).

Salinas moved quickly. He set out to consolidate the power transfer to the technocrats within the PRI and to build the muscularity of his own presidency to proportions not seen since the days of Porfirio Díaz and Lázaro Cárdenas. He brutally repressed the social movements that had supported Cárdenas as well as the PRD—some 280 PRD activists were gunned down or "disappeared" during Salinas's tenure.[100] But Salinas's true legacy, the emblem of his entire project of state power and the coalescence of his various strains of brutality, was the North American Free Trade Agreement (NAFTA). And with the birth of NAFTA—the maximum expression of new forms of conquest—from the last corner of the nation would also surge the deepest manifestation of new forms of resistance, the Zapatista Army of National Liberation, EZLN.

2

THE RULE OF LAW

In the name of the "Rule of Law" they impose economic measures, they assassinate, they imprison, they rape, they destroy, they persecute, they make war.

—Subcomandante Marcos

In the helicopter is where they began to beat us. The soldiers said that this would take the whore out of us, that we were going to hell, that they were the law.

—Sara

IN WHAT APPEARS TO BE BLOOD, the poster board sign reads: "This happened to me for making an anonymous call to the authorities: and they were the very ones who did it."[1] And this is what the sign refers to: a person's body lies twisted on the blood-soaked dirt, the sign covering half of the back, shoulders, and the place where the head should be; the ankles are handcuffed together, feet lying sideways, one shoe off, the other half on, in a pool of deep red. It is not only a message of death, of violent death, but a performance, a spectacle of bodily destruction. We cannot know what that person lived through, what he felt, during his last moments. But the message is clear: drug lords are the authority because they can do this to you, and because those on their payroll answer the phone when you call the police.[2]

Another image, this one published on the front pages of newspapers across Mexico on April 21, 2006. On top of a shoulder-high, white stone wall with the words "State Government" painted in blue, there are two severed heads and an orange poster-board sign that reads, in curly handwriting: "So that you learn some respect."[3] One of the heads lies sideways in a small pool of blood behind the white metal rail design on top of the wall. The other head is upright on that metal grating, facing the camera lens, with two trails of blood traveling down the white paint. The heads and the sign lie just above and below, respectively, the word "Government." The heads belonged to two police officers, one a commander named Mario Núñez Magaña. This commander had participated in a gunfight with presumed drug traffickers from the Sinaloa Cartel on January 27, 2006. Local police killed four of the presumed cartel members that day. The shootout took place only a few feet away from the Guerrero State Treasury Building in Acapulco, where the severed heads were discovered in the predawn hours of Friday, April 21, 2006. Police found the two decapitated bodies later that morning on the side of a road, bundled in green and blue packages. Here too the message was not just the threat of death, but of torture, the complete and calculated destruction of one's body. The message is also dense with subtext: the government might talk bad about drugs and drug traffickers all it wants, but if they attack us, we will obliterate them.

Such photographs, widely published in Mexico's national and local press, are not isolated or rare. While the case of the Acapulco police officers was sensational, drug-related executions have become a daily affair in Mexico. Drug violence claimed the lives of more than 3,000 people during Vicente Fox's six-year term in office (2000–2006).[4] Only a few days after his inauguration on December 1, 2006, President Felipe Calderón mobilized over 20,000 federal troops to battle the wave of murders. With that gesture, the already high number of executions tripled—and began to reach higher and higher into the echelons of government, targeting local, state, and federal police chiefs and prosecutors. During Calderón's first six months in office, organized crime assassins executed 1,455 people, an all-time high of eight executions per day on average.[5] And while the gory photographs somehow magically disappeared from the front pages in July 2007, the executions continued. By the end of the year, drug trade assassins had executed 2,794 people.[6]

Drug trafficking from Mexico into the United States, at its current level, is largely a by-product of the U.S. war on drugs in Colombia during the 1980s, that and the U.S. people's insatiable desire to get high.[7] With the United States thwarting Colombian cartels that delivered cocaine into the country directly, Mexican cartels have jumped in to fill the gap, establishing connections with the Colombian cartels to receive and move their cocaine along with Mexican-grown heroin and marijuana. In the 1980s, Miguel Ángel Félix Gallardo emerged as the "boss of bosses," controlling a loose country-wide federation of drug traffickers.[8] Taken prisoner in 1989, Félix Gallardo relinquished power and divided up the national territory between various local bosses, a city for each.[9] But the agreement did not last long; soon rival bosses sought to destroy each other and gain control of the various routes necessary for moving Colombian cocaine and Mexican marijuana, heroin, and methamphetamines into the United States. The killings then began to escalate, and with the killings, the increased involvement of politicians and police from the lowest to the highest levels of government.[10]

Mexican police and government officials have participated in drug trafficking for decades, but the nature and extent of their participation changed in the 1990s, evolving from protection and the turning of blind eyes to direct participation in executions.[11] Soldiers under the command of General Jesús Gutiérrez Rebollo carried out executions and kidnappings against the Tijuana Cartel, and the general received perks from the Juárez Cartel. Between 1997 and 1999, scores of elite anti-drug Special Forces officers—many of whom received training from the U.S. military—abandoned the army to form an armed wing for the Gulf Cartel known as Los Zetas, the Zs.[12] According to Mexican government sources, between 1996 and 2001, an average of forty-six soldiers a day deserted the army, a total of 99,767.[13] Official involvement in drug trafficking reaches high into the government, implicating multiple army generals and even extends into the office of the president himself: one of Vicente Fox's schedulers, Nahúm Acosta, was a spy for the Juárez Cartel.[14]

The idea of corruption implies an aberration—someone breaking the rules to feed their own private greed. When activities thought of as corrupt become so prevalent in a government that it is impossible to speak of an institution free of them, when corruption ceases to be an aberration and becomes an integral part of the system, it is then no longer accurate to speak of corruption as such.

The idea of corruption is, oddly enough, a tactic to save legitimacy, to stifle and channel moral outrage against the theft and violence of those politicians whose deeds are made public. It is not that Mexico is a narco state controlled by men who don mink coats and emerald necklaces, but rather that the participation of police, military, and government officials in drug-trafficking networks has been so extensive and so persistent over time that the idea of corruption ceases to hold descriptive power. Drug trafficking in Mexico is a massive business, turning over around $30 billion a year. A 2007 U.S. government study found that Mexican drug cartels earn about $23 billion in revenue, making illegal drugs Mexico's num-

ber-one export, bringing in more money than either oil or the
remittances sent home by Mexicans living in the United
States.[15] A study by the Mexican government found that the
country's economy would shrink by 63 percent if the drug
business were to disappear.[16] Mexico is the largest foreign
supplier of marijuana and methamphetamines to the United
States and is responsible for 70 to 90 percent of all the
cocaine that enters the country.[17] The fact that drugs and
their international transport are illegal is simply one of the
market factors. Illegality increases risk, and risk justifies high
prices. The cost of illegality—not all that different in kind
from a corporation's advertising budget—is the maintenance
of the public appearance of official opposition: the commer-
cials, the speeches, the special new police units, the
helicopters, the drug-sniffing dogs, the occasional arrests.
Meanwhile, the real battle is for control of the drug routes,
and police and military training and hardware all filter into
use in the service of one or another cartel. The scale of drug
violence and government collusion leads some analysts to
conclude that "the viability of the Mexican State is now at
risk."[18] But no, it is not that the state is at risk, but rather that
its true nature is exposed.

Cocaine, marijuana, heroin, and methamphetamines are
illegal both in Mexico and the United States. But carrying
these drugs from Mexico, or any other country, into the United
States is *very* illegal. So illegal, in fact, that drug trafficking
inspired first the United States and later Mexico to declare a
"war on drugs"—a war waged not only along the U.S.-Mexico
border but thousands of miles away from it as well, a war with
a multibillion-dollar budget, advanced military technology, and
a vast collection of federal armies and militarized police forces
in multiple countries.[19] Drug trafficking has ceased to be a matter of crime that requires police maneuvers to stop it. No, drug

trafficking so gravely offends the integrity of the state, the politicians say, that it requires nothing short of war. Of all the threats to the state in Mexico, there is really nothing so demonized, so dreaded and despised in the public discourse of politicians, as drug trafficking. And yet, in Mexico, drug trafficking on its present scale is only made possible through the active participation of government employees, elected politicians, army generals and commandos, police chiefs and patrol officers, prison guards, and local and federal judges by protecting one set of drug traffickers from another and, importantly, from incarceration. That is, a portion of the state—not just a few "bad apples" but a deep and extensive network of government employees—aids and abets the greatest proclaimed threat to its integrity; government employees protect the most wanted criminals from the law while at the same time carrying out a war against these criminals and even against the members of the state who get caught with them.[20] In one of the most shining examples of this curious schizophrenia of the state, Mexico's first ever antidrug czar, the same General Jesús Gutiérrez Rebollo mentioned above, was on the payroll of one of Mexico's biggest drug traffickers, Amado Carrillo Fuentes, a.k.a. The Lord of the Skies.[21]

The law exists primarily in three interacting realms: written law, practiced law as interpreted by the rulings and actions of the political class, and perceived law—the perception of legitimacy or illegitimacy in broader society. Written law consists of federal and state constitutions and the volumes of local, state, and federal codes that are all written by the political class—though their content may be disputed and altered by forces outside the ruling powers. Written law is presented as *the* law, but words on paper do not pull triggers or lock prison cells. Without people to interpret and enforce it, written laws have no more sway than poetry anthologies. Those who wield the authority to interpret and enforce the law are the ones who make it real. Police officers, soldiers, judges, and those to whom they owe allegiance and/or favors make the law real. In Mexico, though the idea of democracy has been clumsily paraded through society since before the Revolution of 1910–1920, a small political class has always run the country, written its laws, and governed their enforcement. The laws were meant to cement forms of class control, and at times to strengthen the perceived legitimacy of the rule of law. The idea of the rule of law—that impartial laws govern society and enforce social order—is the ideological underpinning of the contemporary Mexican state, the discourse used to legitimize its actions. The ideology of the rule of law masks, or is meant to mask, the fact of class rule.

LATE AT NIGHT AFTER THE MURDER of PRI presidential candidate Luis Colosio on March 23, 1994, *New Yorker* reporter Alma Guillermoprieto—a Mexican who has reported for decades from across Latin America and written some of the most elegant prose in English about the region—called up a "wealthy businessman and PRI member" who, Guillermoprieto informs her readers, "is close to the ruling circle of technocrats."[22] "At last," she writes, "my friend was speaking frankly, his reserve—like the national myths—undone by Colosio's murder."[23] In just over 100 words, quoted in Guillermoprieto's article, the "wealthy businessman and PRI member, . . . speaking frankly," provided a rare glimpse into the ideology of the Rule of Law in Mexico.

Here is what Guillermoprieto offers of her friend's comments from their phone conversation that night:

> This country does not obey the law, it obeys author-
> ity. And authority disappeared in Mexico as of the first

of January [1994]. It's time for the president to act like a man and grab the bull by the horns, so that all the people, the opposition, and all the sons of bitches who are wandering loose out there, know that there's a rule of law here. If the government sits down to bargain with a handful of bastards wearing ski-masks, there's no law—there's only an atmosphere in which anyone can feel free to do whatever he fucking pleases, and you get disasters like this.[24]

In a striking admission, the rich PRI businessman tells his friend that in Mexico, the law and the "rule of law" are not the same. "This country does not obey the law," he says, and the remedy is precisely for the president "to act like a man" so that there can be "a rule of law here." The law does not work in Mexico; it does not keep the rabble from provoking national disasters. Mexico "obeys authority," not the law. Thus, according to him, the "rule of law" has nothing to do with the integrity of political institutions, due process guarantees, or checks and balances between the branches of government— no, the "rule of law," in Mexico, is the exercise of authority.

And what is the nature of this exercise of authority that the country and the "sons of bitches wandering loose out there" obey? Authority implies a complex web of social relations of domination; a threat at any location can jeopardize the entire web. In the political realm governed by authority, there is no space for social protest. Questioning authority—which simply means questioning the rule of the political class, then mostly concentrated in the PRI—is tantamount to chaos and disaster. Authority is the violent exercise of power, and it is the exclusive property of the political class.

The law itself is not good enough, for the law alone implies open participation. Anyone can study law and become a lawyer or judge, and in theory anyone can run for legislative office and write new laws. The law, if abstracted from a strict system of class control, could provide "the sons of bitches" and the "bastards wearing ski masks" with the tools to advance their own interests, such as defending their land. The law alone will not do, which is why the wealthy PRI member distinguishes law from rule of law. The emphasis here is really on "rule." The law is the mechanism with which the political class exercises its rule. Without appealing to a hereditary or divine right to rule, and without going so far as openly declaring military rule, it uses the rule of law is a kind of ideological middle ground. Justice is anchored in the law, but only authority may interpret and exercise the law, and hence administer justice. When Guillermprieto's friend says that Mexico "does not obey the law, it obeys authority," his statement is prescriptive rather than descriptive. He is not revealing his view of how things work so much as how things are meant to work.

In Luis Estrada's brilliant film, the 1999 political satire *La ley de Herodes* (Herod's Law), a seasoned PRI politician sends Juan Vargas, a low-level PRI functionary who deeply believes in the PRI's mission to bring Mexico "modernity and social peace," to the troubled village of San Pedro de los Saguaros— where locals recently decapitated the last mayor as he attempted to flee the village hefting a suitcase stuffed with cash.[25] Vargas and his wife arrive in the mostly indigenous hamlet to find villagers shouting about local land conflicts, a PAN doctor threatening to ruin Vargas if he doesn't shut down the brothel on the outskirts of town, and the brothel's owner answering Vargas's demand to close her business with the choice of a bribe or a machete blade. Vargas goes back to the state capital within just a few days asking his mentor first for some kind of a budget to work with, hoping to build a school as a first step toward bringing modernity to San Pedro and assuaging his critics. Vargas's boss tells him that all state resources are going into the PRI's electoral campaigns; there are no funds for schools. Distraught, Vargas then asks for some advice. The PRI politician—the second-highest in command in the unidentified state—pulls from his office bookshelf a dust-ridden compendium of Mexican law and places it on his desk. He then opens his desk drawer and chooses a revolver from among three pistols and places it on the book: "With this little book and the pistol, you're off to exercise authority," the politician advises.[26] The camera rests for a moment on the visual metaphor of the pistol lying on the law book. With the gun Vargas manages to turn the law into the rule of law. By threatening, bribing, and executing his enemies, Vargas is able to amass a significant fortune from both the destitute villagers and the local elite in San Pedro. He shoots the brothel owner and her bodyguard, tortures the town drunk into confessing to the crime, and then, instead of closing the brothel down and freeing the women trapped there, takes it over and becomes the new owner. The law text and the pistol in the hands of authority: this is the rule of law.

"IN THE HELICOPTER is where they began to beat us," Sara Méndez, a 17-year-old who had just been released after a week in military detention, told me. "They threw me really hard into the helicopter," she said. "They kicked me all over my body. Then one got on top of me; I could hear the other girls screaming. The soldiers said that this would take the whore out of us, that we were going to hell, that they were the law." Sara, three other girls ages 16 and 17, and Carmela Martínez, a 32-year-old woman who owns a restaurant where two of the girls worked as waitresses, were all hooded with their hands tied behind their backs on the floor of the military helicopter when the soldiers began to undress them.[27] "They kicked me, they bound my hands so tight that my blood could barely circulate. That day a friend and I were wearing miniskirts, and they raised them up, they lowered our underwear and they were touching us," she said. Two of the girls told members of the governmental National Human Rights Commission that during the helicopter ride, after being threatened, beaten, and molested, the soldiers placed warm rags over their mouths causing them to lose consciousness. One girl awoke with vaginal pain and bleeding.

On May 1, 2007, a drug gang was driving down the only paved road in the tiny town of Carácuaro, Michoacán—home of the hero of Mexican independence José María Morelos—when a group of soldiers in civilian clothes apparently backed into their truck, causing a minor fender bender that erupted into a gun battle lasting over twenty minutes. Locals ran for cover and the town police stayed indoors, everyone thinking it a gunfight between two rival gangs. Five soldiers, including a colonel, died, and three more were wounded. One member of the gang was killed; the rest escaped. Within hours, the army mobilized over 1,000 soldiers to comb the Tierra Caliente region of Michoacán looking for the killers. The army raided houses in Carácuaro, neighboring Nocupétaro, and surrounding villages. Soldiers beat, detained, and tortured dozens of rural farmers who had the misfortune of sharing one of the same last names as the dead gang member. The National Human Rights Commission gathered more than fifty complaints of human rights violations during the army's operation around Carácuaro. It was during these roundups that, on Tuesday, May 2, 2007, the army detained Sara and her friends.

Sara's lot has been a hard one. She left school in the middle of fifth grade to follow her parents in search of work in Chicago. She had her first child there at age 11 and moved back to Michoacán with the 16-year-old father soon after. Then, after she gave birth to her second child the father left, and she was forced to look for work. A single mother of two at age 14, she became a waitress in a restaurant owned by Carmela Martínez, that the Mexican Army now claims was a cover for prostitution. But Sara had left that job more than a year earlier and had moved to Cuernavaca with her new husband. She was back visiting family and had gone to say goodbye to Carmela Martínez at her house when the army stormed the town. Police with close connections to the army said that Sara and her friends were "connected to the Zetas," a notorious gang of assassins working for the Gulf Cartel and created by ex–Special Forces from the Mexican Army. One police official told the Mexican national newspaper *El Milenio*: "No, look, these girls even have kids and like to party. I don't think the soldiers raped them; I'm sure they just grabbed them in a few places, just a couple of touches here and there, but no rape—they were even ugly." Sara said she didn't know anything about the Zetas or the clash between soldiers and a drug gang. She had just come to visit from Cuernavaca and was set to leave the next day. After her detention, she said she did not know what to do or where to go, because one thing the soldiers told her haunted her. "They said that if the Zetas don't kill me then they would." Now she does not know whom to fear more, the soldiers or the drug traffickers, she said.

The day after soldiers detained Sara and her friends, they moved on to the nearby village of Las Guacamayas. Soldiers arrived in seventeen trucks and three helicopters, all because the last name of many of the villagers here matched the last name of one of the drug traffickers killed in the shootout with the army in Carácuaro. The village is a collection of twenty houses spread on either side of a single dirt road. There are no stores, schools, or hospitals. Surrounded by dry earth and cornfields, the residents of Las Guacamayas live in adobe and concrete houses. María's family's house has only one wall, a dirt floor, and a corrugated tin roof held up by branches and adobe brick columns. They have electricity and one small TV set, but they cook in an adobe oven and on a cast-iron *comal* (hand skillet) suspended over a wood fire.

On May 3, 2007, soldiers with machine guns drawn approached everyone in the village, first asking for their full names. All those with the last name Mondragón were immediately beaten to the ground, taken to María's house by the road, laid facedown in the scorching earth, and then one by one beaten again, burned with cigarette lighters, and interrogated about the Carácuaro shootout. "A 2-year-old girl tried to get up, and a soldier put a gun to her head," María told me. Over a week later, Pedro Mondragón still had burn marks on his back, a huge scab and swelling on his right knee and throat pain where a soldier had rammed his machine gun barrel in his mouth. "I was eating when they arrived and asked me my name. I told them and they said, 'Ah, you son of a bitch, you are the very one we're looking for,'" Pedro told me. One soldier then stuck his machine gun barrel down his throat, forced him to the ground and beat his face and body. He was bleeding badly, he said. The soldiers then took ten villagers off in helicopters to the military base near Morelia; nine of them with the last name Mondragón. "There in the base they treated us real bad," Pedro said, referring to unrelenting beatings. "They asked, 'Why did you kill them?' We had no idea what they were talking about," he said. One soldier pointed to the bloody right side of Pedro's face and told him: "On this side I am not going to hit you anymore, but this other side is free game." After the interrogation sessions, the soldiers gathered all the detainees from Las Guacamayas and other villages in one room and told them that they had found two kilograms of marijuana in their village and wanted the seventeen of them to agree on whom to blame for it, that is, to choose one person to take the fall. But the villagers said no. One official from the Federal Agency of Investigation (AFI) beat many of them to try and force them to comply. In the room where the soldiers beat and tortured them was a sign on the wall saying torture was against the law. But in Las Guacamayas the soldiers had told the complaining villagers, just as they told Sara and her friends, that they were the law.[28]

DRUG TRAFFICKING IN MEXICO OFFERS a particularly evocative vantage point from which to reflect on the ideology of the rule of law, but not the only one. The violence of authority necessary to uphold class rule is built into the Mexican legal system, woven into the very fabric of Mexican governance. Human rights documents offer a vast and rich territory for exploration in this regard. In their detailed reports and analyses human rights organizations consistently point out and decry the various points where the pistol overrides the letter of Mexican law. But these organizations never really investigate why this happens. To do so would lead them to condemn the legitimacy of the ideology of the rule of law, and these organizations are, for the most part, firmly committed to this ideology.[29] Hence, they blindly consider the systematic human rights violations as aberrations rather than defining characteristics of the Mexican state. Let us take a look at the conclusions of the two largest and most frequently quoted international organizations: Amnesty International and Human Rights Watch.

First an excerpt from the Mexico chapter of Human Rights Watch's 2007 *World Report*:

Among Mexico's most serious human rights problems are those affecting its criminal justice system. Persons under arrest or imprisonment face torture and ill-treatment, and law enforcement officials often neglect to investigate and prosecute those responsible for human rights violations. . . . Mexican police forces routinely employ excessive force when carrying out crowd-control operations. . . . Torture remains a widespread problem within the Mexican criminal justice system. One perpetuating factor of the practice is the acceptance by some judges of evidence obtained through torture and other mistreatment. Another is the failure to investigate and prosecute most cases of torture. Over 40 percent of prisoners in Mexico have never been convicted of a crime. Rather, they are held in pretrial detention, often waiting years for trial. . . . The criminal justice system routinely fails to provide justice to victims of violent crime and human rights abuses. The causes of this failure are varied and include corruption, inadequate training and resources, and a lack of political will. . . . A major shortcoming of the Mexican justice system is that it leaves the task of investigating and prosecuting army abuses to military authorities. The military justice system is ill-equipped for such tasks. It lacks the independence necessary to carry out reliable investigations and its operations suffer from a general absence of transparency.[30]

Human Rights Watch is telling us that, according to their truly exhaustive research, they have come to the conclusion that in Mexico the authorities may arrest, beat, torture, and hold in prison whomever they want, whenever they want, however they want. Human Rights Watch ventures that the criminal justice system "routinely fails to provide justice to victims of violent crime and human rights abuses," and, in a striking phrase, allows that the causes of this failure include "a lack of political will."

Amnesty International, in slightly less staid language, comes to basically the same conclusion as Human Rights Watch. Here are two excerpts from reports published in 2003 and 2007, both specifically on human rights in Mexico:

> Torture is the most flagrant in a chain of abuses committed against many individuals caught up in the Mexican criminal justice system. From the moment an individual is arbitrarily detained to his or her conviction on the basis of a confession obtained under torture, fair trial procedures that conform to international standards ratified by the Mexican Government are routinely and consistently undermined. Such injustice is compounded by the fact that the judicial mechanisms to enable individuals to seek an effective remedy and challenge a conviction on the grounds that the confession was coerced are limited and in practice, woefully inadequate. At the same time, the impunity afforded to those responsible for torture and ill-treatment remains the norm. . . . All branches of Mexico's various police forces, whether federal, state or municipal, regularly resort to torture or ill-treatment as a method of policing or crime prevention. . . . In addition, the increasing role of the armed forces in combating drug trafficking and armed opposition groups has resulted in soldiers—either acting on their own or in joint operations with federal and state-level police—illegally detaining and sometimes torturing or ill-treating detainees to obtain confessions or infor-

mation. Increasingly, torture is also used as a means of extorting money, to intimidate perceived criminal suspects or to serve the direct criminal interests of corrupt police officials.[31]

Amnesty International continues to document cases of arbitrary detention, torture, ill-treatment, denial of due process rights and unfair trials, particularly at state level. The human rights abuses that occur in the public security and criminal justice systems are not primarily due to lack of resources. As evidenced in this report, the inadequate legal recognition of international human rights standards, the widespread failure to enforce existing legislation and continuing political interference in the administration of justice, prevent full respect for human rights across the country. Furthermore, deficient accountability mechanisms result in widespread impunity for those responsible for human rights abuses.[32]

Again: arbitrary detention, systematic use of torture by *all levels* of police and the armed forces, and total impunity for officials. Can such widespread and enduring practices be considered irregularities in the system? No. They *are* the system. In the 2007 report "Mexico: Laws without Justice: Human Rights Violations and Impunity in the Public Security and Criminal Justice System," Amnesty International writes, "There is a wide gap between legal principle and the reality of those who come into contact with the law."[33] In other words, the actions of the authorities bear little relation to the legal codes; they use violence as they please, regardless of the law. Amnesty International also notes that "victims of these violations disproportionately come from the poorest and most marginalized sectors of society—members of indigenous communities, peasant farmers, women, children, migrants and socially excluded urban communities." The systematic use of arbitrary detentions, torture, sexual violence, and executions is designed to maintain class control; these are not "violations" of the law—or human rights—they are the law made real through practice: real and symbolic violence meant to crush resistance to exploitation and reproduce authority across the national territory.[34]

Take the case of torture. Torture is the desperate attempt of authority to play out its social and political quest for domination of individuals perceived as their enemies. I say desperate because the act of torture violates the principles that authority claims to defend in its public discourse. Thus the private, hidden recourse to torture illustrates above all else the fractured legitimacy and resulting violent desperation of authority. The continued use of torture as a standard technique in the exercise of state authority follows a consistent pattern: when the legitimacy of a faltering power is directly challenged by an opposition movement with broad public support, authorities of the state torture anyone suspected of participating in the opposition. Edward Peters, in his history of torture, links the practice of torture to the "colonial experience" and the nature of the modern state with its combination of accumulated power over vast territories and particular vulnerability to internal threats to its legitimacy.[35]

Torture is more than coercion by inflicting physical and psychological pain on a person under the pretext of extracting information. Torture is a tactic of state power. Herbert C. Kelman—professor emeritus at Harvard and coauthor with Lee Hamilton of the groundbreaking study *Crimes of Obedience: Toward a Social Psychology of Authority and Responsibility*—writes, "The essential phenomenon of torture . . . is that it is not an ordinary crime, but a crime of obedience: a crime that takes place not in opposition to the authorities, but under explicit instructions from the authorities to engage in acts of torture, or in an environment in which such acts are implicitly sponsored, expected, or at least tolerated by the authorities."[36] Torture is not an aberration within a system, but an integral part of a system. Kelman again:

> The conditions conducive to the rise of torture as an instrument of State policy are the authorities' perception of an active threat to the security of the State from internal and external sources; the availability of a security apparatus, which enables the authorities to use the vast power at their disposal to counter that threat by repressive means; and the presence within the society of groups defined as enemies of or potential threats to the State. . . . The recourse to repression is particularly likely in situations in which opposition represents a challenge to the legitimacy of those in power and thus a fundamental threat to their continued ability to maintain power, such as States in which the rulers' *legitimacy* rests on a unitary, unchangeable ideology (political or religious), or States run by a ruling clique with an extremely narrow population base (in socio-economic and/or ethnic terms) but with the support of military forces.[37]

The two key points of Kelman's analysis are, first, to understand torture as "an instrument of State policy" directly sanctioned by authorities, and second, to see the authorities' justification for the use of torture as a defense against perceived threats to their legitimacy

Elaine Scarry, in her remarkable book *The Body in Pain: The Making and Unmaking of the World*, defines torture as "the conversion of absolute pain into the fiction of absolute power."[38] Here the physical act—inflicting pain on a defenseless person—and the verbal act—the interrogation—combine to form a "grotesque piece of compensatory drama" the purpose of which is "the production of a fantastic illusion of power."[39] The interrogation is neither the true motive nor the true goal of torture. The information obtained is secondary to the fact of breaking the will of the prisoner.[40] Rare are the documented cases where tortured prisoners actually had information useful to the state's intelligence desires, but the key here is the very nature of the state's intelligence desires, namely the drive to crush any perceived threat to its legitimacy.

In Mexico, torture is an everyday affair. Even though Mexico has both signed and ratified the United Nations Convention Against Torture and other Cruel, Inhuman, or Degrading Treatment or Punishment, torture is built into the way law is actually practiced.[41] Judges give confessions extracted under torture greater evidentiary weight than a prisoner's testimony or even *physical proof* of torture, such as court-certified medical studies.[42] In fact, Mexican courts have decided that a confession obtained under torture may be admissible in trial if that confession is "corroborated by other evidence."[43] Human Right Watch calls torture Mexico's "open secret."[44] Half of the Mexican federal and state doctors interviewed by Physicians for Human Rights in 2003 said that torture was a major problem in Mexico.[45] Mexico's own National Human Rights Commission acknowledges that torture is common practice in the country.[46] Even the U.S. State Department wrote in their 2006 country report on Mexico: "Although the law prohibits such practices, they persisted, and torture in particular continued to be a serious problem. . . . Authorities continued to use torture with near impunity in large part because confessions were the primary evidence in many criminal convictions."[47] It is a mistake however, to believe that torture is so deeply woven into the Mexican legal system and police practices simply because it makes a lazy interrogator's job easier, eliminating the need to investigate and find out who really may have committed the crime, because they can just assault someone into confessing.[48]

Torture is endemic to Mexico precisely because the practice of law is founded on the violence of authority, thus people constantly challenge the state's legitimacy. Soldiers tortured farmers when looking for drug traffickers. Police tortured bus drivers to create convictions and thus the semblance of justice in Ciudad Juárez. Oaxaca state police tortured volunteers at a protester-controlled university radio station as part of a campaign of state terrorism. Mexico state police tortured prisoners from Atenco during the drive to prison, raping women in the buses filled with prisoners. But even in the most banal of cases, where police literally pull some random person off the street and torture them into confessing to a nonpolitical crime, the practice of torture can be seen as an attempt to consolidate the legitimacy of the rule of law through the projection of "absolute power."[49]

"THIS DRIVER IS REALLY GOOD," says the father as his right hand seeks for signs of life over his son's motionless shoulder.

There are eight people in the taxi van: the driver and a journalist in the front, and in the back two pallid journalists, the father and son, and two men who hold the son's body in place, stretched out on the long bench like seat directly behind the driver. The two men take care that the son's limbs don't fall off the seat, that his head, now wrapped in blood-soaked bandages, does not bump against the seat or walls.

The taxi van travels at astounding speed, more like a

motorboat on some wide river than an old Volkswagen on the Texcoco–Mexico City highway at 5:00 p.m. The father is right: the driver is amazing. The father maintains an equally astounding control. He does not scream or cry, he does not lose himself in the desperation attacking him implacably. It seems as if he does not realize it, but every five or six seconds his face contracts and his head leans violently to the left. His body shows the brutal impact of having watched his son bleed into a makeshift bandage, stretched out on a concrete floor, trapped inside a tiny house with more than thirty people for nearly eleven hours. The father keeps speaking, his voice does not waver or crack, but his body cannot take it anymore.

"I only hope he makes it to the hospital alive, that my son can make it to the hospital. Do you think he can? Can we make it there in time? I can't believe how good this driver is! Just make it to the hospital. How is he doing? Is he going to make it? Will we get there in time?"

A cell phone is ringing. I hear the sound, but do not assign to it an origin or meaning. The taxi van continues its strangely fluid journey through the grinding chaos of the highway. We wind through vehicles like a star athlete dodging opponents; we dip into oncoming traffic just for a second to pass someone; we veer over to the other edge of the highway, drive along the shoulder, come to a stop only when a red light coincides with an impenetrable current of traffic. The phone keeps ringing.

"Answer it," the father says to me.

It is my phone that is ringing; I fumble for it in my pockets, pull it out and answer. It is the radio program *Flashpoints* from KPFA in California. They want to interview me live about what is happening in San Salvador Atenco. I cover the phone with my hand and tell the father this, as if to ask if it is okay that I speak.

"Talk, yes. Tell them what you are seeing here"—he motions to his son's slender, motionless body, arms without strength, bandages soaked with blood—"tell them what you saw in Atenco, what the riot police did. Tell them; let them know so that the word can get out. But please, don't mention our names; his mother still does not know what has happened."

On May 3, 2006, the Day of the Cross, about forty outdoor flower vendors arrived before dawn at the Belisario Domínguez Market in Texcoco, twenty miles or so outside of Mexico City, to find the market surrounded by 200 riot police.[50] The police were there to back a local cacique, Alejandra Rodríguez Mendoza, in her efforts to evict flower vendors associated with the People's Front in Defense of Land (who had defeated the illegal expropriation of their lands for a federal airport project in 2002) from the sidewalks around the market. The flower vendors attempted to protest together with residents of the neighboring town of San Salvador Atenco who were also members of the People's Front in Defense of Land. They marched up to the police line with their flowers in hand and the police stepped up and started swinging their clubs. Chaos ensued. The police beat and arrested dozens of people. Others, including the leaders of the People's Front, ran a few blocks and took refuge in the house of one of the flower vendors.

In nearby Atenco, people blocked the federal highway that borders the town to demand the immediate release of those just taken prisoner in Texcoco. The government responded by sending over 800 federal and state riot police to forcibly lift their highway blockade. For hours the police battled the people of Atenco on the open highway. National television networks filmed from helicopters the clashes between the

People's Front and the police: protesters kicking an unconscious police officer in the groin, groups of officers huddled around fallen protesters raining blows upon them with their police batons. The newscasters repeated over and over again the scene of the police officer being kicked, trumpeting the need for a stronger police crackdown to "finish these people off." The newscasters failed to inform their viewers that the protesters had beaten the fallen police officer moments after learning that the police had shot and killed 14-year-old Francisco Javier Cortés Santiago. In Texcoco, federal police stormed the house where the flower vendors and leaders from the People's Front had taken refuge. The police beat everyone into semiconsciousness and submission. When they left the house they doused its walls, staircase, and floors with red paint to cover the pools of blood. Ignacio del Valle, leader of the People's Front, was pummeled and then taken to maximum security prison, his face swollen and disfigured, blood soaking through his pants from where police beat him repeatedly on the groin. A year later a judge would give Ignacio del Valle a sixty-seven-year jail sentence for "kidnapping," more than twice the sentences given to the nation's most notorious drug traffickers. In Atenco, the protesters called the International Red Cross in the evening and released the police they had taken prisoner to the Red Cross. They then called on the government to release their prisoners and settle the conflict through dialogue.

It is 6:00 p.m. in Mexico City's Tlatelolco Plaza of the Three Cultures on May 3, 2006. Subcomandante Marcos of the EZLN declares a red alert and calls for national and international solidarity with the people of Atenco. Atenco must not be left alone, he says.

Ángel Benhumea is with his son, Alexis, and a number of

friends and colleagues, standing in the sun, listening to the words of the subcomandante. After Marcos leaves the stage, they talk among themselves. They decide to go to the campus of Chapingo University, where people are said to be gathering. Chapingo is a few miles outside of Mexico City, about halfway to San Salvador Atenco. When they get to Chapingo, they find a lot of people but little organization. No one is giving orders. Groups form and discuss among themselves how best to stand in solidarity with the people of Atenco. And they wait, for hours. Little by little groups trail off. Some go home, some go on to Atenco. When Ángel, Alexis, and their friends decide to go to Atenco themselves, it is almost 6:00 a.m. They arrive in Atenco minutes before over 3,500 local, state, and federal riot police. They walk not even half a block before they see the black wave of riot shields, hear the violent clack of truncheons against shields, of boots against asphalt.

"We put ourselves right in the front lines," Ángel told me later, "to keep the police from repressing the people of Atenco."

But in the very first moments, with the entrance of the first police troops and the first shots of tear gas grenades, in the front lines, Alexis falls. Ángel is standing just a few feet away when the gas grenade hits Alexis in the head. He falls, but is able to stand again with his father's help; he even says, "My glasses . . . my glasses fell off." But the police are charging forward and they have no choice but to run. Two men see Ángel and Alexis struggling and rush to help, practically lifting Alexis off the ground. Luckily, in one of the first houses they come to, someone is hurriedly waving people in to hide and take shelter. Ángel, Alexis and the two men enter the ground floor of a two-story, concrete box of a house with just two rooms downstairs and two rooms upstairs.

Over fifty-five people are hiding out in the house, about

twenty upstairs and just over thirty downstairs. Some of them are residents of Atenco, others are from Mexico City, some just came from Tlatelolco to help without really knowing what was happening or whom they would be helping. One medic, known as El Doctor Selvas, is the first to recognize the severity of Alexis's wound. Alexis wants to speak now, tries, but cannot. His mouth fails him, won't respond to his commands. El Doctor looks at his head, carefully clearing away his long, thick mat of hair, and can see that his skull is fractured and brain matter is exposed, that he is beginning to bleed intensively. El Doctor Selvas decides to leave the house to seek help. El Doctor never comes back. El Doctor would remain in prison for over a year and a half.

Ollín Alexis (by both his names) can no longer sit up. He lies down on the floor. Another medic, a local resident also seeking refuge in the house, moves over to look at Alexis's wound; he is shocked. He pulls gauze from his backpack and tries to stop the hemorrhaging. Alexis no longer responds. He begins to shake.

In the downstairs floor with Alexis are a few people who, like Ángel, participated in the student protests of 1968 and 1971. They ask the owner of the house for detergent and vinegar. They spread the detergent in the doorframe and windowsills. They then ask for cups. The men move into a corner and urinate in the cups and then mix their urine with vinegar. Then they drip their cocktail in the doorframe and windowsills.

The police have dogs with them. And when they come, later in the morning, the dogs run straight up the winding metal stairs on the building's exterior to the second story of the house. The dogs do not smell the sweat of thirty people in the downstairs rooms. The police break through the door and begin tearing people out of the second floor. They push them down the stairs, and when the people reach the ground, the police beat them to their knees with clubs. Ángel and all those on the bottom floor hear the screams and beatings. The police take family members from the house and all those who had been hiding upstairs. The police take—beating her with every step—Mariana, Doctor Selvas's daughter. Mariana would remain in prison for over a year and a half.

One riot cop bangs on the door of the ground floor, but no one answers.

"The tension was overwhelming," said a young woman who had been hiding in the same house. "The father said that he wanted to turn himself in with his son, that it did not matter what happened, that he wanted to take him out into the street so that the police could take them to a hospital. But if that were to happen, well, we would all have to go out, so no one wanted him to turn over his son. Everyone said no, because no one could be sure what would happen to us. No one could guarantee that they would simply take the young man. Our safety was also caught up in the decision. The father endured so much, and he did not turn over his son. But the pain, you could see it all over him, but he didn't cry, never, not once, until by the end we all kept quiet. We were all very afraid, we kept silent."

When I see him for the first time, stretched out on the concrete floor, I cannot distinguish the features of his face due to the bandages, discoloration, and blood. I can see that he is young, thin, with long hair. He seems kind of familiar, as if I have seen him around, but I cannot make anything out, I cannot tell if I know him or not. There is a man standing over him, to my left. I ask him, "Who is he?" gesturing down at the body caught in the grip of deep breathing and the quick jerks of small seizures.

"He is my son," he answers.

Silence.

"We have a taxi van," I tell him. "The federal police would not let the ambulances into town. We can take him to a hospital now in the van."

"Where is the van? Bring it please."

His first name, Ollín, I would learn later, means "movement" in Nahuatl. Ollín Alexis. He was 20 years old and had studied dance since he was 9. At the National Autonomous University of Mexico he double-majored in math and economics and studied advanced Russian. He played guitar. He read insatiably; he always had books with him, in his backpack, in his pockets. He wore glasses. In photographs you can see him dancing or standing quietly behind Zapatista commanders in the rebel community of La Garrucha, listening to the preparatory meetings for the Other Campaign, the Zapatista rebels' national organizing effort launched in late 2005.

I woke up on the morning of May 4, 2006, at a friend's house in Mexico City. It was a few minutes before six. We turned on the television. Within minutes we saw the police entering San Salvador Atenco. We watched footage shot from a helicopter as the black wave of riot police shot tear gas, aiming at the bodies of protesters. Very few people were in the streets. We left immediately.

Traffic outbound from Mexico City was moving at a crawl; it took an hour to move three miles. We tried to hire a taxi, but none would take us. A *combi*, I thought.* Perhaps we could hire a *combi* driver. We walked to the *combi* stop a few blocks

---

* *Combis* are a form of collective transport common all over Latin America; most are part of the so-called "informal economy." They usually are old vans of one sort or another, their insides fitted out with benchlike seats to squeeze in more people. They have established routes and charge low fares; kind of like minibuses.

away, and after a bit we were able to find a driver willing to take us. It was almost noon and the sun was oppressive. I sent a text message to my friend Diego Osorno, a writer for the Mexican national newspaper *Milenio*, who had covered the clashes in Texcoco and Atenco the day before and had spent the night in Atenco. I wanted to let him know we were en route.

"Be very careful," he wrote back, "The police are ripping people from houses door-to-door; they are running around like rabid dogs."

On May 4, 2006, over 3,500 federal, state, and local police surrounded and invaded San Salvador Atenco. Hundreds of members of the Other Campaign had traveled throughout the night to stand in solidarity with the people of Atenco. Most of these people, however, were caught off guard when the church bells rang in warning at 6:00 a.m. People scrambled up to defend the entrances to the town with rocks and a few Molotov cocktails, but were immediately overwhelmed by the sheer numbers of police firing tear gas grenades at head level. The police pummeled all those caught in the streets upon their entrance. Over twenty police beat Jorge Salinas Jardón—on camera—continuously for nearly two minutes. But the beatings in the streets were just the beginning. Once the police had taken control of the town, masked locals led them house to house to beat and arrest known participants in the People's Front and members of the Other Campaign who had sought refuge in people's homes. The police violence was indiscriminate. Arnulfo Pacheco, a disabled man who has been confined to a wheelchair for years, was pulled from his bed, beaten, and then ordered to get up and walk. When he did not comply, he was beaten unconscious. Police then carried out a sadistic ritual of violence: they piled bleeding bodies into empty buses and the backs of pickup trucks and drove them out into the countryside for further beatings. During these six-hour drives, police systematically sexually attacked and in some cases raped the women they had taken prisoner. The riot police had even included condoms amongst their riot gear.

When we arrive at the hospital Alexis is still alive. We carry him—his body warm but motionless—through the emergency room doors. I hear a doctor comment to a colleague as we rush past, "Ooh, that one's hopeless."

By pure luck, a neurological surgeon was just coming off his shift. They take Alexis to an operating room and within minutes begin surgery that lasts five hours. Alexis holds on, but in a coma. The internal hemorrhaging, from eleven hours of bleeding without medical attention, eleven hours trapped by thousands of police and by thirty people terrified of being discovered, had already damaged some 80 percent of his brain.

His family—father, mother, sister, brother, uncles and aunts and cousins—all stay, camped out first in the waiting room and later, when Alexis is moved to a different hospital, outside in the parking lot. There they sleep, when they are able to sleep. There they eat, when they are able to eat. There they speak with Alexis's friends, classmates and fellow dancers, who visit daily. There they remain, day after day, hour through hour, clutching at every moment to threads of hope rubbed raw.

But Ollín Alexis does not rise up. He sleeps. The dancer of solidarity dies on June 7, 2006. No one is held responsible for his murder.

THE WORD IMPUNITY is useless in Ciudad Juárez. Phrases like "human rights violation" or "discrimination against women," pale and fall apart. Here women are killed for sport. Women—their lives and their bodies—are hunted, raped, and butchered with such frequency that no one seems able to even keep count. The women are young, most under the age of 18. They live in shantytowns without running water or sewage. They feed their children under tin roofs. The women come from all over the country, from broken villages and the deteriorating edges of cities. They come to work. They come precisely to survive, drawn by the fierce pull of promised wages, wages that enclose these women firmly in the grip of destitution. Some work for $2 an hour; some work for $35 a week. They work making the products sold at the "everyday low prices" so celebrated in the United States.

The women are found in the desert, in the road, in the ditch. They are found strangled. They are found cut apart. They are found with their nipples bitten off, pieces of their faces bitten off. They are found so badly decomposed that their names and their histories will never be known. In Ciudad Juárez women are killed, destroyed, and obliterated under the careful watch of the state. Forensics experts charged with collecting evidence boil women's bodies to destroy the DNA. Prosecutors torture bus drivers who happen to drive by a ditch where women's bodies are found. The bus drivers are later released, and the killings continue.

The very letter of the law shelters the killers: the statute of limitations for murders in Mexico is fourteen years. The first of these ritual killings, which took place between 1989 and 1993, no longer constitute punishable crimes. Government officials deride women for provoking men with evocative desert dress: miniskirts and tank tops that bring out some inexorable instinct to abduct, handcuff, rape, strangle, and mutilate. Police shoot investigating lawyers in broad daylight and then claim mistaken identity. The U.S. companies that own the maquiladoras where the women work deny that anything abnormal takes place in Ciudad Juárez: it is just business as usual.

The Chihuahua state government pays for advertisements smearing journalists who criticize the fifteen-year stretch of unsolved killings. During that time, more than 400 women have been murdered and hundreds more disappeared. Can you imagine this? You live in a city. In your city, a woman's mutilated body is found every week. Most of the victims were last seen on the exact same street corner near an industrial part of town. Nothing happens to change this. The city government does not hire more police and create permanent patrol shifts on this street. Nor does the state government. Nor does the federal government. Nor do the owners of the various factories hire private security guards. Nor do they provide company transportation for employees. No one does anything. Every week another woman destroyed. A new president takes office. The new president creates a special federal prosecutor's office to investigate the killings. The president's term ends. The special prosecutor has found nothing, has solved nothing. The killings continue. But not only that, they spread to other cities, to other states. More than 300 women have been raped and slain in Mexico state in the past ten years. In the state of Veracruz, more than 200 have fallen to the same fate, and in Oaxaca 90 women were slain between January 2005 and May 2006. In other states they have not started counting yet. It is an epidemic of brutality that goes unchallenged and unpunished.[51]

The Washington Office on Latin America, a D.C.-based human rights organization, has researched the murders in Ciudad Juárez for years. In a May 2006 report, they write: "But impunity for the murders goes deeper than a lack of resources or investigative skills. There has been a profound lack of political will to solve the murders, owing to corruption in the state police and attorney general's office."[52] Again we find the phrase "lack of political will," a somewhat dignified or face-saving way of saying, "They do not want to change this." Again, those few who have been publicly charged with murders claim that they were tortured into signing confessions, some were held without trial for five or eight years, then sentenced out of the blue.[53] Amnesty International decries the killings and impunity, as does the United Nations Committee on the Elimination of Discrimination against Women.[54] And the killings continue. Today, as I write these words, the headline, buried in the far left corner of page 18, reads: "Another murdered woman found in Ciudad Juárez."[55]

ON MAY 31, 2007, President Felipe Calderón published his 2007–2012 National Development Plan in the federal official daily. The first of the plan's five "spokes" (*ejes*) is "The Rule of Law and Security." The plan states: "The government should be the first to comply with and enforce the law so that an authentic Rule of Law may exist. . . . The government's actions should be exemplary for the citizenry. If the government is clearly committed to following the law, then this will generate the correct incentives for the citizens to order their common affairs." Who could this possibly be written for? International investment firms and staffers for U.S. members of Congress? Or perhaps the orphans of Ciudad Juárez who only know their mothers through expired case files and photographs of bones piled in the desert? Or perhaps the thousands of local, state, and federal police said to be aiding and protecting the various Mexican drug cartels? The Mexican armed forces who routinely use torture and sexual violence against the civilian population? The human rights organizations and international reporters who keep crossing their fingers for a democratic transition?

3.

THE ǰULF

Global poverty is an entirely new and modern construct. The basic materials which have gone into the construct are essentially the economization of life and the forceful integration of vernacular societies into the world economy . . . the new fetish of a healthy global economy destined to save the world's poor, not only helped the pauperizing economic and political systems to reinforce and legitimize their positions, but it also led their victims to perceive their own situation in the same terms. . . . Eradication of global poverty was thus considered yet another reason for consolidating the present structures of governance, both at the international and national levels.

—Majid Rahnema, *Poverty*

Underdevelopment is not a stage of development. It is its consequence.

—Eduardo Galeano, *The Open Veins of Latin America*

Hunger is the dynamite of the human body.

—Carolina María de Jesús, *Child of the Dark*

POVERTY IS AN IDEA that imposes realities more than it describes them, an ideological construct designed to legitimize and safeguard economic domination of the very people whose supposed condition of deprivation it laments. That so many people—in various conditions of hardship, toil, repression, and suffering—across the planet now use the idea, calling themselves poor, testifies to the fantastic missionary zeal with which economists and politicians set out to convert the people they exploit to a shared ideology, to an ideology that transforms exploitation into market factors, land theft into physical geography, racism into cultural barriers, politics into technology, imperialism into poverty. It is a relatively new ideology with roots in the colonialism and industrialization of the past two centuries, but truly coming into its own with the creation of the International Bank for Reconstruction and Development (the World Bank) in the post-1945 era of colonial reconfigurations, when the dominant post–World War II regimes established early guidelines for the economic domination of those still unborn nation-states on the cusp of breaking the military grasp of direct colonial rule.[1]

The shift from military to economic domination has been both incremental and incomplete: the world's front-running imperial power, the United States, serves as a key example. While the United States has built an economic empire across the world, it has used its military to protect that empire; since 1945 the United States has "intervened militarily" both overtly and covertly in dozens of countries across the world (Guatemala, Iran, Cuba, Korea, Vietnam, Chile, El Salvador, Nicaragua, Panama), still maintains huge military bases in former conquered territories across the world (Japan, Germany, South Korea), and unabashedly continues to send massive military forces to subjugate new lands (Afghanistan, Iraq). The shift has also concurred with the development of forms of internal military imperialism, in which a country uses its military against its own population to protect the economic domination of foreign powers in conjunction with an emerging class of post-independence nationalist elites. The ideology of poverty has served both the foreign powers and the nationalists well, leading to its brushfire spread across the globe.

But what is this, one may reasonably ask, about poverty being an ideology, an idea? Isn't poverty a condition, and a bad one at that? Isn't poverty about living without nutritious food, without electricity and indoor plumbing, without access to adequate medical care, drinking water, good roads? Wouldn't it be insulting to say these conditions don't exist or aren't bad?

Excavating poverty's ideological content does not deny the existence of harsh and brutal living conditions, or insinuate that such conditions reflect a wiser, truer way of life than modern industrial capitalism (a typical red herring used to counter critics). The excavation is meant to show how people ended up in horrid conditions, why they are seldom able to change those conditions, and who is responsible for pinning them there; it is meant to help understand both historical and present human actions that forced (and continue to force) people into miserable situations. The ideology of poverty performs a kind of discursive illusion to obscure both historical and current human responsibility for the creation of destitution and suffering, and thus to convince the hundreds of millions of people who are destitute that no one is really to blame for their state, and that national governments and international economists are the best ones to figure out how to help them in their toil.

Perhaps the most recent updating of the ideology of poverty comes in a book published in 2005 titled *The End of Poverty: Economic Possibilities for Our Time*. Written by an economist with twenty years' experience as an economic adviser to more than 100 governments across the world, the book proposes measures to end "extreme poverty" by the year 2025.[2] While the author's goal seems noble, the imperialist logic that drives his arguments makes his desired end forever unreachable.[3]

The argument goes as follows: all places in the world were once poor (p. 29); contemporary poverty is the result of slower economic growth in specific places (p. 31); economic growth is completely distinct from and independent of culture, thus the same recipes for economic growth may be applied universally (p. 31, underlying assumption throughout); the economists, scientists, and politicians of the economic powers have performed the right steps to achieve modern economic growth already and thus are best suited to propose the right steps for others (underlying assumption, e.g., pp. 24, 33–35, 43, and 56); and finally, if underdeveloped countries follow the advice of developed countries and get on the path of economic growth, they can end their extreme poverty in twenty years (p. 24).

This argument is rich with ideological magic. The first step is to place everyone on the same starting point: "All regions were poor in 1820" (p. 29). This statement is both conceptually and historically false. It is a logical fallacy to impose a contemporary, culturally specific standard to define past reality. Since the material conditions the economist now defines as necessary did not exist (or prevail) in 1820, then everyone everywhere was poor. Moreover, by saying that everyone was poor in 1820, the economist strips rural life, and particularly indigenous communal life, of all its complexity, wealth, and even legitimacy (why should one maintain such a culture if it is synonymous with poverty?) and sets the stage for ineluctable, "benevolent" imperialism. As for history, this 1820 leveling ignores 300 years of European colonialism. Look at aristocratic sections of Madrid or London and then slave dwellings in the Americas or Africa in 1820, and see if both were comparably "poor."

The second step in the magic is to deny the historical role of imperialism in creating conditions of destitution across the world and to grant the idea of "modern economic growth" a quasi-spiritual dimension as both the motor and the destiny of world history. The economist writes that "today's vast inequalities reflect the fact that some parts of the world achieved modern economic growth while others did not" (p. 29). This is a key point in the ideology of poverty, and one the economist returns to explicitly:

> Let me dispose of one idea right from the start. Many people assume that the rich have gotten rich *because* the poor have gotten poor. In other words, they assume that Europe and the United States used military force and political strength during and after the era of colonialism to extract wealth from the poorest regions, and thereby to grow rich. This interpretation of events would be plausible if the gross world product had remained roughly constant, with a rising share going to powerful regions and a declining share going to poorer regions. However, that is not at all what happened. Gross world product rose nearly fifty fold. Every region of the world experienced some economic growth (both in terms of the overall size of the economy, and even when measured per person), but some regions experienced much more growth than others. The key fact of modern times is not the *transfer* of income from one region to another, by force or otherwise, but rather the overall *increase* in world income, but at a different rate in different regions (p. 31, emphasis in original).

First of all, note his disregard: "Let me dispose of one idea right from the start." What does he want to do with this idea? Does he want to consider it, engage with it, and reflect upon it? No. He wants to "dispose" of it as one disposes of refuse, waste, trash. The idea that European and U.S. imperialism caused conditions of destitution through open genocide, slavery, and land theft and that these conditions have evolved into contemporary poverty, is an idea for this economist akin to intellectual trash. In fact, according to the economist, the idea has no basis in historical reality but is based on mere assumptions: "Many people assume that the rich have gotten rich . . . they assume that Europe and the United States used military force." The arrogance is, of course, historically vacuous and insulting if not implicitly racist, for the "assumptions" that merit "disposal" are precisely those developed, held, and argued by the exploited classes descended from the oppressed of European and U.S. imperialism.[4] Consider Frantz Fanon's voicing of the idea:

> The European opulence is literally a scandal for it was built on the backs of slaves, it fed on the blood of slaves, and it owes its very existence to the soil and subsoil of the underdeveloped world. Europe's well-being and progress were built with the sweat and corpses of blacks, Arabs, Indians, and Asians. This we are determined to never forget.[5]

In Eduardo Galeano's words:

> But it so happens that those who won, won thanks to our defeat: the history of underdevelopment in Latin America consists in, as has been said, the history of the development of world capitalism. *Our defeat was always implicit in the other's victory; our wealth has always generated our own poverty in order to feed the prosperity of others: the empires and their native caporales.* . . . Development develops inequality. The strength of the entire imperialist system rests in the necessary inequality between its two parts.[6]

Mexican economic historian Enrique Semo sums up the case of Mexico this way:

> The following is key: the means necessary to found the economy of the conquerors (the Republic of the Spaniards) stem from the exploitation of the indigenous community. The Spaniards do not bring capital or means of production with them. The only source available is the labor and product coming from the communities. The historical role of the *encomienda* [a form of indentured servitude to the Crown] is precisely this: to transfer production from the communities to the Spanish estates, plantations, workshops, mines. . . . Without products flowing from the indigenous communities and a mechanism for transferring and transforming them, the economy of the Republic of the Spaniards would never have evolved.[7]

But the arguments developed in these and so many other books, constitute only "assumptions" that need to be "disposed of."[8] Apart from his arrogance, the author of *The End of Poverty* dismisses imperialism as a root cause of contemporary destitution with flimsy reasoning. He calls wholesale slaughter, enslavement, and land theft a mere "transfer" of economic goods and then asserts that it did not account for uneven economic growth. For him, the historical record of overall economic growth disproves such a transfer. But really, what could he mean? Does he doubt the trans-Atlantic slave trade took place? Does he deny the existence of silver, gold, copper, and tin mines throughout the Spanish empire in contemporary Latin America? Did the ships never set sail, the goods never move from South America, Africa, India? Did the Europeans never displace and kill millions of indigenous peoples?

The economist does not deny these historical facts (p. 39); he denies them historical meaning, and thus denies them contemporary meaning. For the economist, technology, democratic institutions, and market forces fueled the Industrial Revolution and opened up the era of great, though unequal, economic prosperity (p. 35). Racism and brutality, for the economist, were sad consequences of mistaken individuals caught in the frenzy of modern economic growth (p. 39).

The author's need to hide the brutal history of his cherished economic prosperity is so urgent he makes amazing associations in his argument. Consider the following two short examples:

> The Americans, for example, believe that they earned their wealth all by themselves. They forget that they inherited a vast continent rich in natural resources, with great soils and ample rainfall, immense navigable rivers, and thousands of miles of coastline with dozens of natural ports that provide a wonderful foundation for sea-based trade (57).

The Americans "inherited a vast continent." From whom did they inherit it? "A little matter of genocide," conquest, slavery, racist and bloody "manifest destiny," and systematic treaty violations are all airbrushed clean and packaged as an ahistorical, nonpolitical inheritance.[9] Here is the economist's summary of world affairs on the eve of the first World War:

> By the early twentieth century, Europe largely dominated the world. . . . This was the first age of globalization . . . what would seem to be an era of inevitable progress. . . . This imagined natural order gave rise to the infamous "white man's burden," the right and obligation of European and European-

descended whites to rule the lives of others around the
world, which they blithely did with a contradictory
mix of naiveté, compassion, and brutality (p. 43).

European domination was the first era of globalization, the
first era of "inevitable progress." This is one of the more honest statements in the economist's argument, for it acknowledges
that "progress" is a European creation, though it still assumes
that the creation is destined and fit for all, even if at the point
of a gun. The economist's description of imperialism as a "contradictory mix of naiveté, compassion, and brutality," also
affirms his conclusion that "European domination" was not all
bad; it had some compassion mixed in with it. Is there compassion in slavery? Perhaps for the slave owner, not for the
slave. Imperialism leaves little room for neutrality—one is
either on the side of empire or against it.[10] The economist and
the ideologues of poverty are firmly on the side of empire.

This leads us to the third step in the ideological magic:
masking economic intervention and domination as the uni-
versalism of modern economic growth. The economist's
formulation is that all regions experience economic progress,
though the rich regions experience more of it (p. 29). Thus
the poor regions need only catch up by following the lead of
the rich regions. Economic growth is put forth here as a force
independent of culture rather than as a concrete cultural construct of European and U.S. imperialism. For a very particular
kind of economic growth is espoused, industrial capitalism,
and pushing "modern economic growth" is simply another
way of describing the imposition of industrial capitalism on
every corner of the world, whether people want it or not. The
implied imperial logic is this: if people resist industrial capitalism—clothed as modern economic growth—it is precisely
because they are mired in poverty and unable to properly diag-

nose their social ills and act correctly upon them. It might be that huge numbers of people across the world long for industrial capitalism—though that has not been my experience in Mexico—but that is another matter, for the ideology of poverty does not conceive of asking them, to find out. It imposes one interpretation from the start: you are stuck in poverty and only modern economic growth can get you out.

THE PRIME DISTINGUISHING characteristic of the Mexican economy is inequality: Mexico contains one of the greatest, most obscene, gulfs between its wealthiest and most destitute citizens of all the nations on the planet. This gulf has both a past and a present populated with specific people making deliberate decisions, those who opened the gulf on purpose and continue to manage its widening reach, and those who rebel against it.

The history of Spanish colonialism is complex, but not vague: the Spaniards invaded, took land from the indigenous communities, enslaved the indigenous people, and then, over the course of three centuries, adopted various forms of forced labor to the moral and political needs of the day. This is where contemporary "poverty" begins. During the first two centuries of colonization, "the majority of the [indigenous] communities that were able to conserve themselves experienced a process of economic regression: the disappearance of commercial specializations, artisan and intellectual activities, and a reversion back to the most primitive agrarian life."[11] In the first half of the eighteenth century, Mexico's economy, especially in the countryside, remained largely precapitalist, based on subsistence farming and regional trade. The *encomienda** system

---

* The *encomienda* system granted Spaniards "trusteeship" over the indigenous people they conquered. In exchange for spreading Catholicism the Spaniards could "tax" the indigenous people's labor, forcing them to work on the Spaniards' plantations. The system quickly evolved into slavery.

evolved into debt peonage, semi-free forced labor: "With their lands having been expropriated, the indigenous could not avoid regular or sporadic work on the plantation."[12] While the Spaniards drove the indigenous off their land and into forced labor, Mexico became the first colony to develop millionaires.[13]

With the War of Independence and the Revolution, Spanish imperialism broke down and evolved into a form of nationalist internal colonialism.[14] Porfirio Díaz opened the economy to massive foreign investment (and forms of corporate control), ruling Mexico as if it were "a capitalist preserve for his Mexican and foreign friends."[15] After the turmoil of the Revolution and its aftermath, Lázaro Cárdenas implemented a series of measures that very concretely addressed Mexico's mostly rural destitution—namely, a huge redistribution of land and the enshrining of communal property rights in the Constitution—which doubled as mechanisms to establish a government-party monopoly over both the economy and the political process. In the fifty years following the Revolution the percentage of the total population considered marginalized dropped, but the absolute numbers of people living on the margin in various degrees of destitute conditions increased.[16]

During the period of the PRI's consolidation of power, between 1940 and the 1970s, the Mexican economy grew annually at a rate of over 6 percent, leading admirers to proclaim this growth the Mexican Miracle.[17] However, the overall growth rates coincided with a drastic increase in the disparity between the wealthy, on the one hand, and the excluded and destitute sectors of society, on the other: "In 1958 the incomes of the richest five percent of all Mexicans were twenty-two times those of the poorest 10 percent; by 1980 the gap had more than doubled, and the rich enjoyed incomes fifty times greater than those of the poorest sector of the population."[18] And the 1980s were even worse. Foreign debt skyrocketed with the crash of international oil prices, and the International Monetary Fund rushed in with an "austerity program": hundreds of thousands of people lost jobs, unemployment in the countryside doubled, millions of rural people were economically displaced into both internal and international migration routes, the minimum wage lost over half its value in ten years, and almost 60 percent of urban households fell beneath the poverty line.[19] Between 1983 and 1988, the cost of living rose over 90 percent while the per capita income fell by 50 percent, from an estimated $2,405 to $1,320 (both in U.S. dollars).[20]

Enter Carlos Salinas de Gortari. It is 1988 and Salinas has lost the election, but the PRI controls the vote count and, after an unexplained computer meltdown, the PRI announces, fresh printouts in hand, Salinas's decisive triumph. What instruments we have agree: the day of his inauguration was a dark and horrid day.[21]

Carlos Salinas eliminated Article 27 of the Mexican Constitution (ending the Revolution's program of land redistribution and opening the way for the privatization of communal lands) and signed NAFTA, two actions designed to knock small farmers off their land, crush micro-enterprise, and consequently cull from the Mexican countryside a mobile harvest of migrant day laborers and maquila workers—two actions designed to create poverty. And at the same time, between 1989 and 1992, Salinas privatized 989 state-owned companies,[22] an action designed to further concentrate wealth in a super-elite class. The *Wall Street Journal* describes Salinas's privatization scheme thus: "The privatization process created a new class of super-rich in Mexico. In 1991, the country had two billionaires on the *Forbes* list. By 1994, at the end of Mr. Salinas's six-year term, there were 24."[23] Twenty days after Salinas left office on November 30, 1994, the Mexican economy crashed; on December 22, the peso fell by 20 percent, $5 billion left the country in forty-eight hours.[24] By the time the benefits of Salinas's economic design had time to trickle down, two million farmers had left their land, poverty had risen from 45 to 50 percent of the entire population, and some 3,300,000 children under the age of 14 had been forced to work.[25]

THEY CALL IT POVERTY, the economists and the politicians. But it is not; it is violence. More than half the world's population, including some fifty million Mexicans, do not suffer from an innate lack or from geographical bad luck, from bad weather or bad choices that all spiral into destitution. Their villages are open-air prisons. People did not choose to live in the arid highlands over the fertile valleys; imperial invasions pushed them there at the point of a lance, the barrel of a gun, and then unleashed the first and most devastating tactic of biological warfare: hunger.

There is no corresponding *Forbes* listing of the world's poorest people, no algorithm to estimate the pace and ferocity of hunger and malnutrition, and if death by destitution were considered poverty's end-of-the-road there would, of course, be no single annual world's poorest—millions would share that doleful distinction. Thus for every *Forbes* billionaire with their glossy photographs and charitable foundations there is, at the other end of the spectrum a corresponding underworld, perhaps a fourth world, of millions of emaciated, shunted-aside people, most of them not yet kindergarten age. This—not the construction of a cushiony intermediate class plugged in to computers and cell phones, fashion, hybrid cars, and other delicacies of disposable income—is the achievement of the Age of Economic Imperialism. One writer said that you could gauge a democracy by the conditions in its prisons—so too can you gauge an economy by the nature of its extremes.

Consider Carlos Slim Helú, the Mexican-born son of a

Lebanese immigrant who made an early fortune buying downtown property in the aftermath of the 1910–1920 Revolution.[26] Carlos Slim, at the age of 26, after graduating from the National Autonomous University of Mexico with a degree in engineering, had about $400,000 from inheritance and early investments. Not a bad start for a youngster. Slim played the stock market in the late 1960s and early 1970s and then went on the lookout for cheap companies to buy and turn around. Slim's strategy proved sound: between 1970 and 1995, the Mexican economy collapsed three times, and each time the United States stepped in to bail it out with loans that hit Mexican taxpayers a generation down the line. Each time the economy tanked, Slim bought up bankrupted companies. In 1981, Slim bought stake in a major tobacco company. He turned his winnings around and, after the massive 1982 economic crash, he "picked up dozens of firms at bargain-basement prices."[27] But, as we have seen, Slim's big break came when Carlos Salinas—his friend of several years—opened the floodgates on privatization, allowing Slim to buy the controlling share in the state telephone company, Telmex, with a government-granted seven-year period of guaranteed monopoly. Slim blocked competition from using the Telmex networks for years and charged some of the highest phone rates in the world. With Telmex and later Telcel, his capital increased exponentially, enabling him to buy somewhere around 200 different companies, many of which produce goods for the state: highways, oil rigs, and the like. In 2000, President Fox appointed one of Slim's former executives to head the agency charged with regulating his industry. Now, fifteen years later, Carlos Slim is number one on the *Fortune* list, the richest man in the world, with an estimated worth of $59 billion. In the years 2006 and 2007, Slim gained an average of $27 million *per day*. At age 67, he has turned over much of his empire's administration to his three sons, beefed up his charitable donations, and now enjoys reading books about the military strategies of Ghengis Khan late into the night.[28]

Slim may be at the peak, but Mexico's super-elite class includes at least twenty-four billionaires and 85,000 millionaires. And at the bottom?

According to official government statistics published by the National Population Council (CONAPO) from a survey conducted in 2005, three entire states have "very high" marginalization and another eight states have a "high" level of marginalization.[29] The numbers are fuzzy, but both the government's national statistics and the United Nations Development Program statistics—both highly problematic and typically conservative in their estimates—tell us that about fifty million Mexicans live in "poverty," on less than about $4 a day, while about fifteen million of them live in "extreme poverty," on $1 or less a day.

If the millionaires of Mexico possess an average of $5 million apiece (a very low estimate), then their total wealth would reach about $425 billion, more than the amount that half the country— fifty million people—lives on in a year. But these numbers are impossibly high: who can make sense of "$59 billion," or "fifty million live in poverty"?

"Like an open wound in the folds of the Guerrero mountains, San Pedro El Viejo is far from everything."[30] There are no paved roads, no money to pay for the four-hour trip standing in the back of one of the oversize and uncovered pickup trucks known as *redilas* that roam the forgotten dirt roads winding through the mountains. During the rain season the trip takes twice as long, eight hours standing in the rain, and between August and September, at the height of the rains, the roads become rivers of mud that even the trucks cannot navigate. "That is why the sick don't try to leave anymore," says

Paulino, the only resident here who speaks a bit of Spanish. "They know that they'll get sick on the road, that they won't be able to make the trip, they'll die. They will force their families to spend money for nothing, and then have to spend even more to bring the body back." Even if an ailing resident of San Pedro El Grande were to reach a hospital alive, once there he or she would have no way to explain what ails them—the hospitals do not employ interpreters for any of Mexico's different indigenous languages—nor would they be able to afford either consultation or medicine.

The people of San Pedro El Viejo have one food source: the tortilla. They call it "tuberculosis," death by malnutrition. Health care is a luxury as inaccessible and otherworldly as Internet shopping. The decrepit "health clinic" holds no medicine, no medical instruments, no doctors, no nurses, only a discolored poster from the national health secretariat that reads: "Wherever you are, your health is there." San Pedro El Viejo is part of the newly created municipality of Cochoapa El Grande, formed by a Guerrero state government decree in 2002. When Vicente Fox took office as president of Mexico in 2000, Metlatónoc was the poorest municipality in Mexico. But in 2006, when Fox stepped down, Metlatónoc was ranked number six and Cochoapa El Grande was the new number one. Cochoapa El Grande has 15,600 inhabitants living in 120 communities over 690 square kilometers of barren southwestern highlands; all of them spent their whole lives in Metlatónoc until a politician waved his wand and they became Cochoapa El Grande. After all the promises and photo ops, they are still the poorest communities in the country; the only thing that has changed is the name of their municipality. Anthropologist Abel Barrera, who runs a human rights center and free legal clinic for the people of the Guerrero highlands, summarized the health care situation in the indigenous com-

munities of the highlands like this: "For them the right to health is a straw mat on the ground; that is, a right to death."
Andrés fell a year and a half ago and now he only has enough strength left to watch. "His body is rotting." They don't know what else to say. He lies on a mattress of old clothes and mountain grasses believed to be curative. His mother, Micaela, feeds him mashed corn mixed with boiled water. It has been three months since he last stood up. In the eighteen months since he fell, no doctor has come through the village of El Carmen in Santiago El Pinar, Chiapas. Micaela walks in silence, her hands clenched into fists. She traveled to town to bring back a doctor, but the doctor refused to come because Andrés and Micaela are not enrolled in the federal health assistance program, "Opportunities." Santiago El Pinar is the second-poorest municipality in Mexico, according to the United Nations Development Program statistics. It costs about $40 to travel to the nearest city, San Cristóbal de las Casas. There are no kitchens, no bathrooms, no floors besides the cleared dirt surrounded by adobe brick walls. There are thirteen communities here with a total population of 2,174 people. The annual municipal budget is $300,000. Children begin working when they are just 5 years old.

She is 4 years old and she picks coffee beans on Yetón Mountain. With cracked feet and broken sandals, María walks an hour and a half to elementary school, an hour and a half back, and then out to the fields to help her parents pick coffee. The renegade scouts who buy coffee from indigenous communities cut off from roads and markets pay between 90 cents and $1.40 per kilogram of coffee, about a tenth of what that same coffee will cost in a grocery store or café in Mexico City or the United States. Federal subsidies go only to those coffee producers who provide sales receipts. Most residents of Aldama and Xulumó, Chiapas, do not speak Spanish; they do not know how to read or write; they do not have electricity; they do not have sales receipts. In Mixtla de Altamirano, Veracruz, Nahuatl indigenous communities have no roads to connect them to the municipal seat or other market towns. For years they have petitioned successive state and federal governments for a road. Recently Senator Pedro Montalvo visited—flying in and out by helicopter—and promised to build a road. No road has been built. According to official government statistics, Mixtla de Altamirano is the sixth-poorest municipality in Mexico. All the municipalities with a majority indigenous population in Veracruz are considered "highly marginalized" by the National Population Council.

David Cilia, the photo editor at *Contralínea*, showed me his photographs upon returning from Oaxaca and the Raramuri indigenous communities of Chihuahua state. He flipped through his digital contact sheets: A man with a rotting leg eating a bare tortilla. Families whose sole possessions consist of a few blankets and a plastic bucket living in half-formed caves in the mountainside. Families grinding corn between river rocks. A woman stretched out on a makeshift bed in a one-room dirt house, her face contorted in pain, her skin sunken in around her bones, is dying of worms. A boy, now blind, with both eyes swollen to the point of bursting, covered with bacteria. A young family whose one piece of corrugated tin balances not a meter high on four piles of rocks to provide their only shelter. A boy who can no longer speak, walk, or chew with an untended tumor erupting from his head. Children without teeth because their bodies do not have enough calcium to make the second set.[31]

The photographs bring us in too close, there is too much light, the actions are clumsy and exaggerated, done without finesse. If I were a novelist I would cross out the words I used to describe them and start again. They do not describe characters engaged in imagined lives. The people shown in Cilia's photographs, and so many more, do not suffer from the arbitrary brutality of nature. They do not suffer from a cruel world. They fight against the most devastating weapon of modern times—hunger. Hunger is not simply the body's lack of nutrients; it is an assault. In the world of antibiotics, e-mail, and commercial air travel, a world where money moves faster, farther, and in greater quantities than ever before, hunger is not accidental; it is a preventable form of genocide. No, poverty is not a state of nature, not an accident of history, poverty is both callous neglect by a complicit society and an ideological instrument used to decontextualize and naturalize forced destitution and new forms of political domination and social control;[32] hunger is biological class warfare; hunger is a weapon of mass destruction.

4.

THE HEIST

In our communities we've only got elderly people, young
people, and kids. Many stay over there [in the United States];
some die on the way, while crossing. Over there they are not
treated well. They are just cheap labor, and they are dis-
criminated against. Mexico is becoming just a nursery for
poor people who will go to work in the United States.

—Dominga Maldonado, La Veracruz, Querétaro

Colonization sets the stage for later migration.

—Aviva Chomsky

The border is so large because we are on our knees.

—Painted on the border wall in Nogales, Sonora

THIS IS THE LAND of stolen futures; the land of stolen families, stolen villages; this is the land of the eviscerated present,
where possibilities hang dry and collapsed in the air, still visible, haunting, unattainable: here all paths lead through the
desert, across an invisible line drawn in the heat, into another
world—a world known here as "*el otro lado*," the other side—
a world where survival implies at least tacit acceptance of the
law of transnational apartheid. No one is spared. The theft
bleeds in the streets, in every home, in the countryside. Empty
streets, empty rooms, fields empty, entire houses empty. The
missing mark their absence by what they leave behind, what
they leave empty, and what they leave undone. Families are

cracked and broken, the towns are stunted, the future suspended in its dependence on the very force that has crippled the present. This is the land of open theft—the theft of humanity, rationalized, naturalized, and trapped in a timeless, apolitical concept of human migration.

The town of Guadalupe lies on a stretch of hillside a few miles outside of the small city of Acámbaro in the far southern corner of Guanajuato state, about 100 miles north of Mexico City.[1] Driving from Acámbaro, one turns right up a hill and starts to climb narrow streets, some paved, some unpaved, leaving one's vehicle to slowly navigate the crevices and rock edges of the road. There are no stop signs, no traffic lights. One-story adobe houses stand next to new, two-story concrete houses freshly painted and equipped with balconies and satellite dishes. Doña Lupe, the *delegada*, or person elected to represent the town before the municipal government in Acámbaro, is the only authority in Guadalupe. There are no police officers, no judges. There is no fire station, no hospital, and no health clinic. There is an elementary school, but no junior high or high school. Houses have electricity and running water (a few liters a day), but no sewage or drainage systems. I have come to Guadalupe to ask people here about their experiences with migration.

ADELA
"*Uy, los pueblos . . . los pueblos están tristes*" (Uy, the towns . . . the towns are sad). Her daughter left for the United States ten years ago and has never returned; she is still trying to get a work visa so that she can safely come visit.

RODRIGO IBARRA, AGRONOMIST FROM ACÁMBARO
"People don't have chickens anymore! They don't produce because there is no workforce left. People live of off the remit-

tances. Before, we grew corn and sold corn to the tortilla shops in Acámbaro, there was a network of local production in Acámbaro, a local economy in Acámbaro, and this is what has been completely destroyed. When I was a kid the countryside was filled with small plots of land planted with corn, squash, beans, chiles, and all of this was seasonal farming, depending on the annual rains. Now no one grows corn or anything without irrigation. There are no more *milpas*,* no more *milpas* in the countryside, and they are gone because you have to spend more than you can make to grow locally. And so local species of corn have disappeared in Acámbaro, and this is something that has happened in just the last two decades. The local networks of production-consumption are completely gone now in Acámbaro; there is no more corn here, it is all Maseca now [Maseca is Mexico's largest corn flour company], and it is that way with everything. We have a perfect climate here but we no longer produce anything that we consume. Acámbaro is famous across the country for its bread, and we produce a lot of wheat here, but there is not a single grain of wheat grown in Acámbaro to be found in the bread of Acámbaro. And what is more, now more people eat Bimbo [the Mexican equivalent of Wonder Bread] than the locally made bread of Acámbaro. I recently went with my family to a small village out in the countryside and thought that I would buy some chickens and come back with chickens to cook, but nobody had any chickens!"

DOÑA LUPE

The only governmental representative in Guadalupe, Doña Lupe has a fierce and cautious stare. She is on duty twenty-four hours a day, receiving only $40 a month from the

---

* *Milpa* refers to the traditional indigenous method of farming where corn is planted together with squash and beans.

municipal government. She is responsible for advocating on behalf of Guadalupe at the municipal level in an unending battle for funds. Guadalupe, like all tiny towns in Mexico, has no set annual budget allotment—the people must fight for every dime, year after year, at the municipal level. This legacy of the PRI's iron grip on government funds now fuels bitter fights between rival political parties. The first year that Doña Lupe won election as a PRD candidate, the PAN municipal president in Acámbaro refused to allocate "even a single bag of concrete" to Guadalupe. The PAN then tried to force Doña Lupe out of office, but the residents of Guadalupe who had voted for her fought back and defended her position. The PAN municipal president recently told Doña Lupe he would send twenty tons of cement to Guadalupe if she would fill a bus full of people wearing PAN T-shirts to attend his first state of the city address. "I told my people to put on the shirts and keep their mouths shut, that's the only way we'll get that road paved," Doña Lupe tells me, disgusted with the game. "The political parties are all crooks. It shouldn't be about parties, but about the needs of the community. But what can we do?"

I ask how many people are in United States. "The majority of young people are over there. In every family two or three people are there," she says. Her 24-year-old son has been in Florida working in construction for four years. His wife went to join him, leaving their 5-year-old daughter in Guadalupe. "It is sad that she is growing up without her parents," Doña Lupe says. "One can't survive here, because in the countryside you earn a $1.50 per day. All life in the countryside is drying up. My other son tells me that he isn't going to keep studying [after junior high] because there aren't any jobs and anyway he'll end up over there." Doña Lupe has three brothers and three sisters; all of them work in the United States, one in Texas and five in Florida. They all have families in the United

States now. Some come to visit because they have visas, but those who are undocumented stay; the years go by and they do not see their relatives. Lupe's husband is a highly skilled carpenter who built their home by hand after working for a year and a half in the United States. He then went back to work for another seven months to save up and build a one-room convenience store in Guadalupe. The convenience store's main attraction is a Harry Potter slot machine that the kids in town line up to play. "Here you can't make in one week what you can in a day over there," Doña Lupe says, "All the rural communities are abandoned. The land is full of sorrow."

MARGARITA AND JAVIER

The couple has five children living in the United States, one daughter in between trips, and one son still in school. Three of Margarita and Javier's sons are in Florida, one in Chicago, and one in California. Several years back, in 1999, Margarita decided to venture north to visit two of her sons whom she had not seen in seven years. One was working in Salinas, California, as a truck driver. Margarita and her daughter Esmeralda, then 16 years old, paid $1,800 each to a coyote to take them over the border. They walked through the Arizona desert for four days, two of them spent in a canyon hiding from the Border Patrol. The coyote gave them canned tuna without a can opener. The best they could do was to make tiny holes in the can by banging it against the sharp edges of rocks and then rush to drink a few drops of the water before they spilled onto the sand. After they made it through, the coyotes on the other side grouped about 160 people into four vans, stacking up to forty people in the back of each van, literally on top of each other. Near Wilcox, Arizona they crashed. Margarita had cuts all over her back and head. The police sent her to a hospital in Phoenix in a helicopter. Esmeralda, her daughter, was left behind at the hospital in Wilcox. A doctor born in Mexico saw Esmeralda, bruised, bleeding, and crying in the parking lot and asked her what was wrong. She said she couldn't find her mother. The doctor soon discovered that her mother had been taken to Phoenix; he hid Esmeralda and after work drove her to Phoenix. At the hospital in Phoenix the doctors wanted Esmeralda to sign organ donor releases for her mother, but she refused, saying she would not sign anything before her brother arrived. The doctors had given up on Margarita until Esmeralda arrived and cried that her mother was still alive, not dead. She called her brother in Salinas, who then flew out to find them. Another doctor in Phoenix hid Esmeralda so the Border Patrol would not deport her. Days later, Margarita was still recovering from serious head and back injuries, but the Border Patrol began searching the hospital to deport her to Nogales. Doctors helped sneak her out the back. She still could not walk. She drove with her son to Salinas, fainting during the drive. In Salinas she was seen by doctors who wanted to amputate one of her legs. She could not walk alone. She refused the amputation and decided to return to Guadalupe. She and her sons paid her Phoenix hospital bills in full. She underwent physical therapy in Acámbaro and after months was able to walk again.

Her husband Javier also has a crossing story. He got caught on a train entering the United States through Ciudad Juárez in the early 1990s. Their train was carrying brand-new cars from Mexico to showrooms in the United States. Scores of migrants jumped the train and were riding in the unlocked new cars, many in the driver's seats, having a ball, pretending they were at the steering wheel. "But some got a bit carried away and started flashing the lights and turn signals and honking the horns, and the immigration police got wind of what was going on and stopped the train. When the train stopped we all went running in different directions, looking for a place to hide." Javier got sent back, but he gave it another shot and made it through, eventually getting a job picking fruits and vegetables in California. I ask Javier if he was able to save any money when he worked in the United States. He laughs. "No. Between the rent, rides, food, telephone, and sending money back, I returned to Mexico with $300 after a year."

I ask the last time the whole family was together. Margarita answers that their youngest son Pancho, now 16 years old, has never met three of his older brothers. Her sons left when they were 17 years old. Now they have adolescent kids who don't know their grandparents. When they call on the phone and Margarita tries to pass the phone to Pancho he says: "What do you want me to say to them if I don't even know them?"

"My family has been broken since 1990," Margarita said. "My family broke, it ceased to be and from there the tears came. About ten years ago the migration began to be so exaggerated. Where before you probably knew someone whose husband worked over there, not anymore, now everyone goes. What one does not do here, one does over there, and what is really sad is that they are barely able to make ends meet. Yes, they send us a little bit, but we know what they suffer over there. You lose your son and gain just a little support. So now people's houses are pretty and well decorated, but the streets are empty. When people come back in December to visit they bring pretty gadgets, appliances, but there are few people here to use them. The town progresses, but only in the sense that it has nicer little houses." Their house has a cracked concrete floor, metal and glass doors, tin roof, and concrete walls. It is sturdy and clean, but humble by any U.S. comparison. "You lose your son; the family disintegrates, everyone is leaving, and the family is decomposing. I think this is a crime."

PRETTY HOUSE

Walking an unpaved stretch of road—the section waiting for twenty tons of cement to come after the state of the city address—I see a very attractive new two-story house with a green lawn, flowers in pots, fresh paint, and a monster satellite dish on the front balcony. I knock on the closed outside gate and no one answers. I knock again and a woman walking down the street calls out: "No one lives there, they are up north."

A second woman, Rosita, walks by and stops to ask whom I am looking for. The owners of this house, I say. She responds: "They are all over on the other side."

Rosita lives across the street in a one-story adobe house. Her husband was killed in a robbery while working in Mexico City and her sons all work in construction in St. Louis. She works as a housekeeper in neighboring Acámbaro, where, she says, "the ladies don't even give me a drink of water, much less a lunch break." Rosita makes ten dollars a day.

OLIVIA AND CARLOS

The two are walking past the church at 10:15 a.m., pushing a wheelbarrow filled with Tupperware containers covered in cloth. The containers hold enchiladas, tacos, and sandwiches. Olivia and Carlos are walking across town to the elementary school, Emiliano Zapata, where they sell their homemade snacks to hungry students during their recess, which starts at 10:30. They, and five others like them, are the mobile school cafeterias. Carlos is 18. I ask him if he thinks of going to the United States.

"Yeah, I think so, but only for a year or so, to work for a while and come back, because I don't really want to stay over there."

"That's what they all say," his mother, Olivia, joins in. "My sister said the same thing, that she would only be there for a bit, and ooh, now it has been years. They say they can't make enough to build their houses if they stay here, that they barely make enough to put food on the table. But now they go, and then they stay."

Olivia's two other children work in the United States, one in Florida and one in Ohio.

FIFTH GRADERS

I walk into a room filled with twenty-seven fifth graders and ask them: What is migration?

"Those who go north!" a voice shouts out. "The ones who don't have papers," comes another.

"And why do people migrate?"

"To work!" "To support their families!" the kids shout in staggered unison.

"Why do people go to work over there and not here?"

"They earn more!" "There are no jobs here!"

I ask who has a relative in the United States and every hand in the room shoots up. Every one. Total, including the teacher: twenty-eight.

Ten have brothers or sisters in the United States. For ten, either their mother or father is in the United States.

"Who has an uncle or an aunt in the United States?" Every hand goes up.

I ask the kids to take out a blank sheet of paper and a pen or pencil, and to answer two questions: What is migration? Why do people migrate?

Francisco Javier, 10: "Migrants are the ones who go to the United States and later to other places and there are young men who go and leave their families behind in Mexico. People migrate to the other side to send money to their families so that they can get by."

José, 11: "Migration is when some men are chased by the police when they go north and so they have to go about hiding from the police. People go *de mojados*"—as wetbacks—"to be able to feed their families and to be able to eat and survive."

Jesús, 10: "Migration is when people travel to the other side. They go to make money for their families."

Anayeli, 10: "Migration is when people go north without documents. They go to make money for their families."

Geovani, 12: "Migration is when people don't have money."

Diego, 10: "Migration is when a person goes to the United States to support their family."

Juana, 11: "Migration is someone who goes to the other side without permission from the authorities risking a lot of danger to support their family. They go to support their family and also so that people know that everyone can do it, not just the men."

THE SIXTH-GRADE CLASS

I walk across the basketball court and into the sixth-grade class, twenty-six students in all, between 11 and 12 years old.

I ask them: what is migration?

"When people go to another country," one student ventures.

"Is there anything special about why they go to another country?"

"They go to work," all the voices say.

I ask them to raise their hands if one of their family members lives in another country. All the hands go up, including that of the teacher. Where? "The other side," and "the north," all the voices say.

I ask them to raise their hands if their brother, sister, mother, or father works in the United States. Twenty-three hands go up. I ask them if an uncle or an aunt works in the United States, and again every hand goes up.

I hand out blank sheets of paper and ask the kids to write down what they would do if they had a magic wand.

Jimena, 11: "I want to change the Mexican State so that there will be more employment and all people can have a better life."

César, 12: "I want to use my magic wand to make more jobs."

Norelli, 11: "I want there to be a better life in Mexico so that all the people won't go to the United States and the families do not separate and they don't leave Mexico."

María Guadalupe, 11: "I want to change Mexico so that there can be more jobs, so that all those whom I miss can come back and they don't have to leave again."

Mariana, 12: "I want all my relatives to be here in Mexico and that there is work in Mexico so that they don't have to go to the U.S.A."

Sheila, 12: "I want to change things so that my brothers can be with the family and we can be happy, because on Christmas it is very sad for my family because we are not together; that is what I want to change with my magic wand."

Arturo, 12: "I want there to be work in Acámbaro so that all those in the United States can come back. I want Acámbaro to be a place where there are jobs."

Xochitl, 11: "I want to change that all my aunts and uncles and my mother come back and that they don't go away forever."

SCHOOLTEACHERS

The director: "Ten years ago in a nearby school there were eight teachers in the morning shift and eight in the afternoon shift. Now the school is gone and the entire community is following close behind." He begins to count on his hand the nearby schools that have closed: four.

The P.E. teacher: "Before only the fathers would go, but not anymore. Now since it is so hard to cross without papers, the fathers go, save, and then send for their kids, then another two or three kids disappear from the school."

The fifth-grade teacher: "My son works in a plant store outside of Chicago. He has worked there for eight years, since he was 18 years old. He crossed without papers and came back once a year. But the last time he left, about five years ago, he nearly died in the desert. They made it through, but they were sick and their feet were completely blistered beyond recognition. I spoke to him over the phone after he crossed. His voice was weak, without any strength at all; he told me that they had had problems, that they had run out of water. After that he stopped coming home. Two years later he had his first child. On the one hand, I am happy because my son is getting ahead, but on the other hand, it hurts because, well, he's far away. And then due to their legal status without documents the bosses exploit them, paying less than normal, not giving benefits. The exploitation continues; it is a kind of modern slavery. Just think about it, even though they live in harsh conditions over there, in our own country things are so much worse that they prefer to live over there where they have to fit three families into a single house in order to make the rent."

WOMAN IN THE STREET
Walking under an umbrella to protect her from the brunt of the early afternoon sun, an elderly woman stops, hesitant, to answer a stranger's questions: two of her sons have worked in California for fifteen years; they both have visas and work in restaurants.

MANUELA, SHEILA'S GRANDMOTHER, ACROSS THE STREET
Manuela is 84 years old. Sheila, from the sixth-grade class, takes me in to meet her. She has three—no wait, she counts on her hand—four children in the United States. And why did they go?

"There is no work here. Nothing, there is nothing here. So

they have to go, here there is nothing left but to die of hunger."

YOUNG WOMAN WORKING IN AN EMPTY CONVENIENCE STORE HALF A BLOCK AWAY

Two of her brothers are in the United States. She wants to go but is scared of crossing the desert.

NEW TORTILLA SHOP OWNER

"We are going to build a monument to the gringos. Thanks to them we are alive over here." He says that the majority of his family works in the United States. He points to a cluster of 11- and 12-year-olds in the doorway: "All these kids are just waiting to get old enough to cross. The whole town survives by what people send back from the United States."

LUPITA'S MOTHER

Lupita, one of the fifth graders (a cluster of fifth and sixth graders adopted me in the street and led me through the town) takes me to meet her mother. Lupia's father works in lawn care in St. Louis, Missouri. He has gone to the United States with a work permit every year for the past eight years. He stays nine months and comes back. Lupita's mother sells enchiladas at the school during recess. "Here there are no jobs, you can't earn a living, that is why people leave, for necessity, no one goes because it's fun."

JORGE, 50, AND HIPOLITO, 84

Jorge is painting a car jack on the sidewalk step and Hipolito is sitting in the shade. I ask them why people go north. "People all go for the same reason," Jorge says, "because there is no way to survive here. There are no jobs and at the same time prices keep going up and up."

Jorge says that there used to be vegetable farms all around Guadalupe: broccoli, tomatoes, celery, lettuce, squash, and, of course, corn. When these farms all went under about ten years ago, all the jobs dried up. But the migration rates really shot up after the fields of cempasuchitl flowers were removed about five years ago. The only people who still grow crops—corn and sorghum—are the wealthy, the ones with large plots and irrigation systems. For poor folks, he says, there is nothing left.

"Before, people had a few cows, and now? What cows? There is nowhere to graze them. Most of the countryside is abandoned, unplanted, but it has all been bought up by the rich."

Jorge worked in restaurants and mowed lawns in California about twenty years ago. I ask if there is a restaurant in Guadalupe.

"There are no restaurants here, with the level of poverty, who is going to pay for a meal in a restaurant? I hope something helps us put things back together, because if not we are going to start dying of hunger, just look at me," he says, pointing to his gaunt frame.

YOUNG WOMAN IN A PAPER STORE DOWN THE STREET

Elizabeth is 21 years old. She sits behind the counter in a closet-size office supply store with only a few pens, pencils, notebooks, and paper clips to offer. I ask if any of her family members have migrated.

"Well, practically my whole family is over there, my uncles, my mother. They've been over there for about ten years. Only two uncles come to visit because they have papers."

Her mother works in Florida; she has not visited in nine years.

What does she think about all the migration to the United States?

"Well, I blame the Mexican government more than anyone. There is no work here and the lack of jobs is what makes people emigrate. Look at me, for example, I just graduated six months ago with a degree in business administration and I can't find a job."

The office supply shop is a family business run out of the entryway to their house.

What is she going to do?

"I am going to look for work in Celaya, Morelia, or Querétaro, but not in the United States. The United States has already taken too many of my family members away."

CONSIDER THE NUMBERS. In 2000: 389,616. In 2001: 392,003. In 2002: 394,120. In 2003: 396,129. In 2004: 397, 988. People. Every year, nearly 400,000 people leave their homes across Mexico to seek work in the United States. From nearly every corner of the country. They walk. They pay or indenture themselves for up to $3,000 for a stranger to lead them through the desert to a land where, in the summer months, the human body needs about a gallon of water every three hours to survive.[2] But these are the successful ones, the ones who cross. Every year the United States Border Patrol arrests and deports about a million people; and every year hundreds die in the heat, drown in the Rio Grande, or fall under the trains or to the bullets and machete blades of drug traffickers and bandits.[3] As many people from Mexico are currently seeking economic asylum in the United States as are seeking political asylum in the entire continent of Africa.[4]

The United States has the world's largest economy and the world's most powerful military. It also has the world's largest immigrant workforce, a huge number of its members (over ten million) undocumented. Mexico, the United States' southern neighbor, sharing a 1,952-mile border with it, generates more migrants than any other country on earth, regardless of population. More people flee Mexico every year looking for work in the United States than do people in China or India, each of which has over a billion citizens. Mexico and the United States signed a so-called "free trade" agreement in 1994. Since Mexico began the wave of privatizations and economic "restructuring" necessary to pass NAFTA, emigration from Mexico to the United States has more than doubled, and it continues to grow each year. In 2003, Mexican migrants sent home over $13 billion, but those same migrants during that same year contributed around $395 billion to the U.S. economy.[5] Mexican laborers pick most of the fruit and vegetables grown in the United States. Mexican laborers also build houses, office buildings, and roads; they clean people's homes and offices; they serve meals and wash dishes. Meanwhile, their hometowns back in Mexico are barely kept alive with the remittances they send back. New houses sprout up, but the roads that lead to them remain unpaved. No new schools, clinics, shopping centers, or cultural centers are built. Relative prosperity in the United States and increasing destitution and marginalization in Mexico are intimately linked, bound in a complex relation of circular influences and impacts. Forced labor migration is an engine of wealth and poverty.[6]

The anti-immigrant Right in the United States conceives unauthorized border crossings as a kind of original sin, a criminal act that forever marks its perpetrators with a criminal identity: "If these people were capable of breaking the law once," their logic says, "they will be prone to breaking it again and again; they will have no respect for the law, thus introducing into this country a wave of criminals." The U.S. economy with all its marvels, privileges, and excesses is kept aloft—and always has been—by exploited migrant labor. Industrial agriculture as we know it would not exist without migrant labor. Development and construction companies are largely depend on migrant labor. The insolence of those who view Mexican (and other migrant) workers as invaders testifies to the deep legacy and continuing prevalence of racism in the United States, as does elected officials' vicious opportunism when they employ jingoism in the hope of scaring up the votes needed for another term of office.

In the War of 1846–1848, the United States invaded Mexico and snatched half its territory—land that later became California, Nevada, Utah, New Mexico, Arizona, half of Texas and Colorado, and bits of Arkansas, Oklahoma, and Wyoming. All of this land had first been invaded by the Spanish and claimed as part of New Spain. General Zachary Taylor invaded Mexican territory in the spring of 1846 in a "calculated violation" of the Mexican border.[7] Two years later the U.S. doctrine of "manifest destiny" was indeed made "manifest" through the conquest of what is today the U.S. Southwest. U.S. capital invaded deep into the Mexican heartland during the Porfiriato, and again after the 1940s.[8] And then came NAFTA. The wave of privatizations and economic restructuring carried out by presidents De la Madrid and Salinas in the years immediately preceding the signing of NAFTA ushered in an unprecedented wave of U.S. capital invasion.[9]

The disaster of NAFTA is well-known and well-documented.[10] Still some squirm and fudge when it comes to holding NAFTA accountable for its devastating impacts on Mexican emigration.[11] They hold out as proof over 100 years of lower levels of migration and the rising migration statistics from the 1980s and early 1990s before NAFTA went into effect. However, NAFTA is more than the agreement signed in 1994: it entails the entire economic restructuring of the 1980s that was necessary to pass the agreement. NAFTA itself is shorthand for the dominant economic model—economic imperialism—that has been foisted on Mexico (and so many other countries). This is the basic argument of the world-renowned Mexican expert on migration Raúl Delgado Wise. He writes, for example:

> The intensification of commercial ties between the two nations as part of a new strategy of imperialist domination controlled by financial capital and the large U.S. multinational corporations has restructured binational work processes and strongly affected the labor force. I . . . argue here that the reigning model of economic integration is sustained by the role the Mexican workforce—both in Mexico and outside its borders—has played in the industrial restructuring of the United States.[12]

Mexican economist Juan Manuel Sandoval develops a similar argument. He writes:

> The relationship established between free trade and labor migration (one as a problem, the other as the solution) by both governments is a false link. Free trade has mainly benefited U.S. capitalists. With this strategy, the U.S. seeks to secure a controlled and regulated cheap labor migratory flow into the economy. . . . NAFTA . . . has become one of the mechanisms for the creation of the new U.S. labor transnational reserve army, by displacing people from Mexican industries and agriculture, which unevenly compete with U.S. big corporations.[13]

The processes of economic competition and domination create a system of transnational apartheid in the midst of so-called democratic countries. NAFTA creates incentive for big business to relocate to Mexico, where labor and environmental protections are lax and seldom enforced. It also uproots Mexico's small farmers and manufacturing workers and carries them off to the maquilas and to the United States, where they labor without the documentary sanction of the state—thus becoming "illegal aliens." NAFTA creates a transnational underclass of economically destitute people, in many cases indigenous, who become second-class citizens both in their own country and in the United States. The migrants' very illegality guarantees their exploitability as workers: few migrants will seek justice when contracts are broken or legal obligations of employers go unmet, fearing deportation. In the United States, migrant laborers are subjected not only to "legitimate" legal discrimination on the basis of their undocumented migratory status, but to institutional, cultural, and personal racism as a matter of daily life. Meanwhile this forced expulsion of the economically destitute releases social pressure from the Mexican elite, annually shaving off about half a million upset, unemployed people clamoring for economic opportunities.

CERRITO DE AGUA IS A PLACE mostly defined by what it lacks.[14] There are no paved roads within or leading to this small town of just under 3,000 people. There are no restaurants here, no movie theaters or shopping malls. There are no middle schools, high schools, or colleges. There is no cell phone service, no hospital. There are no factories, no bookstores, and no cafés. The fields that surround the town are dry and untended. The streets are empty.

The explosion of emigration from Mexico over the past fifteen years has emptied much of the central part of the country and reached into the southernmost states like Chiapas and Yucatán, but it has simply devastated Zacatecas state, a dry, rolling agricultural region located about 400 miles northwest of Mexico City. Just over half of Zacatecas's population—about 1.8 million people—now lives in the United States, especially in areas surrounding Los Angeles, Chicago, and Atlanta. Between 2000 and 2005, three out of its four municipalities registered a negative population growth. A 2004 state law created two new state legislative posts for migrants living in the United States. In 2006, depopulation cost the state one of its five congressional districts.

"Well, you've seen what this place is like," says Dr. Manuel Valadez López, gesturing out the door of his small private clinic, when I ask him how emigration has impacted the town. "There has not been even minimal development here. There is not a single yard of pavement. The few people who have sidewalks in front of their houses built them themselves. Most people defecate outdoors."

Dr. López, a 40-year-old native of Cerrito de Agua, is one of the very few to have left the town and returned. All of his six brothers now live and work in the United States, spread out between Southern California, Aurora, Illinois, and Atlanta, Georgia. All four of his sisters married men who left to work in the United States, mostly in Southern California. Dr. López moved to Guadalajara (about five hours southwest of Zacatecas) in his teens to attend high school and university. He stayed on to study medicine and receive a specialist's training in gynecology.

"I came for a visit and there was so much work to do here that I stayed. That was eight years ago," he says. "The whole culture now is that people grow up and go to the United States: their parents, their uncles, their brothers and sisters, everyone goes. The kids who are strong and smart, they all go to the United States. There are no basic services here; the government has not carried out a single project. Here in the clinic we put in our own sewage system. There is running water, but it's not clean; people get all sorts of infections, typical Third World situation. But the biggest impact, the worst of all, is that the people who could possibly stay here and do something, they all go."

But the emptiness in the streets and the untilled stretches of sun-bleached fields speaks of more than simple abandon. Those who are missing here, those whose land goes unplanted, whose roads remain unpaved, are laboring in the United States, building shopping malls and factories, washing dishes in restaurants and cafés, picking grapes and pulling lettuce: creating within the U.S. economy precisely the goods and services that their hometowns lack.

A January 2008 report by Richard Nadler, president of the conservative Americas Majority Foundation, found that the strongest state economies in the United States are those with high numbers of migrant workers. Nadler writes: "An analysis of data from fifty states and the District of Columbia demonstrates that a high resident population and/or inflow of immigrants is associated with elevated *levels* and *growth* in Gross State Product, Personal Income, Per Capita Personal Income, Disposable Income, Per Capita Disposable Income, Median Household Income, and Median Per Capita Income."

"I think that the United States' plan is to make Mexico into a kind of colony," says Dr. López, with a half smile. "People go to the United States to work and earn dollars. They come back to Mexico and spend their dollars on American products. It's a nice, round business. Everyone here depends on the United States. If this isn't a colony, then how do you define colony?"

The makers of U.S. immigration policy never stop to ask, "What is this doing to Mexico?" Anti-immigration groups attack immigrants for speaking Spanish while immigrants' rights activists laud their work ethic. Debates rage over legalization and guest-worker programs. The driving questions behind U.S. immigration policy are: "How many will be allowed in?" and "How are they to be processed into the system?" But who is asking, "What is happening to Mexico?"

With nearly half a million Mexicans crossing the border every year to look for work in the world's biggest economy, Mexico has become the largest exporter of its people in the world. The word "migration" makes this all seem somehow natural—people moving, people looking for better lives. But the sheer scope of Mexican migration is so massive and its impacts inside of Mexico so devastating, that the simple idea of people moving about hardly does justice to the reality.

"Theories of migration always show the interests of the North," says Raúl Delgado Wise, who is also director of the Graduate School of Development Studies at the Autonomous University of Zacatecas. "We need to create different categories to make visible what is happening. We are using statistics from the United States to show that migrants born in Mexico contribute 8 percent of the U.S. Gross Domestic Product, about $900 billion, which is more than Mexico's entire Gross Domestic Product. That should give you an idea of the scope of what we're talking about, the cost to Mexico of migration."

Professor Delgado Wise is one of a small but busy knot of researchers studying Mexican migration at the University of Zacatecas. They publish an international journal called *Migration and Development* and are laying the groundwork for an alternative think tank to the World Bank, to be called the Consortium for Critical Development Studies.

"With all of this we need to see really how much it is costing Mexico, how much Mexico is losing," Wise says.

To understand the mass migration from Mexico to the United States, Delgado Wise argues, one must demystify the nature of the U.S.-Mexico economic integration that began in the 1980s and reached its maximum expression with NAFTA. What Mexico really exports, Wise argues, is labor. The supposed growth in Mexico's manufacturing sector is a "smoke screen," he writes, when almost half of all manufacturing exports come from maquiladora assembly plants that import production materials and export their final products and their profits. Mexico only adds the labor.

The policies implemented in the 1980s and through NAFTA, often bundled under the term "neoliberalism,"* cut government investment in public works and agriculture, privatized key state enterprises, and created interest rates attractive to foreign capital. These policies opened the way for a twenty-five-fold increase in maquiladora sales between 1982 and 2003. However, just from 1994 to 2002, Mexico lost over one million agricultural jobs. And, from 1980 to 2002, the same time period that maquiladora sales soared, migration from Mexico to the United States grew by 452 percent, up to over 400,000 people a year.

"In Mexico, we have exported the factory of migrants," says Rodolfo García Zamora, a professor along with Delgado Wise at the Graduate School of Development Studies and author of the book *Migration, Remittances, and Local Development.* "Mexico is mortgaging its future with migration and remittances. Look at the statistics: in the ten states with the longest migration histories, sixty-five percent of municipalities have a negative population growth. This means that in the future these communities will not be able to reproduce, either eco-

---

* I use the terms "neoliberalism" and "neoliberal" to refer to the conservative and capitalist ideology that "free markets" will enhance the greater good of the world, and thus that social enterprises such as health care, water provision, and education should be privatized; the ideology obscures the fact that no markets are free, and that neoliberal markets in particular are structured so as to privilege large, often transnational, corporations.

nomically or socially, because the demographics of migration have condemned them to disappear."

García Zamora, who helped write the Zacatecas state development plan, is fiercely critical of government programs to address the impacts of migration. "There is only one political party in Mexico: the PRI," he says. "There is the PRI of the dinosaurs. And there is the PRI with hepatitis, the guilty-feeling dinosaurs contaminated a bit with the Communist Party; that is, the PRD. And then there is the blue PRI, which is just as inept, as corrupt, and has nepotistic as the old PRI; here I am speaking of the PAN.

"The PRD government in Zacatecas now acts just like a PRI government," he says. "The same improvisation and nepotism. It spends its time mainly implementing federal programs. They drafted a good development plan, but they never implemented it. They have relied on assistance programs, populism, and handouts. They have never carried out a serious regional economic development policy that seeks to diminish the massive exodus of forty thousand Zacatecas residents who abandon Mexico every year."

Fernando Robledo, director of the Zacatecas state government's Migration Institute does not really see the problem. "The United States economy demands cheap labor," he says. "Mexico has an excess of laborers. We complement each other."

Robledo dismisses talk of depopulation and an abandoned countryside as "fatalism." "Zacatecas has a one-hundred-and-twenty-year history of migration," he says. "Migration is historical."

Robledo describes the state government's development priorities, all of which are variations on the "Three for One" program, meaning that local, state, and federal governments match each dollar provided by migrant organizations in the United States for local development projects. Robledo mentions the state's top development priorities as building interstate highways north, to the United States, and constructing greenhouses for cash crops to be exported to the United States.

"If you had fifty million dollars in the budget," he asks, "would you use that to increase production in the countryside or to build an interstate highway? It is a political and economic decision."

I reference Delgado Wise's argument that the number of Mexicans migrating shot up after neoliberal economic policies uprooted small farmers from the countryside and sent them off to be laborers in the U.S. economy. I then ask: doesn't building more highways toward the Mexico-U.S. border and changing agriculture to a cash-crop export model reproduce on the local level the very neoliberal policies that dispossess migrants in the first place?

"We do not live in a socialist country," he responds bitterly, a bit before I can finish the question. "Please! Just to be clear, we are not in a socialist country where the government controls every aspect of the economy. We are in a neoliberal country; we cannot escape from neoliberal economics. Please! It is easy to criticize from a desk."

When I repeat the statement "we cannot escape from neoliberal economics" back to him, Robledo tries to backpedal, saying that he did not say that, and then that, well, that is not what he meant. He agrees with Delgado Wise's "criticisms of neoliberalism," but the best way forward, he says, is to build more new highways and create export industries—that is, to implement more neoliberal policies.

Mario García disagrees. García, a rugged farmer and construction worker in his early forties, left Zacatecas a few years back to work in Southern California, but after about five months he decided to return to El Cargadero, a tiny town about fifty miles west of Zacatecas City.

"In Mexico, if you work a couple of shifts, you can live okay, I thought, without so many luxuries and freeways, but you can live a more peaceful life."

El Cargadero, with a local population of about 350 and a population in the United States of over 1,000, is supposed to be a success story of local development based on migrants' remittances. Most of the roads in town are freshly paved, a result of the "Three for One" program. García, his wife, and three daughters, ages 3, 6, and 16, live in El Cargadero, but all nine of his brothers and sisters and more than fifty of his cousins live and work in the United States.

"There are many points of view, but as you can see here, this is a community abandoned by migration," García says, standing in front of his concrete-brick home. "I have always related migration to the government; the government should work to keep people in the country, to find jobs, to better living conditions. Here we have pretty streets, but where are the people? We have potable water and electricity, but the people?"

Indeed, driving from Zacatecas City to El Cargadero one sees mile after mile of empty fields, closed-down restaurants, and boarded-up houses. José Manuel, a taxi driver who worked in California for four years, washing dishes and making salads, accompanies me on the drive to El Cargadero. He tells me that this vast emptiness is a common sight now.

"Nobody works most of this land anymore; the owners went to the United States and left the land behind," he says. "I remember when these roads weren't paved yet, but the fields were full of corn and beans."

This is precisely what brought Mario García back.

"The countryside is broken," he says. "The rural economy needs to be reactivated. But we export one of the most valuable things: our workers. And now we don't produce anything."

"We need to analyze free trade more closely," he continues, "because free trade might be benefiting everybody but Mexico. There might be a few new millionaires, but there are a lot more people who are screwed; things are not even. Before NAFTA we produced tons of peaches, and the national markets all clamored for peaches from Zacatecas. But with NAFTA, U.S. companies started exporting peaches from Chile and Brazil and the prices fell. We couldn't sell our peaches anymore, and people starting leaving to look for work in the United States.

"Mexico does not need an open border with the United States that invites Mexicans to go work in that country. People always talk about legalization, but no, what needs to be legalized is the Mexican's ability to stay in his or her own country so that Mexico can grow and produce."

What could U.S. policy do to help, I ask?

"The United States does not have just policies for Mexico," he says. "The solution here would be for the Mexican government to build strategies to put the brakes on this, so that the countryside can produce again.

"I think that if my cousins, brothers, and sisters were here, if my relatives and countrymen were here, we would be producing. But no one takes the initiative; there are no subsidies for the countryside, no workers. This is a problem that has been building for decades, and now we are paying the consequences of migration."

When I first arrive in El Cargadero looking for García, who represents the town on the municipal council, Ángel, age 9, offers to walk with me on the way to talk to Mario. On the walk he offers me a piece of chewing gum from a tiny pack in his pocket. Four of his aunts moved to the United States and have families there. His brother, now 18, has been in Los Angeles for three years working in restaurants. I ask him what his favorite subject in school is. "Spanish," he answers. I ask if he knows what he wants to be when he grows up, and a big light turns on in his face. He nods.

"What?" I ask.

"*Un campesino*," he says, "a farmer."

"A THOUSAND DOLLARS? For a thousand dollars I'll send people out walking through the desert for six days. I don't even charge my family that. If you want to cross here, it's $3,000. If you only want to walk for a while, for $2,000 I'll take you out a bit farther and [you can start] from there. But for $1,000 you'll go through the whole desert," says the *pollero* without the slightest touch of humor.[15] About five-foot-five and thin, he wears a T-shirt with cut-off sleeves exposing a faded tattoo of Christ on his right shoulder; his sunglasses are pushed up in his thick, short hair, and beneath each sun-clenched eye is a teardrop tattoo, one for a grief that he carries with him, the other for a man he killed. He himself is a child of migration. His parents took him back and forth over the border to Los Angeles ever since he was knee-high; it was there that he joined the Maravillas, there that a rival gang member murdered his 11-year-old brother, there that he sought out and shot dead his brother's killer.

Now he stands across a shallow valley perched in the door-way of his red Blazer. He stands on the Mexico side of the border facing a U.S. army tent about a football field length away, where soldiers scan the valley with binoculars, Border Patrol cameras sweep back and forth, Border Patrol agents troll the roads, and the wall separating Mexico from the United States suddenly stops and starts again, leaving a thirty-yard hole through which *polleros* like him guide over 100 people a day into the United States. Using cellular phones they coordinate with guides who hide down below in the bushes and half whisper commands to migrants crouched down on the Mexican side, waiting for the cue to make a break for it. If the Border Patrol spots them as they cross, they hear a shout from behind and come sprinting back to avoid detention, processing, and deportation.

The scene seems straight out of *Looney Tunes*. But there is no comedy here, where the entire ritual farce of the border is played out in cartoonish detail less than ten yards from the main deportation point for undocumented migrants, where in 2006 alone, according to the director of the Sonora state government's Migrant Attention Center, Antonio Rivera Cortés, the Border Patrol deported 160,000 people. Here, all together, are the elements of a grotesque comedy of errors. The hole in the wall. The army tent. The Border Patrol jeeps and camera towers. The tattooed gangsters. The corrupt Mexican police wearing gold rosaries and dark glasses who drive up to take their bribes. And the destitute migrants willing to gamble everything on a chance to work. The *polleros* even have a decrepit, sunbleached couch placed up here on the cliff in which to lounge as they observe the Border Patrol movements on the other side and coordinate the groups of crouching migrants down below. The *polleros* lounge directly in front of the U.S. soldiers who are stationed to protect the border. All this happens in plain sight.

The guides lead the migrants in single file, crouching down, over the border into the parking lot where they hope to be driven off to safe houses in Phoenix and Tucson and wait for family members to wire their payments. They crouch down by the wall or in the bushes and wait. Every day, all day and all night, the *polleros* lead scores of people across the border literally under the nose of the U.S. Army and Border Patrol. The local Nogales police drive up, and the *polleros* signal for them to come back later for their cut. The state judicial police pull up and get out, joking around with the *polleros*, watching the attempts of the migrants down below to cross. I ask one of the state police if a lot of journalists come around here. He replies glibly: "No, they're all paid off, only the foreign press comes. And besides, reporters aren't stupid, they know what they can and cannot say."

One *pollero* offers to take me and two other reporters into the tunnels. He says he can get us an interview with the "real boss" and we will see drugs, migrants, and guns, all for just $500. The man with the teardrop tattoos whispers, "Don't trust him. He might take you into a tunnel with your cameras, but you won't come back out."

The unspoken word on everyone's mind here is *narco*. Drug traffickers, the untouchable lords equipped with private armies composed of special forces soldiers gone AWOL who control both the urban and desert border routes, reap tens of millions of dollars from human trafficking every year. The government not only watches (literally) but also pockets a handsome cut. And the notion of the law, here on the border? Search for it amidst the bones of those who have perished: here only those with money and guns rule.

"They are walking merchandise," says a man who lives behind one of the Nogales soup kitchens for migrants. "Everyone charges their fee: the local police, Mexican immigration officials, the federal investigative police, the politicians, everyone; this is big money. It is an industry, but one built on the pain and suffering of people who may not return to see their families ever again."

Rosario and Guillermo walk across the bridge with their two boys, 6 and 7 years old, and accept the hot rice and beans offered to them at the Migrant Attention Center known as the Centro Mariposa, only a few yards across the street from the *pollero* lounge. They are from San Isidro, Michoacán, and speak to each other in hurried whispers in Purépecha, their native language. They have just been deported after their third attempt to enter the United States and join two uncles working in construction in Florida. They were robbed in the desert two times. The first robbery occurred after six hours of walking. "A coyote told me that we were in the United States and took $2,000 from me and left us in the desert, but still in Sonora," says Guillermo. That was their first attempt to cross.

They tried again. This time thieves caught them in a group of about twenty people on the U.S. side and stole everything. The thieves beat them with gun barrels. Rosario's face is scratched from her right eye down to just beside her lips. When I ask her what happened she tries to answer, but weeps instead. "I think that the guide was in on it," Guillermo says. "At night he lit a cigarette but said that none of us could light cigarettes. When the thieves came they grabbed him—the only one with a lit cigarette—and took him away before robbing us all."

One 21-year-old man, Zack, was deported through Nogales. He took the Altar-Sasabe route. The Mexican police stopped his group and the *pollero* paid the police. Then the Mexican special migration police, Grupo Beta, stopped them again, and again the *pollero* paid them off. They crossed the border and walked for two days and nights. They were finally picked up, driven to Phoenix, and taken to a safe house. Once inside the house the men waiting there beat them at gunpoint and took their wallets, shoes, and socks. One by one they made them call their families and ask them to send money. If the family didn't answer the phone the men would slap them around. If the family said they did not have enough money, then the men shaved their heads (Zack's hair was cropped less than a quarter inch long, he said, pointing to his head as he told this part of the story) and beat them wildly. After holding them for a month in the room, giving them barely a few tortillas a day (Zack was rail thin), the men beat one of their group and then killed him, plunging a knife in his chest repeatedly, all right in the center of the room in front of the others, with armed men standing guard. The Arizona police soon raided the house and deported them all, kidnappers and kidnapped together. The police never asked the kidnapped any questions nor investigated the kidnapping or the murder. And still, Zack is ready to give it another shot. His conclusion: "There are so many stories, so many even worse than this."

The town of Altar is under constant, if almost invisible, siege. One of the principal gathering points for migrants heading into the Arizona desert, drug traffickers, police, and *polleros* constantly monitoring the streets, driving up and down, day and night, in white sedans with tinted windows and no license plates, scouting for newly arrived migrants. They approach groups of men sitting in the plaza with enthusiastic greetings and handshakes. They wait for the buses coming in from the south to drop their passengers on the side of the road—there is no bus station in Altar—and immediately weave through the assembly of wide-eyed newcomers offering half-price discounts to take them across the border that very day.

Everyone here watches everyone. The migrants are obvious by their desert-required uniform of sorts: T-shirt, jeans, running shoes, baseball cap, and backpack, all black (and a jacket in autumn and winter). They walk in groups of four, never alone nor all together. They head out early in the morning from the guest houses where they sleep thirty to a room on a patch of concrete floor, with a blanket if they pay extra, taking turns breakfasting on tamales and coffee sold on the street. They walk to the outdoor stands that line the street where sellers offer backpacks, socks, foot powder, and other supplies; they walk to the grocery store to buy canned tuna and gallon jugs of water. They are easy to spot.

Everyone else drives. The locals drive in or out of town, for there is nowhere to go in town. Those who drive in circles, slowly, around and around the plaza and the single avenue that cuts the town in two and hums around the clock with eighteen-wheeler traffic going to and from the border, these are the *polleros*, the dangerous ones, those who prey on the migrants without contacts and often lie, presenting themselves as the cousins of whomever the migrants are waiting for. Ermelinda, a 53-year-old migrant, widow, and single mother from Veracruz, waiting to meet up with her *pollero*, tells me: "You are in the wolf's jaws here, be careful."

The wolf's jaws. The border. The desert.

In February 2007, drug traffickers, presumably from the Sinaloa Cartel, kidnapped about 300 migrants, hiding them out in a desert ranch near Sasabe. They were going to run drugs into the Tohono O'odham Nation (in Arizona) and did not want the migrants to "heat up" the zone by attracting Border Patrol agents.[16] A local priest managed to negotiate the release of 120 people on February 13, 2007. No national or international media reported on the mass kidnapping. As of the time of this writing, approximately 180 people are still missing. "They had them sitting there near Sasabe, but they only wanted to give me 120, those who had been most severely beaten, who had broken ankles or their heads cracked open from the beatings. I don't know what happened to the rest of the 300, I don't know if they let them loose," the priest told a Salvadoran reporter who had happened to be in Altar the day of the kidnapping.[17] A local official from Altar called the Sonora state attorney general's office a few days after the kidnapping to report that 300 people were missing. Soon thereafter a *narco* called the official and said that he had just received a call from the attorney general's office informing him of the official's complaint. This would be the last time he would forgive such a transgression, he told the official.[18]

In October of that same year, the torched shells of the passenger vans that took the disappeared migrants north still lie belly-up along the dirt road that leads from Altar to the border.

The wolf's jaws.

5·

THE OAXACA
UPRISING

His August Majesty chided the bureaucrats for failing to
understand a simple principle: the principle of the second
bag. Because the people never revolt just because they
have to carry a heavy load, or because of exploitation.
They don't know life without exploitation, they don't even
know that such a life exists. How can they desire what they
cannot imagine? The people will revolt only when, in a
single movement, someone tries to throw a second burden,
a second heavy bag, onto their backs. The peasant will fall
face down into the mud—and then spring up and grab an
ax. He'll grab an ax, my gracious sir, because he feels that
in throwing the second burden onto his back suddenly and
stealthily, you have tried to cheat him, you have treated
him like an unthinking animal, you have trampled what
remains of his already strangled dignity, taken him for an
idiot who doesn't see, feel, or understand. A man doesn't
seize an ax in defense of his wallet, but in defense of his
dignity.

—Ryszard Kapuscinski, *The Emperor*

A SHANTYTOWN OF MAKESHIFT TENTS sprawls across
the plaza with its patchwork of cords and wires tying tarps to
hefty rocks, trees, and light poles, narrow, nonlinear paths
weaving amid collections of pots and pans for improvised
kitchens. The architects of this tent city—*plantón*, as they call
it—are very competent, even graceful, at building with the
barest of materials in the most precarious of circumstances.

They have had a lot of practice; they have been doing it in the same place every year for twenty-six years.[1]

People often think of picket lines when they think of strikes—men and women walking in circles in front of a company building, chanting slogans, handing out flyers, hoisting signs. Business hours are often, though not always, implicit in this idea—the action of the strike is, in many cases, a nine-to-five affair.

Not here. When Oaxaca's Section 22 of Mexico's national teachers union goes on strike it goes on strike all day, every day. Across the state, 70,000 teachers leave their schools, journey to the capital, and build their camp in the main plaza, called the Zócalo, and the surrounding touristy streets of downtown Oaxaca de Juárez. The plaza becomes a city within a city, or perhaps a city balanced on a city.

But this time the teachers were up against a man, Ulises Ruiz, whose gubernatorial campaign slogan had been "No more marches and no more protest camps!" Unlike his predecessors, Ruiz refused to negotiate with the teachers of his state. He refused to cut a deal: instead he decided to play chicken, threatening to force the teachers out of the city center if they did not lift their strike. The teachers held fast, but spent long, wretched nights jumping up to false alarms of predawn police raids.

At 4:30 a.m. on Wednesday, June 14, 2006, the alarm was real. A few were wide awake, chewing on their nerves in silence, but most were fast asleep when over 1,000 police stormed the plaza from two sides, indiscriminately firing tear gas grenades into the labyrinth of tents. Thousands of teachers screamed, tugged at their sleeping companions, hoisted drowsy children up into their arms, and took off running, many barefoot.

The tear gas was maddening, thick chemical clouds from

grenades that landed throughout the teachers' camp. The grenades are brutal; they cause burns, cuts, and concussions upon impact. The gas itself, especially in such copious amounts, is wildly disorienting. It closes your throat like a faucet and shuts your eyes and locks them shut. There are two well-known do-it-yourself remedies: running blindly away from the gas and dousing your face with Coca-Cola (the latter provides immediate relief). If you have recourse to neither you are in trouble; you will feel like you are suffocating until you vomit, and then you will feel like you are suffocating again.

Though the teachers did not know it, the raid on the plaza started moments after Special Forces police had already stormed the teachers union headquarters a block away and the union assembly hall on the edge of the city center. In their search for the union leaders—a local reporter had whisked them out the back and driven them off—the Special Forces police beat dozens of teachers and pulverized the union's tiny community radio station and its volunteer DJs, who were able to broadcast the first seconds of their thrashing before the signal went dead.

The police victory seemed swift and conclusive. By 5:00 a.m. the police controlled the central plaza, had destroyed the teachers' radio station, and had built a huge pyre in the plaza where they burned the teachers' tents and possessions—clothes, shoes, books, and backpacks all left behind in their stampede to escape. But the police victory was short-lived. The teachers had not run away; they had regrouped at a nearby university building and in other smaller plazas to organize and gather stones and sticks. By 5:30 a.m. the teachers were back on the outskirts of the plaza.

Someone in the governor's office did not do the math, for on June 14, 2006, in the early morning, 1,000 underpaid state police faced off with about 40,000 underpaid teachers and several thousand more neighbors who, upset by waking up to their children choking on tear gas, also took to the streets.

Governor Ulises Ruiz Ortiz—a member of the PRI, the party that has monopolized government in Oaxaca for seventy-eight years—monitored the battle from his mansion on the outskirts of town. Getting word of his troops' imminent defeat, Ruiz ordered two private helicopters to fly over the downtown streets so that state police could shoot tear gas grenades at the teachers from the air.

That was a mistake.

"We had pretty much taken the area back after an hour once we had gotten our courage together," one teacher who participated in the fight told me. "That's when the helicopters started shooting the grenades at us. It terrified us until one guy shouted out that we could grab the grenades and throw them at the police."

The predawn raid itself and the excessive use of tear gas had offended the teachers, but the helicopters pushed them over a line.

"On June 14, the government decided to repress, sending police to beat people and to fire tear gas from helicopters," one teacher present that morning told me. "All the years before, the government arrived and announced over a megaphone: 'We are going to lift the encampment,' and on the third announcement, everyone would grab their stuff and run. This time there was none of that. They even attacked us from the air, as if we were criminals."

An elderly indigenous woman who depends on handouts to survive told me that the governor had made a huge mistake by using tear gas: "He shouldn't have used the gas. He could have just grabbed a few teachers and thrown them in jail, like before. But no, he used the gas and insulted them, and that's why we have all this trouble now."

For the teachers—and most of the residents of Oaxaca City—the state's baroque display of force was not just repressive but way out of proportion, an affront, an attack on their dignity. Despite the widely acknowledged talents of the helicopter pilots ("That was one badass pilot," a teacher said) and the police stationed on rooftops and in hotel windows firing tear gas grenades from every possible angle, the teachers proceeded to chase off the police, pelting them with stones, attacking them with sticks and metal tubes wrenched from the wreckage of their tent city. By 9:00 a.m. the police were in full retreat, firing pistols and submachine guns in the air and at the teachers' feet to cover their exodus. The teachers held control over downtown Oaxaca and took several police prisoner, including Margarito López, one of the commanders of the raid. The teachers released their prisoners to the Red Cross later that night. More than ninety teachers checked into local hospitals with injuries ranging from tear gas intoxication to broken bones, gunshot wounds, concussions, and punctured lungs from the impact of tear gas grenades. Two pregnant teachers suffered miscarriages in local hospitals in the hours following the police raid due to intense tear gas exposure.

ULISES RUIZ'S ILL-FATED police raid ignited a deeper social rebellion that would come to control Oaxaca City for over four months and set in motion forms of organized civil disobedience that would recast the dynamics of protest in Mexico, at least for a time, in favor of the downtrodden. But the flagrant use of police violence was far from the sole cause of this uprising.

Located deep in Mexico's impoverished south on the Pacific Coast, bordering Chiapas to the east, Guerrero to the west, and Puebla and Veracruz to the north, Oaxaca has the fifth-largest territory of Mexico's thirty-one states, with a population of 3.4 million people. It is also the state with the most diverse indigenous cultures. There are sixteen different indigenous groups, or *pueblos*, in Oaxaca, and over a million people speak an indigenous language as their native tongue.

Mexico's federal government has largely abandoned Oaxaca, like most of Mexico's southern states, allowing caciques—regional political bosses—to run state governments like personal fiefdoms. While PRI governors and senators amassed fortunes, half of Oaxaca's population, mostly the rural, indigenous communities, lived without any state services. To this day, only half of the state's people—mostly those in Oaxaca City and a sprinkling of small cities in the central valley and coastal areas—receive the basic municipal services: water, sewage, and electricity.

After a wave of national discontent that had been building for over twenty years, the PRI conceded electoral defeat in 2000, when conservative Catholic candidate Vicente Fox won the elections, promising a government of "change" and "democratic transition."

However, with the end of the PRI's absolute presidential control over the federal government, many of the state and regional caciques lost the only real form of oversight they had. In a recent book on the Oaxaca conflict, Oaxaca-based sociologist Victor Raúl Martínez wrote that the breaking of "presidentialism" in 2000 freed state-level authoritarian governments, or *cacicazgos*, to concentrate their local power now that there was no "imperial president" to call the shots from Mexico City. As an example, he cites a report showing that in the last eight years the Oaxaca state governors have failed to account for $920 million in public funds, no small amount in a state where half the population lives without electricity and indoor plumbing.[2]

Ulises Ruiz, long known as a prize electoral "fixer" for the

PRI, took office in December 2004 under widespread allegations of fraud. During his first days in office he tried to have his opponent, Gabino Cue, arrested on false charges, and sent pseudo-union members to occupy the warehouse and offices of the statewide newspaper, *Noticias*, the only newspaper that had been critical of his campaign. Ruiz's government arrested and tortured scores of indigenous organization leaders. Ruiz moved the governor's offices outside of town into a complex that also houses the state police barracks. He then moved the state legislature to a different town, in the opposite direction, both tactics designed to avoid the marches and *plantones* of the state's many unions and social organizations. He tore up beloved old statues and boardwalks in Oaxaca City to build new ones, and, his critics say, to launder state funds into the 2006 PRI presidential campaign of Roberto Madrazo. Ulises Ruiz made few friends outside his party clique.

"Here we hold assemblies for everything," said Alejandro Cruz, a lawyer with a Oaxaca-based indigenous human rights organization, "but [Ruiz] doesn't consult with anybody. Others simulate consultation, but this guy doesn't even know how to simulate. He thinks he is a king."

Marches and sit-ins are standard fare in Oaxaca. And the reigning champion of the sit-in, or *plantón*, is far and away Section 22 of the National Union of Education Workers (SNTE).

Since the earliest days of the PRI, unions have existed more to create and manage crowd reserves to fill PRI rallies and cast PRI votes in exchange for a sandwich or a bit of cash—than to advance workers' rights. The SNTE is the largest and arguably most corrupt union in Mexico and all of Latin America. Beginning in the late 1970s, teachers across the country tried to break union corruption and created the National Coordination of Education Workers (CNTE), drawing large numbers of supporters in southern states like Chiapas,

Tabasco, and Oaxaca.[3] In 1980, the Oaxaca teachers managed to take over their local, creating the dissident Section 22 and initiating a twenty-six-year struggle to democratize the national union and bring greater resources to Oaxaca's abandoned school system. At least once a year since 1980, Section 22 teachers give their list of demands to the governor and the national minister of the interior. When they don't get a satisfactory answer, they build a *plantón* right in the heart of downtown Oaxaca City, and they stay there until they do.

In late April 2006, the teachers demanded pay increases to compensate for the exploding costs of living in tourism-heavy Oaxaca and a higher allotment of federal funds for school supplies, meals, and school repairs. The teachers demanded a special fund to make sure every elementary school student has a pair of shoes—in Oaxaca, many students and even teachers have to walk for hours on dirt paths to reach schoolhouses. But Ulises Ruiz turned down the teachers' demands and refused to dialogue directly with them. On May 1 and again on May 15 the teachers held huge marches, but the governor would not budge. On May 22, the teachers built their tent city in Oaxaca's Zócalo. But still Ulises Ruiz would not give an inch; instead he threatened to remove the teachers' *plantón* by force.

TWO DAYS AFTER Ulises Ruiz's botched raid, nearly half a million people—in a state of 3.4 million—took to the streets to protest. Witnessing this spontaneous outpouring of support energized the union leaders with an idea.

Enrique Rueda, a slick, athletic history teacher in his early 40s, was secretary general of the Section 22 local at the time. He and a group of union organizers called a meeting for June 17, 2006, with a number of social justice organizations across the state, especially groups with the ability to put people on the street.

"We were looking for a way to catalyze the spontaneous support we received after June 14 and to extend it out over time," Rueda told me back in August 2006. "We wanted to take the union's twenty-six years of experience and apply it to society at large."

The teachers called a meeting of the Asamblea Popular del Pueblo de Oaxaca, or APPO—the Oaxaca Peoples' Popular Assembly. They opened the Assembly to any and all who agreed to the single demand of Ulises Ruiz's ouster. The teachers put their original sixteen demands on hold, calling on Ruiz to resign or the federal government to remove him from office before continuing any further negotiations. The ouster of Ulises Ruiz now became the movement's sole demand.

To everyone's surprise, more than 300 unions and social justice, indigenous rights, and human rights organizations all jumped in. The infamously fractious Mexican Left had found something everyone could agree on: getting rid of Ulises Ruiz. But the APPO was not simply a haphazard collection of old-line leftists, as the foreign press would later bill it (though, granted, huge sketches of Marx, Engels, Lenin, and Stalin did grace the reinstalled *plantón* in the Zócalo, thanks to an organization called the Popular Revolutionary Front, or FPR). Across Oaxaca, people who had never participated in a protest or a march, much less a left-wing political organization, pooled together and formed entirely new organizations so that they too could join the APPO movement in pushing for Ulises Ruiz's political demise.

The APPO movement opened up a vacuum, a promise of political participation that almost immediately filled with tens of thousands of people who had never felt as if they belonged in the world of politics, a world that in Oaxaca had been the exclusive property of the PRI since 1929. One of the first acts of the APPO was to change its name to better reflect the cultural diversity in the state. The indigenous members pointed out that there is not only one *pueblo* in Oaxaca, but many *pueblos*. Hence the APPO became the Asamblea Popular *de los Pueblos* de Oaxaca.

The APPO called on people to participate in the July 2, 2006, federal elections by exercising a *voto de castigo*—punishment vote—against the PRI. And indeed, on July 2 the PRI was crushed in Oaxaca for the first time in history. The PRI lost nine of the eleven congressional seats in the state, and its presidential candidate, Roberto Madrazo, was soundly defeated. The punishment vote was a show of force, but also a warning to Ulises Ruiz and his clan: if Ulises were to fall, the PRI would be unable to win elections to establish his replacement.

As one lawyer explained to me: "If [Ruiz] goes before November, the interim governor would have to call elections, and the PRI would never win those elections. But if he makes it through November first, they don't have to call elections, and his group, can put one of their own in office to finish his six-year term."

Ulises Ruiz does not look like a tyrannical despot. I first saw him at a press conference held at an exclusive, guarded hotel on the outskirts of town on July 17, 2006—the only press conference he would give during nearly six months of conflict. The press had been waiting for over an hour when Ulises Ruiz walked in with a fixed smile that seemed to be held in place by some manner of glue, producing an awkward tension between his alert, darting eyes and his frozen, overextended lips. Of average height, thin, and kind of fragile-looking, Ruiz wears a thick mustache that together with his glasses provide the only real detail on his round, almost featureless face. He is not ugly, nor handsome; he does not scowl, nor does he shine. He is simply plain. When he walked in I thought he was an aide of some sort coming to request patience for the governor's tardiness. But no, this was Ulises Ruiz.

The first question to strike the air, before Ruiz could sit down, came shouted out from a reporter from the largest television company in Mexico, Televisa: "Do you feel alone?" "No. I don't feel alone at all," Ruiz responded. "The government maintains absolute disposition to dialogue." "Will you leave office?" "Absolutely not. This has become politicized. We need to rescue the original issues of this conflict," Ruiz said somehow, miraculously, through his unchanging, iron-on smile. "My disposition is to privilege dialogue."

Ulises Ruiz, like any competent politician, managed to reply to questions without saying anything for nearly half an hour, and then left. No one, not even reporters from the progovernment papers, believed his "disposition" to "privilege dialogue." His disposition had already been made rather clear. Everyone knew more blood would come, but no one knew precisely how or when. The reporters' questions were meant to divine the shape of future violence. Of course the governor would not say it directly, so the reporters aimed their questions at his tone of voice and facial expressions, an entirely unsuccessful strategy, as both remained perfectly unchanging.

Ruiz had called the press conference to announce the suspension of the internationally famous Guelaguetza cultural festival.* The APPO had occupied the outdoor theater where the Guelaguetza is annually held, torched the wooden stage, and spray-painted the entire area with anti-Ulises slogans including a giant, cartoonish middle finger protruding next to the words: "Take your Guelaguetza!" They had blocked all the roads lead-

---

* The Guelaguetza, which in Zapotec means a reciprocal exchange of gifts and services, is a state-wide cultural festival held every July in Oaxaca City and dates back to the precolonial era. The APPO members protested that the state government and the tourism industry had taken over the popular festival, charging high entrance fees for the best seats, which inevitably gave priority to international tourists.

ing to and surrounding the theater and filled the area with thousands of teachers and locals. The APPO spray-painted a message in English for the camera-laden and bewildered international tourists who had not yet heard the news: "Excuse us, because of repression we have suspended the function."

The APPO, not wanting to get pegged as a force that cancels parties, organized a "popular Guelaguetza" with no exclusive seating arrangements and no admission fee. But more than a party, it was a show of reclaiming the people's cultural forms of expression from the state government's commercialization. Their Guelaguetza drew a crowd of some 20,000, mostly from areas around Oaxaca, but was completely denigrated by the media.

The local and statewide radio and television stations were extremely hostile toward the teachers and the APPO. They had failed to report the true extent of police violence on June 14, and they now informed listeners and viewers that the "popular Guelaguetza" was a failure. They consistently claimed that leftist "political mercenaries" and vandals ran the movement. The international media mostly ignored the APPO altogether.

In order to combat the hostility of the government-controlled press—the state government directly owns the only statewide television station, CORTV, and two popular radio stations, and it floods other radio stations and newspapers with the advertising revenue that keeps them alive—the teachers of Section 22 built their own community radio station, Radio Plantón. During the June 14, 2006, raid, state police attacked the station and ripped it apart. That same day, a small group of university students walked into the control room of the tiny university station, Radio Universidad, and told the older students and university employees that they were taking the station over in solidarity with the teachers' movement. They began using the airwaves to direct people's outrage against the state government. When the teachers created the APPO and issued the demand for Ulises Ruiz's ouster, Radio Universidad repeated that demand almost every minute. A month later, nearly everyone walking the streets in downtown Oaxaca had a tiny, three-dollar, handheld radio with them, tuned in to Radio Universidad. With hundreds of people calling in daily from cell phones across the city, Radio Universidad had the scoop—and every rumor under the sun—before anyone else.

On July 22, 2006, at approximately 9:15 p.m., two days before the "popular Guelaguetza," 17-year-old Yolanda and a kindergarten teacher known as La Profesora Carmen were at the controls of Radio Universidad encouraging people to attend the festival.

"We were transmitting live," Yolanda told me. "Me and another *compañera* were at the controls when these pickup trucks drove by shooting. People ran into the station and ducked down on the floor. The transmission was cut off. You could hear everything on the air, the gunshots, and then the signal died."

Carmen was on the air when she heard bursts of machine gun fire piercing the windows and hitting the walls of the station. Only a few women, some with their children, were on duty. They all hit the floor.

"I asked for help and was able to say that we were being attacked before the signal went dead," Carmen said.

Witnesses said that the men wore black, had their faces covered with ski masks and bandannas, and traveled in a pickup truck and a compact car. The shooting lasted about fifteen minutes before people—several thousand of them—began to arrive at the station, chasing off the attackers. No one was injured, and volunteers were able to repair the antenna that same day.

Ulises Ruiz accused the APPO of sending people out to shoot against their own in order to create sympathy for their movement. The APPO and the teachers accused Ulises Ruiz of sending thugs to destroy the radio station's transmission equipment and intimidate the volunteer broadcasters.

To step up their protests to a veritable civil disobedience offensive, the teachers union and the APPO launched a campaign to "create ungovernability." In Mexico, there is no recall measure or impeachment process for governors. The only legal way for people to force a governor out of office is to somehow propel the federal senate to declare the "disappearance of powers" in the state, in effect dissolving the executive branch of state government and opening the door for new elections or a political appointee. Nothing like this had ever happened before in Oaxaca. It was never necessary. Since the PRI controlled all branches of federal and state government, the president only had to give the word and an unpopular governor would step down; the president would then name the successor. This happened in Oaxaca in 1977 when a protest movement forced Manuel Zarate Aquino from office.

In 2006, however, President Vicente Fox was a member of the conservative opposition, the PAN, and had come to power by denouncing old-school PRI practices like removing inconvenient governors from office. Fox said repeatedly: "I do not install or remove governors," both justifying his inaction regarding Oaxaca and taking a stab at the PRI. Fox was also quite busy in Mexico City. The left-leaning candidate in the July 2, 2006, presidential elections, Andrés Manuel López Obrador, accused Fox and his party of rigging the elections and was simultaneously organizing huge marches and preparing a several-thousand-page legal challenge to demand a complete, vote-by-vote recount.

The APPO and the teachers' union thus saw their opportunity: they would render the state government useless by physically, though "peacefully," without guns, blocking all state government office buildings. This they called the July 26 Offensive.

The teachers and local residents arrived between six and eight in the morning. They strung up their tarps to trees and light poles. They unfolded their newspapers and pulled out their knitting. And they sat. They sat in front of the state attorney general's office—which was also the state police headquarters. They sat in front of the state legislature, in front of the governor's office, and in front of the state courthouse. They sat in front of the state treasury. They created "mobile brigades" by driving around in commandeered city buses to smaller state office buildings like the state archives and the department of motor vehicles, where they spray-painted the walls and then—after calling all the employees out—jammed the door locks with toothpicks, glue, and spray paint.

Within a matter of days, tens of thousands of schoolteachers and APPO members forced the state government into roaming exile. When the governor and state legislators were rumored to be meeting at exclusive hotels, the APPO sent a commission of a few hundred people to march out to the hotel and demand that the government functionaries be evicted: "If you don't kick them out," they said, "we'll just have to take over the hotel."

On June 14, 2006, people had overcome their fear of repression; they had fought back and won. The massive outpouring of support in the following weeks created a sense of community participation and movement building that made almost anything seem possible, such as organized teachers and local residents completely shutting down state government with nothing more than their bodies, plastic tarp to block the sun and rain, newspapers, knitting, and conversation. No guns. No manifestos. Just direct, organized action. Here the politics of protest favored, for the moment, the downtrodden: the movement had the numbers, the drive, and the coordination. The state only had guns.

In this atmosphere of kinetic political possibility, a group of women camping out in front of the state treasury started talking. They were making coffee and corn tamales over sidewalk fires and joking about how even in uprisings women still got left with the cooking and the cleaning.

"Are we always going to be stuck in this historic role of women, looking after coffee, food, and cleaning?" one of the women said. "We can do better things."

They decided on a march, a women-only march modeled on the Argentine *cacerolas* of December 2001, in which women took to the streets banging on pots and pans. They sent out word to the press and made the announcement on Radio Universidad for women to gather at 11:00 a.m. on August 1, 2006, at the Fountain of the Seven Regions with their kitchenware, ready to make some noise.

Some 5,000 women heeded the call. Arriving in kitchen aprons, clutching soup spoons and skillets, they made a devastating racket, and the noise plugged into the energy of possibility already in the air. These women were charged, shot through with electricity, as if a single word in their collective subconscious was orchestrating their roar: *invincible*. When the 5,000 women arrived at their destination, the occupied central plaza, they were far too jazzed to stop, too jazzed to listen to speeches. Someone yelled out: "Let's go to Channel 9!" The call rang out, echoed through the crowd, gathered voices, gathered volume. And the crowd surged across the plaza, out to the streets. Some women marched. Some women took over city buses. Some women stopped cars, told the passengers to get out, and ordered the drivers to take them to

Channel 9, the Oaxaca state-owned television station CORTV. One woman in her late sixties told an unwilling driver facing a thick crowd of kitchen-tool-wielding women: "Well, if you don't want to drive us, then just leave your keys in the ignition and get out, 'cause this car is going to the TV station."

When Mercedes Rojas Saldaña, the director of CORTV, got word that thousands of women from the APPO movement were on their way, she ordered all employees to start dismantling the station's equipment. She went out to meet the women at the gates. The women asked for an hour on the air to tell their version of what had happened on June 14, 2006, and why they demanded Ulises Ruiz's ouster. Rojas refused. The women asked for half an hour. Rojas refused. The women asked for fifteen minutes. When Rojas again refused, the women seized control of the station.

"All the women who came here, we only wanted a little time, half an hour, an hour," said Estela, one of the women who participated in the takeover, in an interview conducted inside the occupied station in mid-August 2006. "All we wanted was a chance to tell just a little bit of all the truth, of so much truth there is out there. And we said we would leave. But they refused to give us that time, an hour or so, and I bet that now they're sorry."

It took almost three hours for the women to negotiate releasing all the employees in exchange for their turning the cameras and transmission equipment back on. By 7:00 p.m. the women were broadcasting live, on statewide television and two state radio stations, one FM and one AM, which the women renamed Radio Cacerola, or Saucepan Radio.

A cluster of women—some seated in mismatched office chairs, others packed standing behind them, skillets held high—filled television screens across the state of Oaxaca. The lighting was poor, the audio imbalanced. There were no special effects, no artsy pans from one camera angle to another. No makeup, no wardrobe. A group of women in jeans and sweats, in aprons and T-shirts. Women who live their lives in rickety neighborhoods, and abandoned rural villages, women who teach in one-room schoolhouses without heat or electricity. They faced the camera and spoke, but that night they also stood behind the camera, they also sat in the control room.

The women heard nightly rumors that the police were coming to raid the station. The state government lobbied both the president and the senate to intervene. And yet the women did not budge. "This is the people's television now," they said. And their message to the other media was clear: "The rest of them need to tell the truth. If they don't, now they know what awaits them."

In Mexico, the political position of every media source is well known, though a few are schizophrenic. I asked José Manuel Villarreal, a conservative media industry representative, if he could name for me a few examples of balanced radio stations, television stations, or newspapers. He could not. He fudged and hesitated and then changed the subject. I asked again. He said: "After this conflict is solved I think we need to engage in serious self-criticism and work on restructuring the media, creating more connections to society."

Television stations Televisa and TV Azteca, along with the newspaper *Reforma*, solidly support the ruling party—once the PRI, now the PAN. The newspaper *El Universal* is generally supportive of the ruling party, though it will publish some critical stories. The daily newspaper *La Jornada* and the weekly newsmagazine *Proceso* are the most critical national media, and both covered the Oaxaca conflict extensively. (During the Oaxaca conflict, however, *La Jornada* and other newspapers published scores of paid advertisements formatted almost exactly like news stories reporting on an endless string of public works inaugurated by Ulises Ruiz—none of these advertisements were identified as such, the only difference being that the headlines were printed in italics.) And, as an example of the truly schizophrenic media, the newspaper *Milenio* would print editorials denouncing the APPO as a group of violent and radical vandals while the main news story written by their special correspondent, Diego Osorno, would detail the involvement of plainclothes police and state officials in armed attacks against members of the APPO. In Oaxaca, nearly every radio station and newspaper supported the governor, with one exception: *Noticias*, which supported the teachers and later the APPO.

When the APPO took over radio and television stations, the members did not pretend to be impartial or balanced: they wanted to tell their side of the story. And, it turned out, that was precisely what a vast number of people wanted to hear. The occupied media became organization and communication centers for the APPO. Hundreds of people called in daily to express their views, tell about an upcoming protest action, or denounce police movements and attacks around the city. Thousands more were listening at all hours of the day and night and were ready to respond to threats and dangers.

"What was so important about the media outlets that were in the hands of the APPO," said Jill Freidberg, a filmmaker who covered the movement and directed the documentary *A Little Bit of So Much Truth* about the movement's use of media, "is that no one was really making programming decisions. It was the *phone calls* in to the stations that turned those media outlets into the *concovatoria* [call to participate], the *asamblea* on the air. I really think the media outlets in the hands of the movement did so much more than generate support. They were the voice of the people talking *to* each other, organizing, defending, arguing, convoking."

Lynn Stephen, an anthropology professor at the University of Oregon and author of *Zapotec Women: Gender, Class and Ethnicity in Globalized Oaxaca*, wrote to me in an e-mail: "Radio has been the lifeline of the APPO movement. . . . The women behind the radio station do not appear to be militant fighters, but are often longtime residents who have finally gotten fed up with their invisibility and bad treatment by successive state governments that have been promising to improve their lives for decades."

Media really *is* power. And the APPO movement's ability to use television and radio to directly connect with people across the state of Oaxaca, in real time, compounded the movement's growing wave of sympathy and support. And, as Jill Freidberg said, the occupied media opened the political space for the people of Oaxaca to connect amongst themselves, to talk with each other. The first armed attack against the movement was an attack against the media the movement had commandeered, Radio Universidad. It is no accident that the week after several thousand women took over the state television station armed attacks escalated; para-police groups with weapons kidnapped and attacked protesters across Oaxaca City and in other towns.

During the first armed attacks against the movement something very surprising happened. Plainclothes police arrived at rallies and fired into the air to frighten people. But it did not work. Instead of running away, diving to the ground, or scattering in frenzy, protesters quickly pursued and apprehended their attackers. On July 31, 2006, the APPO captured Isaías Pérez Hernández, a state police officer who had fired a pistol during a rally, and then turned him over—unharmed—to federal police. I spoke with Hernández during his detention. He admitted that he was a state police officer, a former solider in the Mexican Army, but insisted that he had not fired at the

APPO; in fact, he told me that he did not know how to fire a handgun, that after years in the army and the state police no one had ever trained him to shoot a pistol. He was lying. A ballistics test carried out on-site by the federal attorney general's office detected gunpowder on his hand, proving that Hernández had fired a handgun within the previous few hours.

Two agents from Mexico's Federal Agency of Investigation (or AFI, the Mexican federal police force most similar to the U.S. FBI) responded to the APPO's call reporting that they had captured Isaías Pérez Hernández as he was shooting at them. The APPO had taken Hernández to the state law school building two blocks from the occupied Zócalo. The crowd outside was so thick it was nearly impossible to move within twenty feet of the door. When the AFI agents arrived—tall, hulking fellows with starched black suits and thick black sunglasses—they hovered on the edge of the crowd and had to wait for the APPO organizers to call on the crowd to open a path for them to get to the door. Once inside the agents immediately checked Hernández for signs of injury, beating, or torture, lifting his shirt, checking his eyes and head. He had no wounds or marks. They asked him if he had been beaten, and he said that he had not. The agents then took him into a separate room for questioning. Soon a federal forensics team arrived to conduct the ballistics test that proved Hernández had fired a handgun within the past few hours.

At no point did the federal agents interrogate, question, or accuse the APPO of any wrongdoing. It was as if the AFI agents recognized the APPO as an independent, belligerent force and thus acknowledged their legitimate control of territory. And, of course, the APPO members were right: they had apprehended a man who had pulled a gun and fired into the air to intimidate a peaceful march; they apprehended him without injuring him; they called on members of the press to be present at all moments during his detention; and they called on the federal police to come and deal with him. What surprises here is that the federal police would accept the APPO's call and engage with them as a legitimate rebel force of sorts. But the AFI agents, in fact, had little choice: the APPO indeed controlled central Oaxaca City.

On August 8, 2006, two students set a bus on fire near the university to create a distraction; they then ran into the radio station and threw acid on the transmitter. Student volunteers caught and detained the saboteurs, who admitted to receiving $250 for the job. Radio Universidad went off the air, and people switched their dials to Radio Cacerola. The next day gunmen busted into the offices of the newspaper *Noticias*, firing Uzi machine guns and wounding six employees with bullet fragments that ricocheted off the ceiling and walls.

Then on August 10, men in ski masks, armed with assault rifles, walked up to German Mendoza Nube, a well-known activist with the FPR, lifted him out of his wheelchair, beat him in the street, and threw his body in the back of a pickup truck. Witnesses photographed the abduction, and hours later the women of Channel 9 showed the photographs and interviewed the witnesses on the air. Mendoza Nube appeared several days later, in a federal prison outside of Mexico City, which implies, of course, federal involvement in the disappearance. That same day, gunmen ambushed members of the APPO on their way to a regional APPO meeting in the Triqui indigenous region of northwest Oaxaca, killing three people: Andrés Santiago Cruz, Pedro Martínez, and Pablo Martínez.

The next day thousands of teachers and APPO protesters marched to demand the release of Mendoza Nube—who was still being held incommunicado. Gunmen fired from the second story of a house into the march, shooting José Jiménez Colmenares in the heart. Colmenares was accompanying his wife, a teacher and member of the Section 22. The following day, August 11, 2006, police beat and disappeared Erangelio Mendoza, a longtime activist in the teachers union; he appeared several days later, hundreds of miles away in a federal maximum-security prison in Mexico City.

Flavio Sosa, one of the APPO spokespeople, called for a meeting with Carlos Abascal, the secretary of Gobernación (Mexico's powerful interior ministry), to discuss possible solutions to the conflict in Oaxaca. "Ulises Ruiz is leading us into a situation practically of civil war, and our movement is nonviolent," he said in a press conference in the occupied town square. "Our movement is nonviolent. In fact, it is a movement against violence, against a system of violence that excludes us, against the violence of police brutality."

While state police were carrying out hit-and-run assaults against people protesting, tourists were still sipping coffee and wandering around the APPO-occupied city center, oblivious to the gunshots a mile or so away. The atmosphere in the protester-occupied Zócalo was peaceful and even vibrant.

Then, on August 20 and 21, uniformed and nonuniformed police drove through Oaxaca City in a convoy of about forty pickup trucks, firing on protesters with machine guns. The first night they targeted the state-owned transmission equipment for Channel 9, wounding those who were camped out by the antennas and completely destroying the transmitter with machine gun and shotgun fire. Channel 9 and Radio Cacerola went off the air. But before the sun rose, thousands of people took to the streets and occupied every commercial radio station in Oaxaca City, twelve in all. They occupied the radio stations without guns, without throwing punches or pushing people around.

"The door was open, there were two guards on duty. We arrived and we communicated to them that we were going to peacefully take control of the radio station," said La Profesora Carmen.

That night the police came back, this time attacking the radio stations. They shot at protesters. They shot at reporters. They shot at people walking in the street. They killed Lorenzo San Pablo Cervantes, an architect who had just walked out of his house to volunteer at an APPO-controlled radio station in his neighborhood. The two national television stations filmed the death squads and showed the footage. Camera operators from the Reuters news agency filmed the death squads. Luis Alberto Cruz, a photographer with *Milenio*, took pictures of men in the back of one of the trucks, dressed in all black, wearing bulletproof vests and ski masks, firing machine guns. Moments later the men shot at Cruz, who was able to take cover behind a light pole. He heard the wood splinter and crack as bullets struck the pole.

In response, thousands of people across the city built barricades to block the death squads. In the following days, somehow, the national television stations talked only about the violent and radical vandals from the APPO. The media filmed and photographed the police attacking and killing people in the street, but somehow the people who built barricades in the street to stop the death squads became the violent ones in the mainstream media.

I walked those streets every night for weeks on end. The men and women tending to the barricades offered me coffee and bread. They offered to walk with me so that I would not be alone. They showed me the altar to the Virgin of Guadalupe they had built atop the sandbags of their barricade. They told me their stories. A 60-year-old Zapotec indigenous teacher who has to walk four hours to get to her school. A 20-year-old university student who just came back from construction work in Michigan to pay for his studies. A 67-

year-old kindergarten teacher who refused his retirement so that he could stay in the union and participate in the strike. Families from across town traveling from barricade to barricade to offer coffee and hot chocolate to those staying up all night on alert. An 8-year-old girl who offered me a cup of coffee as I interviewed six women at a barricade and asked me, concerned, at 2:30 a.m., "Aren't you tired?"

"I have to walk six hours to get to my school," said Estela, a Mixteca woman who had been teaching in mountainside communities for thirty years and had sat up through the night at a barricade near an APPO-occupied radio station. "And then when I get there, I find that half the kids have not had breakfast and the other half don't have pencils or notebooks. I use my salary to buy these supplies, to prepare bread and tortillas. How do you expect children to learn if they have not had breakfast?"

In many ways the barricades were the APPO's most eloquent expression of the movement's commitment to peaceful struggle. "Do they want people to take up arms? Do they want them to arm themselves? Do they remember how the Mexican Revolution started?" asked Antonio, one of the APPO spokespeople the day after police killed Cervantes. Instead, Antonio said: "We call, once again, for a peaceful struggle. We are going to respond with organization, with barricades, with night watches. We are not an urban guerrilla movement; they are trying to provoke us." Imagine: Death squads drive through your neighborhood and kill your neighbor. You don't hide. You don't leave town. You don't grab a gun and shoot back. You get together with your neighbors, build makeshift barricades, and sit up at night on the lookout; you make coffee and sandwiches to share; you talk about what you are living through and what you think should be done. And then they call you violent.

Just as the movement-occupied media became nonhierar-
chical spaces of political participation where the people of
Oaxaca spoke with each other, so too the barricades became a
fragmented, horizontal space of direct political action where
the people of Oaxaca found each other, and again, spoke with
each other. It was high-risk action at that: two people were
gunned down at the barricades. With the exception of a handful of barricades run mainly by young people, the majority of
the barricades were built and maintained by the people who
lived on that particular street, in conjunction with teachers
from around the state, divided amongst different parts of the
city. The night watch became a place for conversation, reflection, and analysis, for sharing experiences and desires, for
organizing revolt and consciousness-raising without imposition from leaders.

The APPO never called for the use of violence. They did
use, however, the *threat* of violence to force behavior. The
"mobile brigades," for example, consisted of crowds of men
and women bearing sticks, pipes, and menacing clubs with
nails, ordering people to get off buses that they planned to
commandeer, or to leave government buildings they planned
to surround or symbolically close. On one occasion, an office
worker upon exiting a government building shouted to the
press: "You don't call this violence? They are forcing us out!
Look at the clubs and pipes in their hands! Is this not threatening?"

Yet while the APPO's threats were menacing, the protesters never carried them out. During one mobile brigade action,
for example, a woman refused to get off the bus, shouting at
the masked men with clubs that they had no right to impede
her free transit. The men persisted, but the woman would
have none of it. After only a few seconds of shouting, the
young men backed down, stepped off the bus, and waved it on.

Then they stopped the next one and tried again, that time successfully.

The movement's civil disobedience offense and constant preparation for self-defense exposed the organization to many dangers: agitators sent in to provoke violent clashes, outbreaks of mob violence, and explosions of built-up rage. The APPO constantly warned of agitators and crowds called out—often unnecessarily—to remove suspected agitators. The danger of boiling rage and mob violence was especially high in the relations between protesters and the press. Members of the APPO felt hurt and betrayed by the local and national press corps, whom they accused of only reporting the government's version of the events, and especially the government's description of the APPO as a violent urban guerrilla movement. (The international press mostly ignored the APPO until the killings in late October.) Protest crowds would shout at reporters, "Tell the truth!" They would approach reporters and demand to see their press credentials. Correspondents from the major television networks Televisa and TV Azteca would be herded away from protest events by mobs shouting jokes, insults, and threats.

On one occasion a local reporter was hospitalized and required stitches after being beaten by protesters who thought he was a policeman. Members of the crowd itself were the ones to hold the attackers back and help get the reporter to the hospital, and within hours the APPO's provisional leadership committee held a press conference apologizing for the beating and calling on all APPO protesters to respect individual reporters, even though their employers and directors may have been hostile toward the movement.

While apologies and calls to change behavior do little to absolve a beating, they show the protesters' commitment to avoid mob violence in the guise of self-defense, while never relinquishing their right to and preparedness for self-defense.

The provisional leadership committee's quick and unequivocal acknowledgment of their mistake—both beating the reporter and allowing the fermentation of such a hostile climate against reporters—also shows a readiness to be self-critical that the state completely lacks. (Two years later no government official has apologized for the assassinations carried out by government death squads.)

Theirs is an odd and little-seen strategy; call it a civil disobedience *offensive*. They neither employed traditional Latin American guerrilla tactics nor espoused philosophical nonviolence. It was—awkwardly and innovatively—somewhere in the middle.

The barricades became the most decentralized, horizontal form of protest during the six months of conflict. Thousands of people of all backgrounds built barricades in their neighborhoods. The barricades became impromptu cultural centers, debate societies, and social clubs. They even inspired an underground hit song—*Son de la barricada*—written in the traditional style of folk music from neighboring Veracruz state, *son jarocho*.

After television reports showing police death squads, the federal government called the teachers and the APPO to mediated talks in Mexico City. At the same time, Ulises Ruiz threatened to recognize López Obrador as the legitimate president of Mexico and denounce electoral fraud in the past July 2 elections. His threat: if the governor of Oaxaca falls, president-elect Felipe Calderón would be next.[4] Rumors ran daily that Vicente Fox was going to send the army or the federal police to Oaxaca. Every night throughout September and October the rumor was the same: tonight they are coming. No one slept.

On September 21, 2006, members of the teachers' union and the APPO began a march to Mexico City to set up a protest camp. The 4,000 protesters walked more than 300 miles through four states, arriving in Mexico City on October 9, 2006, where they set up a *plantón* outside the Mexican senate. On October 16, twenty-one marchers from the APPO began a hunger strike to demand Ruiz's ouster.

"This is an example of people having reached the limit of patience with decades of neglect," said César Mateos, one of the central organizers of the march. "The movement in Oaxaca seeks deep structural changes, and the first step in these changes is the exit of Ulises," he said. "But we want to achieve these changes through a peaceful movement, which is why we have done this march. This is the true face of the APPO."

The march began with more than 4,000 people, dipped to approximately 1,000 on the last few days, but then swelled to at least 10,000 as it entered Mexico City. The APPO protesters walked an average of eight hours a day, through both rainstorms and blistering heat.

Juan Pérez, a thin, 25-year-old teacher from Jocotepec, Oaxaca, walked for nineteen days straight. He wore rough leather sandals, jeans, a hand-woven straw hat, and a shirt with "APPO: a dream in construction" painted in orange letters across the front. "No revolution is going to come from behind a desk," he said as set out from Nezahualcóyotl on the final eight miles of the march. "For the government, the voices of the people don't count," he said, "that is why we have to take to the streets, to do something with the impotence we feel."

The Mexican senate finally agreed to send a commission to investigate the "governability" situation in Oaxaca. On October 11, 2006, the day before the senators were to arrive, plainclothes police fired on an APPO "mobile brigade," wounding four people. When the senators arrived the next day they met with Ulises Ruiz and his cabinet in a guarded airport hangar. Ulises Ruiz delivered boxes of documents to prove that his government had being working as "normal," completely unaffected by the conflict. "This is all documented," he said. "Not one single state agency has stopped working." The APPO, in turn, delivered a box of bullet shells, exploded tear gas grenades, broken police clubs, photographs of death squads, of police beating people in the street, of torture victims with their faces destroyed: this they said, is the proof of "ungovernability."

While the senators were deliberating back in Mexico City, on October 14, 2006, plainclothes gunmen shot and killed Alejandro García Hernández. It was 2:30 a.m. and Mr. Hernandez, together with his wife and son, were taking hot coffee to the volunteers at the barricade near his house when two men opened fire.

"My father was bleeding from the head. I held him and they kept shooting, but now at me," his son Johnatan Halil told a reporter from *La Jornada*. "A *compañero* [Joaquín Benítez] jumped in the way to protect me. That is why they shot him in the shoulder."

The senators kept deliberating.

On October 18, at 9:00 p.m., gunmen in a blue Jetta without license plates pulled up next to Pánfilo Hernández, an indigenous teacher and member of the APPO, and shot him point-blank, three bullets to the stomach. He died an hour later.

That night, on a television screen in the Zócalo a news anchor reported that the senate had voted down the designation of "disappearance of powers." Oaxaca was still "governable." Ulises Ruiz would stay.

By late October the teachers had been on strike, living without wages, sleeping on cardboard boxes under tarps, for five months. The teachers and the APPO together had controlled the city for four months. Plainclothes police had killed eleven people, abducted four, and beaten, tortured, and wounded scores. Thousands of people across the city had built nightly barricades and sat watch until dawn for two months. The tension, fear, and exhaustion were palpable. Many teachers wanted to end the strike and go back to school. And just as many felt the need to press on.

"It is not so easy, after five months and so many murders, to say, 'well, that's it,'" one teacher told me the night Pánfilo Hernández was killed.

Both business owners and workers in the tourism sector—restaurants, cafés, hotels, handicraft shops, bookstores—were at the point of economic collapse. Tourism in June, July, and early August had dropped to a trickle. But in September, after the death squads roamed the city two nights in a row and killed Lorenzo San Pablo Cervantes, the smaller but steady tourism stream dried up. Even so, the business owners I spoke with acknowledged the legitimate social demands of the APPO and blamed the government as much as the protesters for their impending ruin.

"I am not in favor of one side or the other," said Gerardo Vázquez, an engineer and owner of Los Cocos Construction, "but, sadly, in some of the things [the APPO members] do, they are correct. But the government does not pay the slightest attention."

I met Vázquez in the street when he came out of his office to ask the APPO mobile brigade not to paint on his section of the wall or sidewalk, saying that he had spent over $4,000 cleaning up graffiti and fixing broken windows on his properties and that his business, even after laying off over 100 workers, was on the verge of collapse.

"I've got nothing to do with the government," Vázquez said. "Go paint the houses of state officials—they have robbed everybody. Go paint there where all our tax money has gone."

Henry Wangeman has lived in Oaxaca for more than thirty years. He owns Amate Books, a surprisingly good English-language bookstore across the street from the famous Santo Domingo Cathedral. Amate Books has a more complete selection of books on Mexico and Latin America in English than most good bookstores in the United States. Wangeman sold during the six months of conflict what he used to sell in one month. He shipped much of his inventory to Mérida, far away in the Yucatán, to open up a new store and see if he could sell there. And yet, despite the very negative impact the APPO had on his business and his personal income—and his disapproval of the rowdier window-smashers—he supported the overall goals of the APPO.

"When you go out to the marches, you can see that the people are really out there," Wangeman said, "not just a few political groups, and that they are out there to move their ideas, to change their society. I love to see the marches because the families, the young and the old, are all out there. And I didn't see a single march that was well reported on in the press."

"It is an embarrassment that they did not remove Ulises Ruiz," he told me later, after state repression had broken the last of the barricades. "All the people they killed, and that they were filmed shooting! And then the state tries to blame the people from the APPO in spite of all the evidence."

On October 19, as Pánfilo Hernández's family and friends mourned his death, Enrique Rueda, then general secretary of the Oaxaca teachers' union, went on national television in Mexico City and told the country that the strike was over, that the teachers would return to classes within days. Rueda made this statement before the Section 22 state assembly had met to vote. When Rueda arrived at the union hall two days later for the state assembly, huge bodyguards had to escort him into the building. People threw food and drinks at him and rushed to crowd him, shouting insults. One woman who was eating a sandwich as he arrived watched with disgust and then, looking down at her half-eaten sandwich, paused only for a second before throwing it, successfully, at Rueda's head.

The teachers' assembly lasted for about fourteen hours, during which time no one could enter or exit the building. A crowd of several hundred people waited throughout the night for the results of the teacher's vote, shouting slogans denouncing Rueda as a traitor and urging, pleading with the teachers to continue their strike. Groups of masked young men prepared to set the building on fire, but activists from a newly created women's organization formed by those who had taken over Channel 9 stopped them.

Rueda and other union leaders tried to tamper with the vote, but an overwhelming protest forced them to recount the votes, one by one. The recount gave the victory to the strikers, defeating the return to classes that Rueda had called "a fact" on national television. His bodyguards disguised Rueda and sneaked him out of the building the following morning.

President Fox promised to "solve the Oaxaca crisis" before the end of his term on November 30. But the APPO did not buckle. Instead they called for a statewide general strike and highway blockade on Friday, October 27, 2006.

THE AMOUNT OF EVIDENCE is overwhelming. Hundreds of witnesses. Scores of photographs. Video footage. On October 27, 2006, plainclothes police officers and local officials attacked APPO barricades at fifteen different locations across Oaxaca City, killing three people and wounding dozens more. At a barricade in Santa Lucía del Camino, a working-class area of Oaxaca City, police and officials shot and killed New York Indymedia reporter Brad Will.

I first met Brad in January 2006 while covering the launch of the Zapatistas' Other Campaign. I then saw him ten months later, in early October, in the Zócalo. We sat down for a cup of coffee and talked about what was going down. I invited Brad to come walk the barricades with me that night, but he wisely said, "No thanks, I think I want to get a feel for things before walking around too much at night. It is pretty serious here; I mean, they're killing people!"

Police and local officials from Santa Lucía first approached and opened fire on the APPO barricade on Calicanto Avenue. The APPO called for help, and Radio Universidad—back on the air with a new transmitter—announced the call; more than 1,000 people came out to the streets and started to push the attackers back, lobbing rocks and bottles. The gunmen retreated around the corner and back a block or so, and APPO members pursued them down narrow Juárez Street. There, for the first time in the entire conflict, people on the APPO side drew guns, mostly low-caliber pistols, and fired back.

Brad Will was slightly crouched, holding his video camera with two hands, filming, ready to move, when two bullets hit him in the chest and right side. The first bullet pierced his aorta. The national newspaper *El Universal* published a picture of Brad just moments before he was shot. He was facing straight ahead, a photographer crouching right next to him. *El Universal* also published photographs of the police and officials shooting pistols and rifles at the APPO protesters protecting the barricades in Santa Lucía moments before Brad fell.

These gunmen were identified on the front page of *El Universal* on October 28, 2006: Juan Carlos Soriano Velasco, a police officer in a red T-shirt and jeans, firing a machine gun; Manuel Aguilar, police chief, in grey slacks and a black jacket, firing a pistol; and Avel Santiago Zarate, city councilman, in a red button-down shirt, walking briskly with pistol drawn. This photograph was later reprinted in the *New York Times*. Oaxaca's state attorney general said that these men had been arrested. A few days later, Diego Osorno from *Milenio* reported that the men were not to be found in any jail in Oaxaca. The next day the attorney general said, okay, now they have really been arrested, but then a week later she let them go for "lack of evidence."

On October 28, 2006, President Fox sent over 4,000 militarized federal police to "reestablish order" in Oaxaca. The planes, helicopters, and anti-riot tanks began to arrive that afternoon.

Early in the morning on October 29, 2006, the Federal Preventive Police (PFP) prepared to march into Oaxaca City from two points: the airport and the highway that enters town from Mexico City. They had to march, because tens of thousands of people rose at dawn to build barricades throughout the city. There were barricades on nearly every street corner. As the police prepared to march, crowds of men, women, and children, entire families, formed lines in front of them. They offered the police flowers, they waved Mexican flags, they carried paintings of the Virgin of Guadalupe, they walked up to individual police officers and urged them not to repress. The police carried riot shields, clubs, tear gas rifles, and automatic weapons. Helicopters landed and took off. The anti-riot tanks revved their engines. After nearly four hours of standing face-to-face, the police began to advance, firing water cannons and pepper spray into the crowd. People pushed briefly against the police shields, against the blades of the tanks, and then they turned around, ran up a few yards and began to walk in front of the police.

By nightfall, federal police occupied the Zócalo. They tore down the improvised tents, destroyed the life-size papier-mâché sculptures of Ulises Ruiz firing tear gas from a helicopter. They killed three people—Alberto López Bernal, Fidel Sánchez García, Roberto Hernández López—and detained thirty more.

"After hours of smoky clashes in the streets, the end of a political crisis that had left at least nine dead and tested President Vicente Fox came quietly," wrote the *Los Angeles Times* on October 30, 2006.

But the crisis did not end, much less quietly. That same day, once again, the APPO took to the streets. The police had enclosed the Zócalo with razor wire and were guarding every entrance with hundreds of troops and tanks. So when over 10,000 people marched into the city center, they walked right by the Zócalo and established a new *plantón* in front of the Santo Domingo Cathedral, only a few blocks away. That same day the senate passed a nonbinding resolution calling on Ulises Ruiz to resign. Ulises Ruiz submitted a complaint to the Supreme Court arguing that the senate resolution was illegal.

On October 31 and November 1, the APPO built traditional Day of the Dead altars and sand paintings dedicated to the seventeen people killed by police since August. "Our movement is peaceful," said Flavio Sosa, a spokesperson for the APPO. "Our lethal arms against the PFP consist in flowers and sand paintings built in honor of our dead." (A month later Flavio Sosa would be picked off the street in Mexico City by federal police and held in a maximum-security prison for a year and a half.)

At 8:00 a.m. on November 2, 2006, police came to remove the last barricade in Oaxaca City. After clearing away the rubble and city buses used to block the major Cinco Señores intersection, several hundred riot police and Special Forces from the Federal Preventive Police took positions along University Avenue on either side of the Autonomous State University of Oaxaca. Two groups of police forces armed with submachine guns, tear gas grenades, riot shields, and batons prepared to advance, with military helicopters circling overhead and anti-riot tanks behind. Only the charred skeleton of an old bus, stretched across University Avenue halfway between the two police lines, remained.

Inside the walled university campus, students busily readied old soda bottles with gasoline and rags, made impromptu gas masks with orange peels and vinegar, and gathered fist-size rocks in shopping carts, preparing to defend the university against the federal police. The commander of the federal forces, who would not give his name, said that they had no intention of invading the university campus, home to the occupied radio station that APPO protesters had used for months to coordinate their civil disobedience uprising against Governor Ulises Ruiz Ortiz. "They are in their house," the commander said, "and we did not come here to kick them out."

The students saw it otherwise.

Soon, residents from surrounding neighborhoods trickled into the streets to stand before the lines of riot police, talking, pleading, and screaming at them not to advance, not to attack the university. The crowd swelled. By 10:00 a.m., students began to leap over the campus walls and join in, carrying junked cars, old tires, and fallen telephone poles to build a new barricade only ten feet from the federal police. They then set it on fire. The students shouted at the police, waving their sticks, rocks, slingshots, and Molotov cocktails in the air.

Then one of the helicopters overhead fired tear gas grenades inside the campus, and the students unleashed a torrential volley of rocks and bottles. To the west, a morning soccer game froze in mid-play before both teams and the referees ran to gather rocks and join the defense.

Doctora Berta, a 58-year-old physician and professor of medicine had participated in the APPO since June 14, when she volunteered emergency medical assistance to the wounded in the streets. She had started helping out at Radio Universidad in October and just happened to be on the air when the police started firing tear gas inside the campus. Her raspy, calm voice would be broadcast all over Oaxaca and, through Internet streaming, all over the world, as the battle raged out in the street.

"They are attacking us now, as we speak," she said on the air. "Now is the time to come out and defend the university, to defend the radio."

Along the avenue, men and women pushed shopping carts filled with rocks up toward the front line. They shouted to those coming from surrounding streets to bring rocks. An elderly woman advanced into the clouds of tear gas offering water that had been blessed by a local priest to the students.

The protesters pushed the police back, but this only opened the way for a coordinated attack by the riot tanks and helicopters, which blasted tear gas grenades at protesters from the air.

Inside the university grounds, improvised first-aid brigades rushed Coca-Cola and vinegar, their remedy for the immediate burn of tear gas, out to the protesters. Announcers inside the occupied university radio station called for supporters to come into the streets and to bring food, water, and Coca-Cola to the university,

The battle along Eduardo Mata and surrounding streets turned into chaos. Tanks rumbled in to disperse the crowd; three military helicopters flew overhead firing chemical grenades at people in the street. The protesters rushed the police and the tanks with thick volleys of rocks and then ran back to take cover and wash their burning faces in Coke.

"In this struggle I am ready to give my life," said Olivia, a 23-year-old university student, who went straight to work making improvised gas masks out of plastic bottles and vinegar-soaked gauze, "and it will all be so that my children don't have to live on their knees."

Over all, thousands poured into the streets from surrounding neighborhoods and joined the fight: rocks and sticks and Molotov cocktails against anti-riot tanks, tear gas, and federal riot police. By 3:00 a.m. the police retreated and returned to the Zócalo, leaving the university in the hands of the APPO. Some 20,000 people filled the streets and started to rebuild the barricades taken down that morning. More than 200 people suffered injuries during the fight.

After November 2, 2006, Doctora Berta received death threats on a daily basis. Someone sent her a copy of the Bible with all the damnations underlined. (She was forced underground, volunteering as a doctor in another Latin American country.)

"I was calm, scared, I'm not stupid, I thought they were going to grab us, that they would find us in front of the microphones," Doctora Berta said later outside the radio office. "When they say, 'We are not going to enter the university,' one thinks, well, if they say no, it means yes. We can't open the streets around the university: people shoot at us from there. They are the ones who force us to put up barricades all across the city. Do you really think they don't want to shut off the voice of the people?"

Throughout November the police maintained their occupation of the Zócalo and the APPO their protest camp just blocks away. The APPO held several huge marches and a two-day congress with hundreds of delegates from every corner of the state to formalize their organization. The state para-police squads began operating again, beating APPO members down in the street and carting them off to jail.

René Trujillo Martínez, a thin 25-year-old lawyer and volunteer APPO radio announcer, holds the uncomfortable distinction of having survived a disappearance. Trujillo was abducted from his apartment by armed men in civilian clothes, brutally beaten at gunpoint, taken to a safe house and tortured, held for two days incommunicado while being interrogated by federal authorities, and then, miraculously, released on bail.

On Tuesday, November 7, 2006, at about 2:15 p.m., Trujillo and two friends got out of a taxi and began walking up Santo Tomás, the narrow, hilly side street that leads to Trujillo's rented room. They noticed a group of men following them and began to run. The men also broke into a sprint, catching up to Trujillo and his friends just as they were closing the garage door. The men, at least six of them, three large and three of average size, according to several eyewitness accounts, busted into the garage with pistols in hand, firing and beating the three young men, forcing them out into the street.

"I don't know if they were waiting for him or following him, but they came in with pistols and everything," said one witness. (All witnesses interviewed spoke on the condition of anonymity.) "They were dressed in civilian clothes. They came in hitting him; they pulled him out violently. They didn't even talk; it was pure violence."

Trujillo and his two friends, Mauricio Marmolejo and Benito Pereda Fernández, were each held down and beaten in the street by two men. But it was Trujillo they were after, and Trujillo who received the most intense beating: after striking him repeatedly in the face with the barrel of a pistol, Trujillo's assailant stuck his gun into Trujillo's mouth while slamming his head against the wall.

Days later Trujillo's blood was still visible on the rocks outside his house.

Trujillo had participated in the June 14 takeover of Radio Universidad and volunteered around the station until the paid saboteurs threw acid on the transmitter and the station went off the air. But Trujillo hung around, helping maintain the barricade protecting the university station. He then began as program announcer on October 21, when the radio went back on the air with a repaired transmitter. Trujillo ran the 3:00 to 5:00 a.m. program, known as *Barricade Radio*, providing information about police movements around town and barricades that need reinforcement.

The gunmen forced Trujillo and his friends into a yellow rental pickup truck, which they had called for by cell phone during the beatings, according to witnesses. The assailants then covered the men's faces with their own shirts and forced them to lie facedown in the back of the truck, knees pinning down their backs.

After driving for approximately twenty minutes, the gunmen stopped and switched to a white pickup truck, where they placed nylon hoods over the three men and then took them to a warehouse—they think near the airport. At the warehouse the gunmen tortured them, sticking needles under their fingernails (the scars were visible three days later), applying electric shocks to their feet, beating them on the head, and choking them, according to the three men, who were later released.

They asked them to identify militants in the APPO, the most active people at Radio Universidad, and the men who, a few days before, had captured two soldiers and later released them. The gunmen had Oaxaca, Mexico City, and northern Mexican accents.

After some ten hours of torture, the gunmen made them hold guns and then took pictures and filmed them with the guns in their hands. The three men were then taken to the office complex of the Federal Attorney General (PGR) in Oaxaca and charged with the federal crime of possession of illegal firearms. They were held incommunicado at the PGR, where again they were interrogated and terrorized by threats against their lives and against their families. At 6:30 p.m. Thursday, November 9, 2006, they were released on bail. Trujillo had to pay $4,000 for his liberty.

Trujillo's case is rare: he was released within such a short amount of time that the scars from his beating and torture were still plainly visible. His testimony also describes the cooperation between state and federal authorities in carrying out disappearances and torture during the Oaxaca conflict.

On November 15, 2006, the Oaxaca state attorney general, Lisbeth Caña, floated the theory that the APPO had killed Brad Will, shot him point-blank for filming them. She presented a detailed PowerPoint presentation to the press using an audio track from Brad's own camera—pulled from the Internet—in which a voice is heard saying, "Hey, didn't I tell you, dude, not to take photos!" When the voice pronounces the word "take" a metallic sound is heard; Lisbeth Caña said that the metallic sound was that of a 9-millimeter pistol being cocked.

There are many flaws in this theory.

First, according to the autopsy, Brad was not shot at point-blank range, as Caña would have it.

Second, Brad was facing straight ahead and filming at the exact moment he was shot, and the bullet entered his chest from straight on, with a slight downward angle; the APPO members were standing to Brad's left, slightly behind him. No protester appears in Brad's camera frame.

Third, the voice off camera explicitly says, "Didn't I tell you, dude, not to take photos!" (*"Qué te dije güey, que no estés tomando fotos!"*) Brad was not "taking photos," he was filming with a professional high-definition video camera (and the APPO protesters know the difference); however, crouched to his left was a photographer for an international photo agency taking photos of the protesters as they fired slingshots and threw rocks.

Fourth, there were scores of witnesses, both members of the APPO and reporters from across the country, and no one saw a protester shoot Brad. Quite the opposite: "All the shots were coming from the other end of the street. We reporters were all covering the battle from that angle, and just before Brad was shot, a photographer got hit in the leg. We all knew the bullets were coming from the other side," Diego Osorno told me.

Fifth, Brad was well known and liked by the APPO in Santa Lucía, he had been filming there for weeks, and his rapport with the APPO is evidenced by the previous minutes of his own footage—he was running with the APPO, helping them determine where the shots were coming from, using his camera's zoom.

Sixth, Lisbeth Caña said that Brad's second bullet wound came almost half an hour later while the APPO members were trying to get through all the barricades and take Brad to the hospital; the autopsy doctor said that the second wound was produced at the same time as the first, most likely as Brad was still in the process of falling from the impact of the first bullet. Also, a photograph on the front page of *Milenio* on October 28, 2006, shows APPO protesters carrying Brad to the car in which they would try to take him to the hospital: both gunshot wounds are clearly visible in this photograph. The national newspaper *Excelsior* published a photograph and article on March 24, 2007, also showing Brad before he was taken off to the hospital and again with both bullet wounds clearly visible. Lisbeth Caña later sent the case off to the federal attorney general, left her post, and launched a campaign for state senate.

After a march on November 20, 2006, four masked men threw rocks at the police and then ran off. The police fired tear gas, and the APPO responded with more rocks. After a few tense hours, APPO spokespeople gave the order—the first and only one the APPO would issue—for people to pull back and avoid direct confrontation. But five days later the exact same thing would happen: a huge march took place, and this time police provoked the protesters by stealing a cooler of soda from one marcher. The young and rowdy crowd set up a line of impromptu shields and began firing bottle rockets at the police and shooting pebbles from slingshots. The police responded with a barrage of tear gas, and also shooting marbles with slingshots and began advancing block by block until, several hours later, they pushed the protesters out into an open avenue where more troops were waiting.

But that night, November 25, 2006, once the police pushed the protesters out of the city center, they unleashed a wave of violence not seen during six months of conflict: police beat men, women, and children unconscious in the middle of the street; police blasted machine guns at people running for cover; police entered the hospitals throughout the night with their guns drawn, pulling wounded protesters out and piling them in trucks. That night the police grabbed 203 people— at most thirty people had participated in firing bottle rockets at the police, while a crowd of several hundred watched from a distance—and two days later they shipped 141 of them off to federal prison five states away in Nayarit. Most of those who fought with the police escaped down side streets, setting cars and buildings on fire as they fled. Most of the 203 people arrested were charged with arson—which took place at the same time that they were being beaten in the street—and over the following months the charges would be dropped. The APPO charged that the young guys fighting the police were paid provocateurs.

At General Hospital Dr. Manuel Velasco Suárez, armed men came and went throughout the night, looking for wounded members of the APPO, according to multiple witnesses. Hospital director Dr. Felipe Gama said that seven men with pistols drawn forced their way into the hospital, threatening nurses and hospital employees. "The men walked through the hallways and then left," he said. But various witnesses said that armed men who began to search the hospital after police shot at protesters in nearby streets around 8:00 p.m. forced their way into the wards to look for patients. The men threatened the hospital guards at gunpoint and, witnesses say, removed several wounded people between 9:00 p.m. and 2:00 a.m. Dr. Gama said that only three adults had been admitted to the hospital for injuries related to the confrontation between the APPO and the federal police, two for gunshot wounds and one from a projectile wound to the eye. Witnesses in the hospital waiting room said that at least fifteen people arrived at the hospital seeking medical attention for bullet and other wounds resulting from the conflict, but that some were turned away. The night hospital guard's list included names of twelve adults admitted to the emergency room during the night.

After the November 25, 2006, crackdown, two weeks would pass before the APPO could once again take to the streets in protest, this time demanding freedom for the people arrested on November 25. During those two weeks the Oaxaca state police returned in uniform for the first time since June 14 and began a witch hunt for well-known APPO activists, most of whom had gone underground and sneaked out of Oaxaca in trucks traveling through a maze of back roads to avoid police roadblocks. In one particularly absurd case, state police detained, disappeared, and later officially arrested a young human rights activist from Mexico City who had just arrived in Oaxaca that day—for the first time in his life—to help local human rights groups document the disappearances of APPO activists. Twenty-one-year-old Alberto Cilia, a university student and chess champion, came to Oaxaca City to help gather information about the disappeared and within hours was himself disappeared. (He appeared two days later in a Oaxaca state jail and was soon released on bail.)

On December 10, 2006, more than 10,000 members of the APPO returned to the streets, marching in Oaxaca City to demand Ruiz's ouster, an end to the repression against the movement, and the immediate release of all political prisoners. "People are moving beyond the fear," said Fernando Soberanes, an indigenous teacher and member of the APPO who had participated in the movement from day one. "We are returning to the streets."

"THE STRUGGLE IN OAXACA IS, in many respects, a precursor of other struggles yet to come," said Luis Hernández Navarro, an early member of the teachers' movement and now the opinion pages editor of *La Jornada*. "Oaxaca contains the core contradictions in Mexican society and anticipates conflicts that will surge in other states." Electoral fraud, authoritarian rule, and the combination of the teachers' highly organized protests and the governor's unsuccessful raid led to a governance crisis in which the teachers are the backbone of popular resistance, Navarro told me. "This fight will continue; it will not fade away."

A year after Ulises Ruiz ordered the state police to chase the teachers out of their camp at dawn, the APPO led a march of several hundred thousand people who continued to demand justice. While all but three of the prisoners from the movement had been released from jail, not one member of the state or federal police forces had been charged with the seventeen murders and hundreds of torture cases and illegal detentions. The government ignored both the root causes of the conflict—schoolchildren without shoes and illegitimate police violence—and the disastrous social impact of criminalizing dissent. Impunity reigns along with Ulises Ruiz. The governor is an almost cartoonish embodiment of the violence of authority masquerading as the "rule of law." He rigs elections, launders state money through disastrous public works, attacks critical newspapers, and organizes death squads composed of convicted murderers and on-duty police officers to pull ski masks down over their faces and drive through the protester-occupied city shooting and killing people in the street[5]—and Ulises Ruiz is not an aberration. Throughout the conflict in 2006 and since, the federal government has done nothing to investigate and punish his acts of criminal violence; rather, they have protected him at every turn.

The Oaxaca uprising, for all its idiosyncrasies and quirks, tells us this: "History is still very much alive, the story continues; we have more ideas, and we will advance them." The movement that the APPO represents is not a creature of the Mexican Left, as typically conceived, nor is it a creation of any of Mexico's political parties. Rather, the APPO is an expression of the Oaxacan peoples' insistence on pursuing justice, their will to defend their dignity despite the blunt violence of the state. Amazingly, the APPO united almost every opposition group in the state of Oaxaca. And yet even that unprecedented feat pales beside APPO's unique genius: it opened a social space for people who have always been shut out of the everyday workings of politics.

The movement that gave rise to the Oaxaca uprising reasserts that resistance and revolt are not only about articulating real demands and mobilizing thousands to leverage the realization of those demands, not only about throwing rocks at riot police or tending to piles of burning tires at the barricades. Revolt is also brewing coffee and taking it to the tired barricade watchers, or gathering rocks in shopping carts and ferrying them up to the front line. Resistance is also

taking photographs at mobilizations, listening to the movement-occupied radio stations, creating protest stencil art and
painting city walls, holding neighborhood meetings, writing
new protest songs, telling stories of resistance and revolt,
connecting with others. There are many unnoticed battle-
fields that never make front-page photographs or the
morning news. Another aspect of genius in the Oaxaca
movement is the unlimited opening of spaces of resistance
on equal footing—all are members, rock throwers, and coffee brewers alike.

People participating in the APPO rarely speak in the first
person singular when asked about their motivations or their
hopes: they almost always answer in the plural, saying "we." I
would ask, "Why are you out here" or "What do you hope to
achieve?" and time and time again the person interviewed
would respond: "We are here because . . ." or "We are fighting
for. . . ." It is not that particular individuals pretended to represent or speak for others; rather, their most fundamental
ideas about their actions, the meaning of their actions, their
desires, and their inspirations are social, not individual.

I asked Florentino López—one of the APPO spokespeople—on several occasions why he *personally* was risking so
much to participate in the APPO. Florentino and his family
have been repeatedly threatened with death, he has a warrant
out for his arrest, and he has already been picked up off the
street and beaten by para-police units, who threatened to kill
him on the spot. He, as an individual, it would seem, has a lot
at stake, a lot on the line. But he never responded to my questions by saying, "I feel" or "I think" or "I hope," or by telling
me a personal story or anecdote. He always embedded his
individual self deep inside the social: "Because we long for a
real social transformation; because the exclusion and abject
poverty that most of us who are participating in the movement

have suffered in our own flesh has dragged us out here, in a natural way, to become part of this movement."

The voices in the streets of Oaxaca warned many times over that it is the violence of "poverty" and the violence of authority that make revolt necessary. The incredible participation and creativity expressed on the streets during the Oaxaca uprising of 2006 teaches that revolt is not only necessary, it is also possible.

6.

RECLAIMING INDIGENOUS AUTONOMY

We are the product of five hundred years of struggle: first against slavery; then in the insurgent-led war of independence against Spain; later in the fight to avoid being absorbed by North American expansion; next to proclaim our Constitution and expel the French from our soil; and finally, after the dictatorship of Porfirio Díaz refused to fairly apply the reform laws, in the rebellion where the people created their own leaders. In that rebellion Villa and Zapata emerged— poor men, like us.

We are denied the most elementary education so that they can use us as cannon fodder and plunder our county's riches, uncaring that we are dying of hunger and curable diseases. Nor do they care that we have nothing, absolutely nothing, no decent roof over our heads, no land, no work, no food, no education. We do not have the right to freely and democratically elect our own authorities, nor are we independent of foreigners, nor do we have peace or justice for ourselves and our children.

But today we say enough!

—First Declaration of the Lacandón Jungle, General Command of the EZLN

IT IS ONE OF THE MORE BEAUTIFUL stories ever told: thousands of men and women converging in silence, unseen, their movements undetected, walking through mountains of shadow and mist, winding along dirt roads in the backs of rickety trucks, tunneling through underground sewage channels, gathering on abandoned street corners on the outskirts of towns consigned to marginal duties, their invisibility now, after so many broken years, a weapon; no one sees them, no one hears them, no one notices that an army is moving. During the first minutes of 1994, a rag-and-bone army attacks, and while few gunshots are fired, their rebellion sets in motion a tsunami of symbols and ideas that will lash against the shoreline of what is thought to be possible.[1]

Those who are awake are watching their clocks, waiting for midnight and with it the arrival, they have been told, of a unique New Year. In Mexico City, President Carlos Salinas is engaged in a ceremony. He and the luminaries of the Mexican elite, suits pulled taut, white shirts starched, are waiting to raise their glasses at the stroke of midnight to consecrate the president's successful delivery of his nation into the arms of the "First World," to seal his place in history and his future in the folds of power. The president waits for the minute hand to advance its circular, inevitable drive, and as he waits, in the last corner of the country, along its southernmost edge, an army of the forgotten march still unseen against oblivion, their long night's journey a subversion of this midnight, an attack planned not only on the seat of colonial power in Chiapas, but on the "First World," on history, on the electronic mirage of a future for anyone in the folds of power.

A few have machine guns, some have old, bolt-action rifles from decades past, some have sticks painted to look like rifles, some just have sticks, and many have nothing but rage and hunger and the resolute choice to fall to a bullet before living any longer in the destiny of ordained oblivion. After Salinas de Gortari has completed his various toasts and exchanges of knowing smiles, an unlucky group of advisers has to disturb the revelry and deliver the news: indigenous guerrillas have interrupted Mexico's glide into the First World, taking over several cities in Chiapas, including the cobblestone streets of San Cristóbal de las Casas. The president is not pleased and quickly orders the Mexican army to crush the insurgents. But the Mayan rebels, mostly Tzotzil, Tzeltal, Tojolabal, Zoque, Chol, and Ma'am indigenous farmers from the highlands and the jungle regions of Chiapas, have already occupied several cities, trashed the government archives in San Cristóbal, read their "Declaration of the Lacandón Jungle" from the government palace and pasted copies along the walls of the city, kidnapped the loathed cacique and land baron General Absalón Castellanos Domínguez, and captured the attention of a quickly assembled huddle of journalists and photographers, and through them, much of the world.

Since the arrival of the Spaniards, to be indigenous in the land now called Mexico (and throughout the Americas) meant to be frozen in the grip of hunger, trapped in the condition of lack, to be children of an emaciated culture who by their very nature and constitution were seen as deficient and thus simply destined to wade through centuries of want and suffering. Imperial domination has from its beginning and through its evolution depended upon naturalizing in one way or another the horror visited upon the subjects of domination—"inferior" races, the poor trapped in cycles of poverty—to be indigenous has meant to be forgotten, at best, or to seen as an animal locked outside the considerations of ethics, at worst. On January 1, 1994, the Zapatista Army of National Liberation took their hunger, the hunger of the indigenous, the aura of lack, and brandished it as a weapon: the image of the rebel soldiers' thin bodies and tattered uniforms spoke the legitimacy of their rebellion in an unsilenceable voice, a voice that could not be feigned, a voice that spoke first through wordless action. As the Zapatistas would write in one of their first communiqués,

"Our voice began its journey centuries ago and will never again be silenced."[2] The president—in an inept and desperate attempt to combat the rebels' legitimacy—would charge that the indigenous soldiers were led by foreign, blond, and blue-eyed "professionals of violence," because, according to his logic, the indigenous could not rebel themselves, they could not organize and carry out something so complex as a clandestine, armed uprising, they could not become historical subjects on the same stage as a president. Confronted with the audacity of an indigenous rebellion, none could deny the injustices underlying the revolt, hence the elite attempted to deny that the rebels were in fact indigenous, or that they were organized and led by the indigenous. Identity is always contested territory, and in Chiapas the Zapatistas reclaimed theirs.

But what, you may ask, could possibly be beautiful about a war? What could be beautiful about people with guns, soldiers marching and firing, planes dropping bombs, bodies strewn across narrow roads emptied now of life and blood? Nothing. The story of the Zapatista uprising is not a war story, though there is war in it. The Zapatistas' is a story of taking a stand against all odds in the defense of dignity, and a story of trying against all odds to take one's stand by the dictates of its goal—that is, to fight with dignity. In the Zapatistas' words: "We didn't go to war on January 1 to kill or be killed. We went to war to make ourselves heard."[3] From the first day of war, the EZLN called on the International Red Cross to "observe and regulate any combat involving our forces so as to protect the civilian population" and wrote: "We declare that we are now, and always will be, subject to the Laws of War of the Geneva Convention."[4] The EZLN only attacked the military and the police, released prisoners usually within a matter of days, and refused to execute prisoners as the Mexican Army did.

What is beautiful about this story? In the city where for centuries the indigenous were forced to walk in the streets with animals and cars, leaving the sidewalks for the European-descended; the city where the indigenous had to walk with their heads bowed, avoiding eye contact with the "authentic" residents; the city where a blow to the head served to communicate the wishes of the elite; the city down whose stone walls and streets echoed the unspoken law of apartheid: through these streets, into these buildings, in this city the indigenous rebels walked with their heads raised, and so too their guns; with their faces covered in black balaclavas or red bandanas, the Zapatistas occupied the symbolic core of colonial power in Chiapas; and, what is amazing, they did not burn houses and execute people in the street, as one might expect from an armed uprising, but they read their declaration and announced their rebellion with a dash of humor that is now the stuff of legend. Frightened tourists in the occupied town square of San Cristóbal were pestering the guerrillas about their obstructed travel itineraries, whereupon a masked and armed guerrilla quipped: "The road to Palenque is closed. We have taken Ocosingo. I'm sorry for the inconvenience, but this is a revolution."[5]

For twelve days indigenous rebels from one of the poorest regions in the hemisphere faced off with the military machine of the Mexican armed forces: men and women in boots and sandals pitted against tanks, "U.S.-provided counter-narcotic helicopters,"[6] and warplanes; the knowledge of mountain paths against the aerial bombardment of rural villages; the careful attempt to avoid civilian deaths against the command to kill "anyone who looked like a Zapatista."[7] But these twelve days of combat—with over 200 combatants and civilians falling to bullets and shrapnel—opened an unforeseen battlefield: the federal government quickly attacked the perceived legitimacy of the indigenous uprising, once again denying them even the right to be who they are, and to this territory the rebels quickly dispatched an arsenal of fiercely written words, written as if spoken, armed with the rage and poetry of unfiltered honesty. In just a few weeks the EZLN would hold their own in an intensely imbalanced military conflict and then, reading both the government's unease and the swell of popular support for the indigenous call for justice, the rebels would decisively shift the combat into the territory of reason and argument, of history and present, of language and truth, territory where the insurgents' superiority would devastate the facile troops of government logic. The most decisive early battle took place on January 18, 1994, when Subcomandante Marcos responded to President Salinas's offer of a "pardon" for the rebel soldiers:

> Up until today, January 18, 1994, the only thing we have heard about is the federal government's formal offer of pardon for our troops.
>
> Why do we have to be pardoned? What are we going to be pardoned for? For not dying of hunger? For not being silent in our misery? For not humbly accepting our historic role of being the despised and the outcast? For having picked up arms after we found all other roads closed? For not having paid attention to the Chiapas Penal Code, one of the most absurd and repressive in history? For having demonstrated to the rest of the country and the entire world that human dignity still lives, even among some of the world's poorest peoples? For having been well prepared before we began our uprising? For having carried guns into battle, rather than bows and arrows? For being Mexicans? For being primarily indigenous people? For having called on the Mexican people to struggle, in all possible ways, for that which belongs to them? For having fought for freedom, democracy,

and justice? For not following the example of previous guerrilla armies? For not giving up? For not selling out? For not betraying ourselves?

Who must ask for pardon, and who can grant it? Those who for years and years have satiated themselves at full tables, while death sat beside us so regularly that we finally stopped being afraid of it? Those who filled our pockets and our souls with promises and empty declarations?

Or should we ask pardon from the dead, our dead, those who died "natural" deaths of "natural causes" like measles, whooping cough, breakbone fever, cholera, typhoid, mononucleosis, tetanus, pneumonia, malaria, and other lovely gastrointestinal and lung diseases? Our dead, the majority dead, the democratically dead, dying from sorrow because no one did anything, because the dead, our dead, went just like that, without anyone even counting them, without anyone saying "ENOUGH!" which would have at least given some meaning to their deaths, a meaning that no one ever sought for them, the forever dead, who are now dying again, but this time in order to live.

Must we ask for pardon from those who have denied us the right and ability to govern ourselves? From those who lack respect for our customs, our culture, and ask us for papers and obedience to a law whose existence and moral basis we do not accept? Those who pressure us, torture us, assassinate us, disappear us for the serious "crime" of wanting a piece of land, neither a big one nor a small one, but a simple piece of land on which we can grow something to fill our stomachs?

Who must ask for pardon, and who can grant it?[8]

In the space of a few hundred words, Subcomandante Marcos stripped the federal government of its claim to legitimacy, wrecking its drive to force the EZLN to buckle either under pressure or under a rain of bombs. In the space of a few inches of newsprint, the masked rebels flipped the edifice of the state on its back and pinned it there, stunned and squirming. In a political jujitsu move—the language simple, direct, and fearless—the rebels hiding in the mountains won the respect of millions. The chemistry of the EZLN's quixotic military offensive then laced with the poetry, humor, and unapologetic insurgency of their communiqués created a guerrilla force the government was unprepared to confront: one in which most people in the country agreed that the rebels spoke the truth.

ALLAN R. HOLMBERG lived with the Sirionó in Bolivia from 1940 to 1942. He wrote about them in a book called *Nomads of the Longbow*, saying that they were "among the most culturally backward peoples of the world."[9] He described their lives of constant wandering and destitution and concluded that the Sirionó had been frozen in time, trapped in such a life for millennia, examples of "man in the raw state of nature."[10] He failed to research their history—it never occurred to him, it would seem—and thus failed to learn that smallpox and influenza had wiped out their villages in the 1920s and that they had been battling the land invasions of white ranchers, aided by the Bolivian military; when Holmberg lived amongst them, they were on the run, escaping murder and slavery at the hands of the military and the ranchers.[11] Holmberg, writes Charles Mann in his book *1491: New Revelations of the Americas Before Columbus*, "never fully grasped that the people he saw as remnants from the Paleolithic Age were actually persecuted survivors of a recently shattered culture. It was as if he had come upon refugees from a Nazi concentration camp, and concluded that they belonged to a culture that had always been barefoot and starving."[12] Charles Mann takes "Holmberg's Mistake" as a metaphor to describe how Europeans profoundly misunderstood the peoples who inhabited the Americas before them by denying them history, and thus conveniently failing to detect the implication of European land invasions in causing the brutal living conditions that the illuminated anthropologists would "discover, describe, and introduce into history."[13]

Holmberg's Mistake is not a question of some misguided, ambitious graduate student in the 1940s: it pervades political thinking into the present. The indigenous people of Mexico, Holmberg and his followers would no doubt tell us, have always lived like that, in destitution, devastated by hunger and curable diseases; what they need is further state aid, government assistance, further intervention. A convenient ideological platform: in one stroke it erases the history of colonialism, genocide, slavery, and land invasions that caused such misery and continue to do so right up to the present; it also conditions the improvement of the indigenous peoples' lot on the very institution, the state, that has orchestrated their destitution since taking over for the crown. According to historian Enrique Semo, in colonial Mexico "the majority of the communities that were able to conserve themselves entered a process of economic regression: the disappearance of the commercial specialties of the *calpulltin*, the artisans, and intellectual activity, and a regression to the most primitive of agrarian life."[14]

For centuries racism has been the principal ideological tool to explain and justify oppression. In Mexico the Spanish Crown created and maintained social and political separation between Spaniards and indigenous peoples for three centuries: "power and privilege correlated closely with 'racial' identification."[15] Mexican independence liberated the emerging *criollo* and *mestizo* capitalist class from Spanish imperial control, but in no way affected racism. Historian Alan Knight notes that the "heyday of European racist thought—dated approximately from 1850 to 1920—roughly coincided with Mexico's phase of liberal state-building and capitalist export-oriented economic development."[16] This development reached a certain climax with the thirty-year dictatorship of Porfirio Díaz. Knight continues:

> Yet more significant and pervasive, I would suggest, was the inherent logic of the Porfirian model of development, which required the dispossession of peasant communities (many of them Indian) and the creation of a reliable labor force, urban and rural. These trends were not new; they followed old colonial precedents. But the pressures and opportunities were now greater (not least thanks to the advent of the railway) and they lent themselves to new racist and Social Darwinist rationalizations. As in colonial countries, the "myth of the lazy native" was invoked—by foreign and Mexican employers—to explain peasant resistance to proletarianization and to justify tough measures to overcome it.[17]

Porfirian-era racism exclusively targeted indigenous peoples, claiming the *mestizos* were a part of "progress," while indigenous inferiority was "a problem of nutrition and education."[18] The Porfirian regime was obsessed with state-building, and indigenous peoples were conceived as "an antinational element requiring prompt and, if necessary, forcible assimilation . . . the practice of the Porfirian regime was one of Indian oppression."[19]

The 1910–1920 Mexican Revolution, as discussed below, was largely inspired and fought by indigenous peoples and campesinos. The nation-state that privileged classes built on the ruins of the Revolution however, would only recast and more carefully window-dress the ideological constructs housing racism and its practices of oppression. The post-revolutionary regime that culminated in the formation of the PRI took up the Porfirian project of state-building, infusing it with a feverish new cult of nationalism and establishing the official ideology of *indigenismo* as part of its bedrock. The new nationalist ideologues sanctified the *mestizo* as a kind of "cosmic race" and welded the *mestizo* to nationhood, opening the way for a racial manifest destiny where *mestizaje* was the precondition for development and progress.[20] Alan Knight writes: "Again, therefore, *mestizaje*, and nationhood were equated . . . thus the necessary consequence of nation-building was to 'dissolve the Indian element in the mestizo element.' . . . The mestizo thus became the ideological symbol of the new regime."[21]

In 1965, Pablo González Casanova wrote: "The indigenous problem is essentially a problem of internal colonialism. The indigenous communities are our internal colonies."[22] And little has changed in the past forty years. A recent study by researchers at the National Autonomous University of Mexico showed that indigenous people in Mexico—which make up 13 percent of the total population—and in fourteen other countries across Latin America continue to be the "most marginalized, vulnerable, and poor" sector of the population.[23] The exclusion and marginalization of indigenous peoples is a worldwide trend, and this should come as little surprise: to be indigenous is more or less synonymous with being the underdog throughout centuries of imperial invasions across the globe. The United Nations estimates that over 300 million people, in some 5,000 groups and more than seventy countries, are indigenous, and most of them live under the continued invasions and domination of contemporary imperial societies.[24]

The name itself comes from Holmberg's Mistake. None of the more than 100 million people estimated to have been living between Alaska and the Patagonia in 1491 called themselves indigenous or Indian.[25] "Indian" identity is itself a product of conquest.[26] Francisco López Bárcenas, a Ñu Savi lawyer and historian writes, "The Indian or indigenous is a concept invented by the invaders with very clear purpose. . . . they sought to differentiate themselves from those who rightfully inhabited these lands [when they had come] to occupy them without any right to do so . . . thus they invented the Indian and they subordinated them to their interests."[27] The Spaniards further sought to mass the vast diversity of cultures, languages, and peoples that flourished across the Americas into one category: indigenous.[28]

While many peoples have fought to shake the insults that colonial powers used to name them—the Lakota are not Sioux; the Me'phaa are not Tlapanecos—the category *indigenous*, with all its awkwardness, has stuck. In Mexico, non-European peoples across the country reclaim indigenous identity as an instrument of struggle against the continued denial of their autonomy, cultural sovereignty, languages, and history.[29] In fact, one dimension of indigenous identity that links extremely diverse cultures is the explicitly anticolonial stance of indigenous peoples. Consider the following definition "accepted by an international gathering of indigenous peoples in 1996":[30]

> Indigenous communities, peoples and nations are those which, having a historical continuity with pre-invasion and pre-colonial societies that developed on

their territories, consider themselves distinct from other sectors of the society now prevailing in those territories, or parts of them. They form at present nondominant sectors of society and are determined to preserve, develop and transmit to future generations their ancestral territories, and their ethnic identity, as the basis of their continued existence as peoples, in accordance with their own cultural patterns, social institutions and legal systems.[31]

Two sentences: one deals with the past to present and the other with the present to future. The past-to-present dimension captures two salient facts: the historical continuity of both invasion and domination. The present-to-future dimension captures the determination to survive as peoples, maintaining and constructing autonomous culture, knowledge, and governance all on their ancestral territories. This description (better than "definition") is anticolonial, anti-nationalist, and anti-capitalist. Why anticolonial? The peoples are determined to "develop and transmit to future generations their ancestral territories," that is, they refuse to accept past and present land invasions, the sine qua non of colonialism (be it foreign or internal to the state). Why anti-nationalist? The peoples refuse to submit their own "social institutions and legal systems" to the externally imposed systems of the state—the very systems that inherited colonial dominance and carried it into the present upon the dissolution of European monarchies. Why anticapitalist? The peoples will maintain the historical continuity of their territory and cultural practices, meaning, in simple terms, in the autonomous regions, community and territory reign over private property rights and the accumulation of capital; it does not mean, for example, that Zapatistas will not sell coffee and corn and buy medicine and laptops, it means that the Zapatistas will defend their land, culture, and autonomy and decide for themselves how and how much to give and take with capitalist societies.

Many of the indigenous peoples of Mexico have compacted these radical stances into an even shorter expression: *autonomy*. Indigenous struggles for autonomy have lasted for centuries, mostly leading to overwhelming military violence as the state's sole response. In Oaxaca, where such struggles had been particularly fierce, indigenous peoples' de facto autonomy led the Oaxaca state government to recognize autonomy in the state constitution, acknowledging indigenous social institutions and legal practices, including assembly-based elections of local authorities. After 1994, the EZLN opened their negotiations with the federal government to all indigenous peoples of Mexico, leading to the creation of an indigenous rights agreement that would establish federal recognition of indigenous autonomy not only for the Zapatistas in Chiapas but for all indigenous peoples across Mexico.

Critics of indigenous autonomy, including members of the progressive left, argue that such autonomy is impossible, that no one may be extracted from capitalism, globalization, and the world of states. They immediately assume that autonomy means a reversion to some precolonial utopia, a "back-to-the-land" or "off-the-grid" escapism dreamed up and lauded more by the disenchanted middle class than by indigenous peoples. But here again we confront Holmberg's Mistake; these critics imagine the indigenous as peoples without history, subjecting them to the either/or stricture: "Either you are capitalist or you are shut out of everything created during the reign of capitalist production; either you live in a world with automobiles, computers, antibiotics, and electricity, or you do not; and—get used to it—extraction at this point is simply impossible," their logic says. Precisely what is missing here is the critique of contemporary forms of colonialism and imperialism and their historical continuity. Indigenous autonomy does not advocate a world without antibiotics, surgery, and book printing; it argues for specific territories without imperial conquest, without military intervention, without capitalist intervention, for specific territories where the inhabitants may choose according to their knowledge and policies how and when to integrate with other territories, which antibiotics they need, which books they want. Autonomy does not mean isolation; it means sustainability without external impositions—social, political, and cultural sovereignty.

According to Mexican government statistics, there are an estimated 12.7 million indigenous people in Mexico, making up about 13 percent of the national population. Sixty-two distinct indigenous languages—not including regional dialects that often vary dramatically—are currently spoken in thirty of Mexico's thirty-one states and federal district. (Aguascalientes and Colima are the only two states where no indigenous languages are spoken.)[32] Of the 317 municipalities across the country that have an almost total population of indigenous inhabitants, 196 are qualified as having a "very high" level of marginalization and 119 are qualified as "high"; only two predominantly indigenous municipalities are qualified as "medium" and none as "low" or "very low."[33] In its eight-month investigative series on poverty in Mexico, the magazine *Contralínea* wrote: "The words extreme poverty are synonymous with indigenous communities: lack of potable water, sewage, and plumbing; houses without floors or electricity; no basic health or education services."[34]

"Let us say this with all clarity," writes López Bárcenas in his essay on indigenous autonomy in Latin America, "indigenous peoples in Latin America struggle for their autonomy because in the twenty-first century they continue to be colonies. The nineteenth-century independence wars ended foreign colonization, but those who took power continued to view indigenous peoples as colonies, colonies that the hegemonic classes hid behind the masquerade of individual rights and legal equality. . . . All while the indigenous peoples of Latin America suffered and suffer still the power of internal colonialism."[35] At its root, indigenous autonomy is the simultaneous rejection of invasion and the affirmation of sovereign indigenous culture and territory, and thus indigenous movements are struggles of both resistance and emancipation.[36]

The post-independence states in Latin America used the idea of individual rights to systematically violate the rights of indigenous peoples as peoples, particularly their practices of collective land ownership and assembly-based forms of governance.[37] Beyond the obvious conflicts created by state land expropriations and individual claims to private land ownership, such seemingly mundane practices as the drawing of state and municipal boundaries violated indigenous territories and subjected indigenous peoples to the practices of state governance, almost always in the hands of nonindigenous people.[38] Autonomy, which fights against land invasion and legal-administrative divisions of indigenous territories, is the politics of asserting and defending the rights of indigenous peoples as peoples—not the rights of particular communities or organizations, but of the peoples, *los pueblos*. Although such collective, peoples' rights have been formally established in Convention 169 of the International Labor Organization—which Mexico has signed and ratified—they are incompatible with the state's assertion of supreme individual and property rights. Thus indigenous movements for autonomy demand the refounding of the state itself: indigenous autonomy and internal colonialism cannot coexist.[39]

THEY HAD TO COVER THEIR FACES TO BE SEEN.
This was the explanation for why thousands of indigenous
rebels continued to wear black ski masks or red bandannas
long after the gun battles stopped and talks with the government began in 1994. And the same remains true today. In a
country with over twelve million indigenous inhabitants, most
remain invisible to the world beyond their villages. Few Mexicans or non-Mexicans can name more than a handful of the
sixty-two distinct indigenous languages spoken in Mexico. But
almost everyone knows about the Zapatistas.

From December 30, 2006, through January 2, 2007, over
1,000 people from forty-seven countries traveled to Oventik, a hillside Zapatista village about an hour north of San
Cristóbal de Las Casas, for a gathering between Zapatistas
and activists, artists, and curious individuals from across the
world. The Zapatistas organized conference-style panel discussions on indigenous autonomy, health, education,
women's participation and experience in the autonomous
communities, media, art, culture, and land. Representatives
from the five regional governance bodies known as good
government councils (*juntas de buen gobierno*) took turns
speaking on their experiences organizing community life
without help or permission from the federal, state, or municipal governments. Thousands of masked Zapatista men,
women, and children also attended the event, attracting the
eyes and camera lenses of the national and international visitors and showing that their metaphor of the mask as their
cloak of visibility still holds. The event in Oventik was the
first of three international gatherings held in Zapatista territory during 2007.

The EZLN took the nation and the world by surprise on
January 1, 1994, when they rose up in arms, taking over major
cities in Mexico's southernmost and heavily indigenous state

of Chiapas. The rebels' battle cry, "*¡Ya basta!*"—"Enough!"—
resonated with millions of poor Mexicans.

They tried everything. They declared war. They took over
seven cities across Chiapas. They called out for "work, land,
housing, food, health, education, independence, freedom,
democracy, justice, and peace."[40] They fought the Mexican
Army for twelve days. They agreed to a ceasefire. They
released their prisoners of war. They sat down to dialogue with
their enemies. They weathered military encroachments that
violated the ceasefire. They escaped a surprise army invasion
to capture their military leaders. To the government's betrayal
of the ceasefire, the army's invasion of Zapatista territory, and
the displacement of thousands of people, they responded with
words that cut through the might of tanks and helicopters and
compelled more than 100,000 people to take to the streets in
Mexico City, thousands to protest across the globe—and with
their will and their words they defeated an army and forced the
president of Mexico to retract the invasion.

After several failed attempts, the Zapatistas and the Zedillo
administration signed the San Andrés Accords in February
1996, promising greater levels of autonomy and self-determi-
nation to Mexico's indigenous peoples. The EZLN opened its
negotiations to all indigenous peoples of Mexico, declaring:
"*Para todos, todo; para nosotros, nada*"—"Everything for everyone; nothing for ourselves." They and those who came to
stand with them negotiated with the federal government an
agreement on indigenous rights and autonomy, the San
Andrés Accords, that in the end fell far short of what they
themselves had designed. They signed the agreement. And
then they watched as the president refused to implement it.

They convoked the creation of a civil society organization
to open a space for a pan-Left participatory movement. They
held international gatherings. They carried out nationwide

consultations. They survived paramilitary and military attacks and massacres. They wrote reams of communiqués, stories, and analyses. They responded time after time to violence with appeals to reason, to gunshots with words, to betrayals with disposition to dialogue. They did not disarm, but they did not use their weapons to attack. As the government's violence grew more insidious and more devastating—on December 22, 1997, paramilitary troops armed with high-caliber assault rifles attacked refugees gathered in a church in the community of Acteal, slaughtering forty-five men, women, and children, and, with machetes, four babies in utero—the Zapatistas stood their course, calling out for justice, refusing to surrender. They waited and they organized.

In March 2001, they finally packed up their rucksacks, left their arms in the jungle and drove in a caravan, followed by some 3,000 people from across the world, through thirteen states, thirty-three communities, and 3,000 kilometers before arriving—for the first time—in Mexico City. They drew millions to their speaking and cultural events, packed Mexico City's Zócalo, and spoke in Congress, all to call for recently elected President Vicente Fox and the nation's legislators to make the 1996 San Andrés Accords law. However, all three political parties in Congress, PRI, PAN, and PRD, turned their backs, passing a gutted, paternalistic version of the accords;[41] and the Zapatistas again responded to betrayal with resolve: they denounced the eviscerated law and traveled back to Chiapas, cutting off all communications with the government.

In the following years they set about implementing the San Andrés Accords on their own, building the foundations for complete autonomy in their forms of governance and establishing of institutions to provide social services such as health care and education. In 2003, the EZLN helped set up "good government councils," composed of men and women elected in open assemblies, to organize regional and village affairs. The good government councils would replace the military leadership structure of the EZLN in day-to-day regional governance, following the Zapatista first rule of government: *"mandar obedeciendo,"* or "command by obeying."

They tried everything, and at every step the response of the government was violence and betrayal. And then they said: let's try again.

Early in the morning on January 1, 2006, Subcomandante Marcos emerged from the Zapatista village La Garrucha astride a black motorcycle and set out on what was planned as a six-month journey across all thirty-one states and the Federal District of Mexico City. Marcos set out to travel—mostly in cars provided by volunteers—as the EZLN's "Delegate Zero." His assignment: to listen to the indigenous communities, workers, social movements, nongovernmental organizations, students, gays, lesbians, trans, anarchist collectives, and any and all who make up the underdogs (*los de abajo*) of the Mexican Left. The Other Campaign's ultimate goal: to pull all these people together into a national anticapitalist movement.

In June 2005, with no public explanation, the EZLN had sent out a red alert, calling an emergency session with the guerrilla commanders. After a month of discussions, the EZLN released the Sixth Declaration of the Lacandón Jungle (*La sexta declaración de la selva Lacandona*). The Sexta, something like a Zapatista Declaration of Independence from capitalism, lays out the Zapatistas' analysis of the social ills in Mexico and abroad, and what they plan to do about them.

The analysis in the Sexta is simple: capitalism treats people and nature as sheer merchandise, objects without rights, to be used and discarded at the whim of stock markets and speculators. Democracy within a capitalist system is nothing more than window dressing, reiterated false promises, and government aid programs that stifle autonomy, foster dependence, and ultimately conquer social movements fighting for social transformation. The major political parties all serve as the guardians of the capitalist system, with candidates and businesspeople linked through stock holdings and outright corruption, forming a single, capitalist political class. There is no way to overthrow capitalism from within the electoral system; something entirely other must be built, and must be built without the corrupting influence of the capitalist political class.

Hence the first phase of the Other Campaign, a six-month journey across the country to listen. The EZLN does not want to tell their fellow underdogs of the Left how to organize or what to do, but first to ask them, a whole lot of them, what they have already been doing and how best to bridge their efforts. In many ways, the Other Campaign re-creates at a national level what the original small group of EZLN insurgents first did when they arrived in the jungle communities of Chiapas—organizing through listening. Today the Zapatistas are walking their talk, and have set out to spend the next several years building a nationwide movement.

The tour visited rural communities, inner-city slums, and downtown plazas. Marcos often spoke in public to encourage people to join and participate in the Other Campaign, but the backbone of the tour consisted in the hours-long meetings where Marcos—and the ragtag crew of organization representatives and independent media correspondents who followed him—sat listening to the tales of repression and exclusion, of resistance and autonomous governance projects. The listening sessions were long and arduous, stretching for hours, several times a day, seven days a week. Most meetings were held either in boxlike concrete rooms in union offices and public halls or outdoors, sometimes with and sometimes without thatched roofs or tarps to block the force of Mexico's sun and rain. When the agenda was tight, meeting organizers set a time limit for each participant, but most often there was no limit. And while no one ever screened for content, two topics were explicitly unwelcome: speaking in favor of either capitalism or political parties.

The Zapatista effort at first glance appeared rather peculiar. Just as the institutional Left was winning elections across Latin America, the Zapatistas came out repudiating electoral politics in Mexico. Rather than putting their energy and moral authority behind a candidate in 2006, they staked everything on a national organizing effort, calling upon those who were and are cut out of the political system to reject the exhausted promises of the presidential candidates along with their blind faith in the benefits of capitalism and build something entirely different, from the bottom up. One of the mottos of the Other Campaign in 2006 was "Vote or don't vote: organize."

With the Other Campaign, the Zapatistas stepped firmly outside of the dominant political and economic culture in Mexico. Their message was clear: the time for dialogue between the EZLN and the Mexican government was long gone. And another core message, equally clear: the Zapatistas cannot push the national struggle for liberation forward alone.[42]

The winter 2006–2007 gathering in Oventik was the first between national and international visitors and the autonomous good government councils, and an opportunity to hear firsthand from the typically elusive Zapatistas about what autonomy means for them.

"The authority should serve but not serve itself, propose, not impose," said Roel, from the good government council of La Realidad during the workshop on autonomy that was held in a wood and corrugated sheet-metal auditorium with a dirt floor covered in pine needles.

Council members are elected in open assemblies and serve

for three years without salary, though villagers support them with food, child care, and travel funds. In the four years of operating in good government councils, Zapatistas have opened schools in every village and regional center, health clinics, women's artisan cooperatives, and organic coffee cooperatives.

"As Mexicans, we live within the Mexican state, but with the right to our autonomy," said Elías from La Garrucha. "Our way of being, our practice of working in collective, our language, and our ideas are all different."

"Autonomy is not what it says in the dictionary," said Beto of the good government council of Morelia. "Autonomy is not what it says in the constitution of the bad government; it is not what we say here . . . but what is done and built in practice."

For first-time visitors who do not speak one of the six indigenous languages of the region, however, one of the most impressive aspects of Zapatista villages is the mural art that adorns walls throughout the village.

"The murals are another way of expressing, or telling our own history," said Karina, another member of La Realidad's good government council. She then gave an example of how autonomy works in practice.

"At first we had problems with brothers and sisters from other places who came and painted things that we did not understand," she said. "But we talked it over, and now the whole village decides what to paint. We elect mural commissions to work with the painters so that we can explain the meaning of the paintings to all our other visitors."

And the main image in all the paintings is still that of the masked face, with only the eyes visible. The face that covers itself in order to be seen.

The third gathering in Zapatista territory took place in the *caracol* of La Garrucha from December 29 to 31, 2007. (*Cara-*

coles are the communities that house the various autonomous good government councils.) This was the first-ever Zapatista women's gathering: only Zapatista women participated in the panels, only women—from all over Mexico and the world— were allowed inside the auditorium where the panels were held. The Zapatista men cooked, carried firewood, and cleaned the bathrooms and latrines. The men from other parts of the world listened to the panel discussions standing and sitting around the auditorium, outside.

The first woman to speak, addressing the way indigenous women lived in Chiapas before the 1994 uprising, was Dalia, one of the first women to join the EZLN, taking tortillas to the guerrilla fighters in the mountains: "Before, the *patrón* treated us like animals . . . but not anymore; now we are free. . . . The *patrón* raped the young women; fathers had to deliver their daughters in exchange for land to work. We had nothing."

Comandanta Rosalinda:

> We are very content to see us all here in this women's gathering of different sizes and colors, like maize that is yellow, black, red. . . . Before, if we participated in meetings the men would mock us, saying that we did not know how to speak. We could not go out into the street; we only worked in the kitchen. Men had time after working in the *milpa* to rest and have fun in the street. But women only worked; we never had time to rest, much less go for a walk. Men could have fun, but they would not let women leave the house. Women were exploited and raped by the *patrón*. A woman had to be the *patrón*'s lover first and the father could not do anything, because it was the *patrón*. After a while the *patrón* would let her go ahead and get married, but

often with children of the *patrón*. The mother would have twelve or fourteen children and be very weak. And nothing was her own, of her own work; everything belonged to the *patrón*.

Capitán Elena: "On January 1 [1994] we were not afraid to fight the enemy, because we knew that otherwise we would die of curable diseases; it is better to die fighting than of illness." Compañera Rosaura, on the subjects taught in Zapatista autonomous schools: "History: how people suffered in the plantations of the *patrón*. Mathematics: how our grandparents counted and how the government palaces lied. Environmental science: how to take care of the land."

Comandanta Dalia: "Compañeras from the Other Campaign, men are not the main problem, the main problem is the bad governments, that is why it is necessary that we organize to defeat the bad governments and capitalism that exist throughout the world."

AROUND 3:00 P.M. on January 2, 2008, nine shots were fired into the air. The perpetrators withdrew, leaving behind a button-down shirt with the cuffs tied to two lone trees in the cornfield. Machetes had hacked the shirt and cut a thick cross into one of the tree trunks at chest height. A bullet case was embedded at the center of the cross.

"This is an example of what they want to do to us," said José Morales, a 22-year-old Tzeltal. "Grab us and hang us from the trees." Morales is a member of the Zapatista community of Bolón Ajaw, one of dozens of Zapatista communities across the southern state of Chiapas facing almost daily attacks, land invasions, and death threats.

After hearing the gunshots, Pedro Álvarez had run down the mile-long path from the field where he was cutting wood to Bolón Ajaw's center, a cluster of houses made of old boards, corrugated tin roofs, and dirt floors, none with electricity or running water. Álvarez then led the authorities and five observers back to the cornfield, where they found the hanging shirt and the cross freshly cut into the tree.

Since early 2007, aggressions have taken place against scores of communities, affecting 800 families and threatening more than 12,000 hectares of Zapatista-controlled territory, reports the Center for Political Analysis and Social and Economic Investigation (CAPISE), based in San Cristóbal de las Casas.

"This is clearly a systematic counterinsurgency strategy," said Ernesto Ledesma, director of CAPISE. "We haven't seen an offensive this intense for at least ten years."

During the last half of 2007, Ledesma and a handful of CAPISE staff and volunteers have released an average of three reports a month documenting the new "government onslaught" against the Zapatista indigenous communities.

"The Mexican state has reactivated paramilitary groups," said Ledesma. "They are doing what the Spaniards did during the Conquest and what the ranchers and local mafias did after the Mexican Revolution: they are dispossessing the indigenous peoples once again from their lands, from their territory."

In 1994, when the EZLN had risen up in arms in Chiapas, indigenous insurgents forced the ranchers from the land and became collective owners of the very fields they had worked as slaves for hundreds of years. Since then, the EZLN has resettled thousands of landless people on former haciendas, a process the Zapatistas call recuperating the land. Road signs throughout Chiapas announce to travelers: "You are now entering autonomous, rebel territory."

Throughout his six-year term (2000–2006), former Mexican president Vicente Fox built on previous administrations' attempts to divide Zapatista communities by using handouts and government assistance programs. Fox, like his predecessors, also tried to create and train anti-Zapatista paramilitary groups to masquerade as rural indigenous rights organizations, such as the Organization for the Defense of Indigenous and Peasant Peoples' Rights (OPDDIC). Now, with many communities divided between pro- and anti-Zapatista residents, organizations like OPDDIC are using government aid programs to get land grants to Zapatista territories. Once the government provided the grants, OPDDIC would have a "legal" pretext to dispossess the Zapatista families from their lands.

The Zapatistas, in turn, refuse to enter into government aid programs, and they refuse to leave the land.

"We spilled our blood for the land, not for a government handout," said one member of the Zapatista autonomous municipality of San Manuel, which is also under threat.

Morales of Bolón Ajaw says that the aggressions began in 2006 when OPDDIC began to recruit among government sympathizers in the area.

"They are not doing this alone," he said, "they come on behalf of the government. Whenever there is a problem, the helicopters and police come right away, as if they already knew what was going to happen."

During the last four months of 2007, according to CAPISE reports and local press accounts, in Bolón Ajaw the OPDDIC ambushed Zapatista villagers repeatedly with guns and machetes, badly beating four people.

In response to attacks in late November 2007, CAPISE organized observation brigades to camp out in Bolón Ajaw and other communities to document aggression and threats against the Zapatistas.

"In all of the cases we documented," said Eugenia Gutiérrez, a member of the caravan that visited four of the five

Zapatista autonomous regions, "the strategy follows a pattern that combines land invasion, death threats, harassment and physical violence, and the destruction of property and natural resources with a dispossession by law, where the invading organizations act in conjunction with the agrarian and judicial institutions of the state and federal governments."

"This is a new onslaught of the Mexican state, with all levels of government participating," said CAPISE's Ledesma. "They are going for the land. They are going for territory and all the natural resources therein. But now there is an entire movement of indigenous peoples who are opposed to their project and, moreover, developing another, alternative project, autonomous and their own."

While troubled President Felipe Calderón—still haunted by the surrealist vote-count of July 2006—had not so much as mentioned the persistent conflict in Chiapas, his administration set in motion a new phase of counterinsurgency against Zapatista rebel communities designed to strip the Zapatistas of their land and thus uproot and destroy their autonomous municipalities. The series of reports by CAPISE documents changes in military deployment, paramilitary activity, and highway projects that combine to form a counterinsurgency strategy to displace Zapatista communities.

Between 2005 and 2006, the Mexican Army withdrew sixteen military bases from indigenous regions in Chiapas, leaving a total of seventy-nine bases in the state, including fifty-six permanent military bases in Zapatista territory. The military withdrawals seemed to indicate a decline in the militarization of Zapatista and other indigenous regions, said Ledesma, but instead, the opposite is taking place. Now the army is reinforcing the remaining military bases with Special Forces, including elite airborne troops and special elite units from Mexico City without jurisdiction to operate in Chiapas.

These bases completely surround all the Zapatista *caracoles* as well as other Zapatista communities where paramilitary groups threaten to dispossess the Zapatistas from their land. Paramilitaries that masquerade as indigenous rights groups, like OPDDIC, with the cooperation of the Mexican Army, encroach upon and threaten Zapatista communities.

"The Mexican armed forces act as guarantors for the various groups that want to displace Zapatista communities," said Ledesma.

The town of 24 de Diciembre is an example of the process being used for such displacement throughout rebel territory. The community was founded in 1994 on 525 hectares of land reclaimed by the EZLN and distributed to landless indigenous families who had supported the Zapatistas. In February 1995, then-president Ernesto Zedillo (now a professor at Yale) violated the ceasefire and ordered the Mexican army into Zapatista territory to capture the women and men comprising the leadership of the EZLN. The families in 24 de Diciembre fled the army's persecution and lived as refugees for twelve years in other Zapatista communities before returning to their land on December 24, 2006. During their absence, no one inhabited or worked the land.

On July 17, 2007, over fifty members of the PRI-affiliated Union of Ejidos of the Selva, which sells coffee to the Mexican café chain Café de la Selva, marched through the community wielding machetes and threatening the residents. The PRI members built a camp on the edge of the village, blocking the path the families use to walk to their cornfields. They then built small one-room houses with wood stolen from the community, right in the middle of the path. Now, they go daily to the military base located only a few hundred yards from 24 de Diciembre to receive basic supplies and turn in reports on the Zapatista community. They play soccer with the soldiers.

The Union of Ejidos, like the OPDDIC and other PRI-affiliated paramilitary groups, has used bogus legalism to mount a false claim to the Zapatista lands. They create new "ejidos," or communal land holdings, that include Zapatista territories, authorized by the state government, and then use the newly issued land titles to declare the Zapatistas land invaders. Most of the Zapatista land was stolen from the indigenous by land barons like General Absalón Castellanos. As mentioned earlier, Castellanos, a former army general and governor of Chiapas, was taken prisoner by the EZLN in 1994 and released on condition that he surrender land to the land-less indigenous rebels, many of whom had lived and worked as slaves for Castellanos before the Zapatista uprising. The federal government paid Castellanos for his reclaimed lands, but Castellanos then issued separate land grants to the state government. These land grants are now used to authorize the new ejidos offered to PRI groups that have never lived on or worked the land.

"They told us to stop working the land, to leave voluntarily in order to avoid the spilling of blood," one member of 24 de Diciembre told me during an interview in July 2007.

The Zapatistas went on the alert, rotating Zapatista support groups from different communities near La Realidad to stand guard at 24 de Diciembre. Organizations in Mexico City participating in the Other Campaign carried out a boycott of the Café de la Selva chain, publicly denouncing the Union of Ejidos hostilities against 24 de Diciembre. On April 1, 2008, the PRI group finally renounced their claim and withdrew their blockades.

Ledesma pointed out that the counterinsurgency actions in Chiapas involve full governmental support through both administrative and military institutions: the secretary of agrarian affairs, the national defense secretary (the army), police forces at the municipal, state, and federal levels, the transportation secretary, and Congress all participate in overlapping counterinsurgency activities in Zapatista territory.

As a further example, Ledesma showed that the Mexican Congress is quietly building a new "superhighway" through rebel territory to connect military bases and the Montes Azules bioreserve to other national highways. The highway is cutting through mountains, ostensibly to minimize curves for large trucks, and in some cases cutting directly through communities.

"The good government councils constitute the threat of an alternative," said Ledesma. "Now even local indigenous PRI members go to [the Zapatista good government council of] La Garrucha to resolve their land and other conflicts in their own languages, according to their customs, with an honest response to their conflicts. The Mexican Army, with its elite Special Forces, is trying to fracture the entire project of autonomy and the functions of the good government councils."

And the aggressions continue. On Wednesday, June 4, 2008, a military convoy of about 200 Mexican soldiers and federal and municipal police attempted to enter Zapatista villages under the pretext of searching for marijuana plants, something patently absurd in communities that have maintained a self-imposed "dry law" prohibiting all drugs and all forms of alcohol throughout Zapatista territories for more than a decade.

The convoy first stopped at the entrance to the *caracol* of La Garrucha. Four soldiers stepped out into the road, others photographed and filmed the Zapatistas from their vehicles, but the community began to draw people together, shouting at the soldiers to leave. The soldiers quickly got back in their vehicles and continued down the road. The convoy joined a second convoy farther on, where they all descended from their vehicles and set off walking to the Zapatista support community of Galeana. A police officer from Ocosingo, Feliciano Román Ruiz, guided the soldiers through the trails toward the community.

In Galeana, the men, women, and children organized to bar the soldiers' entrance to the community. According to the Zapatista communiqué denouncing the events, the Zapatistas shouted at the soldiers to turn back. The soldiers said that they had come to destroy the marijuana plants they know to be near by. The Zapatistas denied growing marijuana and began to gather slingshots, machetes, rocks, and sticks to defend their land.

The soldiers turned back, but warned that they would return in two weeks and would enter the community no matter what. But they did not leave; they walked to nearby San Alejandro, where some sixty soldiers had already taken up positions around the community, automatic weapons drawn. The people of San Alejandro, a Zapatista support community, also confronted the soldiers and barred their passage. Soon the soldiers withdrew. They did not go back two weeks later as threatened.

"People of Mexico and of the world," the good government council of La Garrucha wrote in a denunciation of these events released on June 4, "it will not be long before there is confrontation provoked by [President Felipe] Calderón, [Chiapas governor] Juan Sabines and Carlos Leonel Solórzano, municipal president of Ocosingo, who send their dogs of repression. . . ."

In preceding weeks the aggressions had escalated. On May 19, 2008, federal agents and soldiers, arriving in helicopters and a military convoy, entered the community of San Jerónimo Tulilja, in the *caracol* of La Garrucha, breaking into houses and pushing people around without explanation. Three days later, a large group of armed men from the PRI invaded the Zapatista *caracol* of Morelia, cutting the community's electricity lines and attacking people in their homes throughout the night. The gunmen wounded over twenty Zapatistas, six of whom were taken to the hospital with serious injuries.

But the aggressions are almost daily: kidnapping Zapatista supporters and taking them to local jails on invented charges, contaminating local wells, invading lands, cutting corn plants, leaving death threats for the community.

"It is as if we are seeing the preparations for what will be another Acteal," said Subcomandante Marcos in a 2008 interview published in Mexico, referring to the December 22, 1997, paramilitary massacre of 45 indigenous men, women, and children gathered in a church in the community of Acteal. "But now they are not looking for a conflict between aggressors and defenseless people, but really a confrontation," he said.[43]

Zapatista autonomy is not only a threat to the perceived legitimacy of the state, it is the very structure of resistance that maintains and protects Zapatista territories, land recuperated through the 1994 uprising and cared for and cultivated since.

"We are not drug traffickers," the good government council members of La Garrucha wrote. "We are what we all well known to be, brothers and sisters of Mexico and the world. It is clear that they will be coming for us, the Zapatistas; they will be coming from the three levels of bad government, and we are ready to resist, and if necessary to comply with our slogan, *Vivir por la patria o morir por la libertad*—Live for the fatherland or die for liberty."

These are brief and dramatic lessons in autonomy. With slingshots and machetes the Zapatistas are ready to refuse entrance to their communities to the soldiers and federal police. Most of the daily work of autonomy goes unseen and unreported: collective land management, autonomous schools and health clinics, community dispute resolution. But autonomy also means rejecting the authority of the state, rejecting the legitimacy of the state, and this rejection comes not only in the form of eloquent communiqués but also in staring down the soldiers with nothing other than a farm tool in hand.

DURING THE FIRST FEW MONTHS OF 2008, if you had been driving through the back roads of western Oaxaca state with the radio tuned to 94.9 FM, Radio Copala, "The Voice that Breaks the Silence," you would have heard a slow, piercing violin trace a melancholy minor chord and then give way to the languid voice of a woman singing slowly in Spanish: "I am a rebel because the world has made me that way, because no one ever treated me with love, because no one ever wanted to listen to me." Then, in the midst of such overwrought sadness, a strong, perhaps slightly hurried young woman's voice interrupts: "Some people think that we are too young to know," and immediately a second young, female voice interjects: "They should know that we are too young to die."

Those voices belonged to Teresa Bautista Merino, age 24, and Felícitas Martínez Sánchez, age 21, two of six young producers and hosts at Radio Copala, the first radio station to broadcast in both Spanish and the Triqui indigenous language, a project of the recently declared autonomous municipality of San Juan Copala, Oaxaca.

That station tagline was recorded in January 2008 and played daily. By April, Teresa and Felícitas were dead.

On April 7, 2008, Teresa and Felícitas were riding in the backseat of their cousin Faustino Vásquez's car on their way to participate in a community radio workshop in Oaxaca City. They held Faustino's 2-year-old son Agustín between them.

In the front passenger seat rode Faustino's wife and 4-year-old son, Cristina and Jaciel.

"We were going downhill, with a sheer cliff on the right," said Faustino. "Before we went down I noticed an access road from the highway and said, 'Look at that new white pickup parked there.' "

Seconds later, as they rounded the curve at the bottom of the hill, Faustino again looked off to the right. "There were seven men up on the hill, and they began to shoot at us," he said.

Bullets immediately pierced the windshield, crashing through Faustino's left wrist and shoulder, grazing his right arm and leg and the back of his head. Two bullets grazed the back of Jaciel's head; he lost consciousness. A bullet shattered Cristina's left arm.

"The motor shut off," Faustino said. "I tried to start it again, but it wouldn't go. I took the key and ran. When I ran Teresa and Felicítas were still alive. I shouted, 'Run! They're shooting at us!' "

Men fired after Faustino as he ran, but they did not pursue him.

State police later collected some twenty spent shells from AK-47 assault rifles by the side of the road: the gunmen had descended the embankment and completely shot out the back of the car. Teresa and Felícitas died almost instantly. Cristina, Agustín and Jaciel survived.

For centuries, the small Triqui indigenous region, about 300 square miles situated in the middle of the larger Mixteca, or Ñu Savi, region of western Oaxaca, has been known for endemic violence. The Triquis largely resisted Spanish colonial incursions and were the first indigenous people to rise up in arms against the recently independent Mexican state in

1823, when a local general, Antonio de León, tried to grant their land to goat ranchers.[44] The Triquis fought for three years and defended their land. In 1825, the government created a free municipality to encompass the entire Triqui region. In 1843, the Triquis rose up against León a second time when he tried to take their land to pay for the community's supposed outstanding debts to the Catholic Church for "services" such as weddings, baptisms, and funeral rites. Once again, the Triquis emerged victorious. As a result of their armed defense, the Triqui region is today a green oasis in the midst of the eroded Mixteca region where centuries of clear-cutting and goat herding have decimated the land.

After the Triquis had successfully defended their land in two separate wars, the Mexican government decided to shift from direct, armed confrontation to a divide-and-conquer strategy, said Francisco López Bárcenas, the Ñu Savi lawyer, historian, and author of over fifteen books on the region, including the forthcoming *San Juan Copala: Political Domination and Popular Resistance.*

From the late nineteenth century to the present, internal divisions in the Triqui region fomented by the state government have led to unending cycles of political killings and massacres, with the federal government twice sending the army into the region.

"Why do they kill each other?" asked López Bárcenas. "Diodoro Carasco, when he was governor, said that it was a cultural problem. Ulises Ruiz [the current governor] says that violence is part of their indigenous customs and practices. No. It is a problem of social decomposition that comes on the heels of the political and economic domination of the state, and it has a history."

That history, according to López Bárcenas, has always pitted state government collaborators against Triqui communities fighting to maintain autonomy. One of the early twentieth-century battles began over control of land for coffee production. Nonindigenous speculators brought coffee into the region in the 1920s. New coffee farmers started to assassinate other Triquis who refused to substitute their traditional *milpa* production for coffee. The nonindigenous coffee buyers fomented the divisions by paying for portions of the coffee crop with guns and alcohol. The violence in the region escalated until the federal government sent in the army in 1940. The coffee wars broke apart segments of the traditional Triqui economy, but Triqui political organization—largely based on the council of elders and villages structured around families—remained strong until, on December 7, 1948, the Oaxaca state government divided the Triqui region into five municipalities in an attempt to break their political cohesion.

"This was a strong blow to politically submit the Triquis," said López Bárcenas.

But in the 1970s the Triqui council of elders tried to end the violence by passing their community powers down to a coalition of young Triqui men pledged to unite the region peacefully. That peace lasted less than two years; one of the newly appointed communal authorities linked up with the PRI and killed off his rivals. In 1978, the army went back into the region, building bases and supporting the PRI band.

The violence escalated with the creation of various political organizations in the 1980s. The most powerful organization, the Movement for Triqui Unification and Struggle (MULT, by its Spanish acronym) evolved from a land-defense organization that directly confronted the state into a quasi-paramilitary group controlled by a non-Triqui man, Heriberto Pasos, with long-standing connections to the Oaxaca state government.

"Heriberto Pasos runs the MULT with a leftist discourse,

but in reality they act in relation to the powers of the state," said Pedro Matías, a Oaxacan journalist who has covered the region for over ten years. "The MULT took over control of the region and the killings started again in this context."

In 2006, more than half of the Triqui region split off from the MULT, creating the MULTI—the added "I" standing for "Independent." When Oaxaca erupted in a civil disobedience uprising in June 2006, the MULTI joined the protesters' organization, the Oaxaca Peoples' Popular Assembly (APPO), while the MULT sided with the state government.

"The MULT participated directly in the death squads in Oaxaca in 2006," said López Bárcenas.

Indeed, the first people killed during the 2006 conflict were three Triquis from the MULTI; they were ambushed on their way to an APPO meeting in Oaxaca City, shot down with AK-47s. MULT member Fortino Alvarado Martínez carried out the first direct assassination of a protester in Oaxaca City, shooting José Colmenares during a march. APPO members detained Alvarado Martínez, but governor Ulises Ruiz later released him, despite the testimony of dozens of people who witnessed the murder.[45]

Inspired by the APPO, the MULTI decided to dissolve their organization, and on January 21, 2007, it created the autonomous municipality of San Juan Copala in the Triqui region, joining together twenty Triqui communities and cutting off all relations with the Oaxaca state government.

"During the APPO conflict we thought about creating a new organization, a new peoples' front to denounce the problems in the region," said Jorge Albino Ortiz, coordinator of Radio Copala. "We asked the council of elders and they said no, that a new organization would not do anything but further divide people. It would be better to make our own authority, they said."

Drawing inspiration also from the Zapatista autonomous municipalities, the proposals for indigenous autonomy worked out in the 1996 San Andrés Accords, and the Other Campaign, the Triquis of San Juan Copala cut off all relations to the state government, kicking out the state police and severing all budgetary ties.

"Government projects were always top-down projects, designed and approved by municipal officials without consulting the communities, and the funds for the projects would never arrive in the communities; they seemed to get lost along the way," said Macario García Medino, municipal secretary and director of the bilingual elementary school in San Juan Copala. "Now we work differently, the people decide on their own projects."

The state government catalogued Copala as a "rebel municipality." But García Medino said that they did not rise up in arms but simply cut off relations with the state. Many of the Triqui migrant communities in California and New York are sending money to the new autonomous municipality to fund local projects, including building a four-mile road to a community that is still unconnected to the local road network.

Lack of communication is one of the main issues facing the region. In San Juan Copala and surrounding villages, there is no cell service or telephone line. Copala has one satellite phone in the municipal office. The idea of the radio station was born of the need to discuss the project of autonomy in villages that are cut off from roads and modern communications like telephones and the Internet, says Albino Ortiz. He participated in the APPO-occupied radio (La Ley) during the 2006 conflict. "We observed how the radio called people to participate in the various actions of the movement and we wanted to do something like that in our region," he said.

The radio, which reaches about a seven-mile radius, was on the air all day, focused on themes of autonomy and indigenous rights. One of the main tasks of the radio was to encourage women's participation in the new autonomous municipality, which is why, Albino Ortiz said, they decided to have three men and three women working at the radio.

"When we started we felt really excited to have a radio station in Copala," said Yanira Vásquez, who worked with Teresa and Felícitas at the radio. "Women do not participate much, and we were just beginning to promote women's participation in assemblies and meetings and to include our perspectives and interviews about how we see what is happening in the region."

"We named the station 'The Voice that Breaks the Silence' because it would provide information to people," said Albino Ortiz.

On April 7, 2008, news of the killing traveled around the globe via Internet in a matter of hours. Dozens of national and international human rights organizations, reporters' defense groups, and even the United Nations and the Inter-American Commission on Human Rights all issued condemnations of the assassination and demanded that the Mexican government conduct a rigorous investigation and punish those proven guilty. But three weeks after the killing, no government official had come to gather testimony from the surviving witnesses. Faustino clearly saw the men who attacked them and can name them. "They are all gunmen for Heriberto Pasos," he said.

But the government, instead of investigating, has followed a well-worn path of insuring impunity by denying the political nature of the crime and attacking the legitimacy of the victims. Oaxaca state attorney general Evencio Martínez told the press on April 18, 2008, "What is clear is that the attack was not directed at the two announcers, but at the person [Faustino Vásquez] who was driving the vehicle."

Perhaps because state investigators had not interviewed Faustino Vásquez themselves, they ignored the fact that Faustino was able to easily escape without being pursued, while Teresa and Felícitas were targeted by the gunmen who descended the embankment on the side of the road, shooting the two women through the back of the car.

On April 21, 2008, Juan de Dios Castro Lozano, a subdirector of the federal attorney general's office, told a group of Mexican and international human rights investigators that the two young women were not really journalists—they had no journalism degrees—but were housewives who just changed the music when callers made requests at the station. Castro Lozano's comments provoked immediate criticism, including from the selection committee of the National Journalism Award, which was given to Teresa and Felícitas posthumously.

Buckling under pressure from the Mexican media, Castro Lozano said that his comments were misunderstood and announced that the federal government would take over the case, on account of the caliber of rifle used in the killing. Still, the federal government is pursuing the same theory put forth by the state government.

"All of this has the mark of the long-standing problems in the Triqui region," said Attorney General Martínez during the April 18, 2008, press conference, expressing the commonly held view that the violence in the Triqui region is a product of inherent lawlessness.

"The intention has always been to strip the Triquis of their land," said María Dolores París, professor of rural sociology at the Autonomous University of Mexico, who has worked with Triquis in Oaxaca and Triqui migrants in California.

"There is no real government in the region," París said.

"On the contrary, the state government goes into the region to foment violence and then washes its hands of it with theories that the violence comes from the nature of the Triquis themselves."

París said that the state's claim that Vásquez, and not the two women, was the real target of the killers is "absurd," though she says that women were not targeted in regional violence before.

"I feel certain that the young women were assassinated for their work with the radio station," she said.

But stripping the violence of its history and context is part of the technique to guarantee the cycle of violence, the cycle that broke the voices of Teresa and Felícitas.

Faustino Vásquez and his family have now been thrust into the heart of this violence.

"I am scared," Faustino said. "I will have to be careful now, no more living life like somebody who can just go wherever he likes. If they see me out there, they'll certainly execute me."

I asked if he has any hope that justice may be done.

"With the help of human rights organizations," he said, "with the help of journalists, radio, television, with all that putting pressure on the state and federal governments, maybe there will be justice."

7.

THE GUERRILLA

Repression, the Veracruz state government, that is what led
me to the armed movement.

—Gloria Arenas Agis

SOMETIME BEFORE DAWN on October 22, 1999, Gloria
Arenas Agis awoke to the sound of gunshots.[1] She rushed to
the window, but then immediately dove onto the floor to avoid
being shot. Within a matter of seconds she was surrounded by
men in unmarked black military dress, their faces covered with
ski masks, all carrying assault rifles. They handcuffed her arms
behind her back and blindfolded her.

"Where are the computers and the party documents?"
someone asked. She gestured toward her computer.

"So you are who we are looking for," one said. And then:
"Where are the guns?"

"There are no guns here," she said.

"Well, there should've been," the man responded.

"What is your name?"

She gave an invented name.

"Or would you like us to ask your daughter or your
mother?"

The man gave the order to gather up all documents, photographs, computers, and computer disks. They took off her
blindfold, grabbed her by her hair and walked her outside to a
waiting truck, forcing her to look down at the ground.

"Now you are going to see your husband," one said, referring to Jacobo Silva Nogales, alias Comandante Antonio.

And yes, there he was, lying on the floor of the truck, with men stepping on him from all sides. She recognized his jacket, but could not see his face. As she strained in the dark to see him, they lifted his head by the hair. His eyes were covered with a thick cloth.

"Here she is, Antonio," one said.

He tried to say something to her, making great effort to pronounce a few words. She could not understand. He had been beaten and tortured and could not speak.

They closed the door to the truck and took her off to another vehicle. Once inside, again they covered her eyes and asked her name; again she gave the false name she had given in her house. She felt the first strike to her stomach and instinctively tried to lift up her legs as if to protect herself, but men on both sides held her legs outstretched and the beating continued. After a time, they transferred her to an airplane. During the flight a man sat next to her, talking at length about internal conflicts between two guerrilla movements, making an obvious display of the information about her and her organiztion they had gathered.

They took her from the plane into a very large room, most likely a hangar, since it was very close to where the plane landed. They took her up a metal spiral staircase and left her in a room. After a while the man who had spoken to her on the plane came back.

"Señora, you will have to tell us everything we want to know, otherwise I will have to send you off to the other guys, and they will not respect you. Whatever happens, we will make you talk."

She said nothing.

"I'll let you think about it for a bit."

He left her in the room with men on guard all around her. After a while they took her into another room and sat her down on a bench. They removed her handcuffs and blindfold and took photographs and video images of her sitting there on the bench; close-ups of her face, eyes, hands, and wrists. No one spoke. Then they put the blindfold back on, but this time carefully, placing cotton balls all around her eyes first. Then they wrapped her wrists in cotton and put the handcuffs back on.

"You'll notice we don't do this like we used to," one man said as they applied the cotton, "now we don't leave scars; we have modernized."

They said that they had located the apartment where her daughter and mother live and that soon they would be bringing them to join her.

They took her to another room. They stripped her and applied electric shocks all over her body. They asked for the names of the leaders of her organization. They asked for the names of people under her command. She gave the names used to sign their communiqués—Santiago, Cuauhtémoc, Emiliano, Hermenegildo—and denied having people under her command. They asked again and again. They threatened to bring her daughter and torture her as well. They asked about her family and upbringing, how she met her husband, who recruited her into the organization. She said nothing. That day they carried out three torture sessions using electric shocks. Then they left her in a room to listen to the torture of her husband in a nearby room. They hung her husband from his wrists, his arms behind his back (ten years later he still cannot do push-ups), beat him on the face and body, and applied electric shocks.

"After the torture I heard them say, 'Well, now we wait to see what the high authority says.' Of course, they meant the

president. He decided to present us to the press and not disappear us."

On October 24, 1999, Gloria Arenas Agis, or Coronel
Aurora of the Insurgent Peoples' Revolutionary Army (ERPI);
Jacobo Silva Nogales, or Comandante Antonio of the ERPI;
and Carlos García—who together with his wife Felícitas
Padilla, maintained a safe house where ERPI members occa-
sionally met—were presented to the press (Felícitas passed out
just before the press conference) from behind a wall of sound-
proof glass. They all wore white baseball caps pulled down low
to hide in shadow the signs of torture; Jacobo's face was so
swollen and bruised that his family could not quite recognize
him when they first saw the images on television.[2] Gloria
raised her right hand to make the victory symbol, but was
quickly suppressed by guards standing behind her, though the
photographers had already captured her gesture.

Almost ten years later they are still in prison, guilty of
rebellion.

The Mexico State Prison of Ecatepec is nestled just below a
trash dump at the top of a sprawling hill where ramshackle
neighborhoods cascade down into the traffic- and smog-
choked valley. Guard towers loom over the high concrete walls
and razor wire next to the parking lot. Just outside of it, every
Saturday and Sunday, street vendors assemble to sell home-
cooked food, telephone cards, and soft drinks to families and
friends visiting prisoners. One woman I spoke with spends her
Friday and Saturday nights chopping meat and vegetables
until midnight, rising only a few hours later, at three in the
morning, to begin cooking huge pots of chicken in green mole
sauce, pork stew, nopal salad, and tomato rice with chopped
carrots and garlic.

At nine in the morning friends and family line up outside

the visitors' entrance to the far left of the building. In line one observes people readying 100-peso bills under their ID cards. Prisoners are allowed registered visits either every other Saturday or every other Sunday, but for the equivalent of ten dollars, anyone can get in on any Saturday or Sunday they choose. The first guard on the inside glances at the registered visitors' passes and collects the 100-peso bills from the others, all in plain sight, with truly minuscule effort to conceal such illegal activity.

You receive a series of special security stamps on your right forearm, and the line then snakes to the left for food inspection. Everyone in the line for food inspection digs in their coat pockets and coin purses to ready the requisite coins. The guards in charge of food inspection make a small play at dismay regarding the quantity of food or the type of container used to carry the food, saying drily, "This can't go in." The visitor makes a tired and futile gesture at protest: "But this is exactly what I bring every week." "Well, not this week," the guard replies. Then a down-turned, closed fist containing fifty cents or a dollar in Mexican coins extends across the counter, transfers its contents to the guard's hand, which mechanically—exhibiting the dexterity of ingrained habit—deposits the coins in a side pocket. No more words are exchanged; the guard pushes the packet of food back across the counter to the visitor and waves for the next person in line. On my first visit I saw another registration line before the food inspection counter and asked a woman if it was necessary to register there as well before proceeding. "No," she said, "that is for people with permanent passes; they'll just take more money from you."

From food inspection one passes to objects inspection. Some prisoners, such as Gloria Arenas, have permits to receive newspapers, magazines, and books. Here again coins are readied and passed. Then on to the body search. Again, one must have a coin or two ready. There is always a pretext. "You can't go in with long hair." A coin moves from hand to hand. Next. "You can't take a notebook inside." The coin. Next. "No pens allowed." The coin. Next. When no pretext may be found the guard will ask, shyly, "Would you be able to cooperate with some change for a soft drink?" On my third visit, as I walked into the body search area the guard dropped the 10-peso coin bribe from the previous person. I quickly knelt to pick it up and hand it to him saying, "Good morning, how's it going?" Visibly embarrassed, he responded with a good-natured, "Still alive, can't ask for much more." He quickly made a caricatured show of frisking me, didn't search my pockets or ask me to remove my jacket, but rather hurriedly moved me on and called, "Next."

Then on to ID inspection. Here prison guards collect visitors' IDs and check their stamped forearms. Newcomers may get caught here as well. I was told on one visit that my passport, my Mexican FM3 visa, and my driver's license were all "inappropriate" forms of identification. I had no coins left after the food inspection, objects inspection, and body search. Hence a 20-peso bill was required as "appropriate" identification, and I was waved on. But then stopped again only three steps later.

"What is in that bag?" A guard asked pointing to a plastic bag in my right hand.

"Newspapers and magazines," I responded, opening the bag and holding it out toward the guard.

"You can't take those in there," he told me. And somehow, naively, I thought he was making some technical mistake.

"But the prisoner I am visiting has a permit for these," I said.

"Let me see it."

"But they collect the permits at the entrance," I answered.
"Then you can't take those in."

"I am sorry, I don't understand, the prisoner has a permit and at the entrance. . . ."

"Not today she doesn't," he said now looking down the hall to those in line behind me.

Ah, then it hit me; I understood but I had no coins. I reached in my pocket and pulled out a 50-peso bill. He opened the door for me and said, "Next."

Once inside the visiting area, the atmosphere among the prisoners is altogether different, joyful and even cooperative. Women who do not receive visits help heat water for coffee and prepare lunch for women who do. No one fights for a location along the two rows of stationary picnic tables. Visiting children run and play all around, couples sit and whisper in corners.

Gloria exudes an instantly contagious excitement on visiting days. She loves to converse. Her energy stands at odds with the drab, colorless, concrete surroundings of prison. After only minutes of conversation one forgets the concrete, the prison guards, the corruption, and becomes absorbed in the jubilant brand of attention Gloria gives to both talking and listening. Her energy stands equally at odds with the mass-media image of the dogmatic guerrilla: Gloria is down-to-earth, expressing herself with an uncommon agility of thought, though always directly and simply, never quoting in conversation Marx or Lenin or Mao or even El Che (though she has read them all), but rather constantly referring to her experiences in Mexico's urban slums, desolate countryside, and marginalized indigenous communities. But it is the depth of her conviction in the urgency of social struggle and people's inalienable right to fight for justice—a conviction that does not rule out armed self-defense or armed uprisings, but does not rule out unarmed social organizing either—that sets her apart and reminds one that she is indeed, what one could quite legitimately and respectfully call a rebel.

She can recall images of their house, of her mother ironing. She was about 3 years old, and she can see herself wearing a flowered dress. The house was simple, humble she said. It was an old house, made of rocks and cement with thick walls and a clay-tile roof. The house is no longer there in Orizaba, in the southern Mexican state of Veracruz. "I remember the house fondly," she said. "An old house, inexpensive, never fixed-up or rebuilt, the cement deteriorating; dirt would fall in from the tile roof. Orizaba is one of the cities that receives the most rainfall in the country, so it is common for roofs to rot with time." With three daughters the family stayed at first in several rooms. But after an earthquake in 1973 knocked down half of the house, they all slept together in the same room. They had to place buckets along the floor to catch the rain as it fell through the unfixed cracks in the roof. "For a child it was fun," she said. "We would shout: 'It's raining, get the buckets!'"

La Calle Real, East 7, #637, two blocks from the San José Church. At the time the buses entering town would come down Calle Real. It was a busy street. Not anymore. "Orizaba *was* an industrial town, it used to be, with textile factories from the era of Porfirio Díaz. There was also an important Moctezuma brewery in town. All that is over; the textile factories all closed down, the brewery got bought out by Grupo México. The economy plummeted.

"My father was a laborer all his life," she told me. "At the age of 16 he started working in a bottling factory blowing glass." He worked in that same factory until retiring. He lived through the presidency of Lázaro Cárdenas in Orizaba, a time of shootouts in the street between rival trade unions. "One union bought a Thompson machine gun and installed it at the front door of their union hall."

She was born in 1959 and lived in Veracruz state until 1984.

"I feel like the region where I grew up had a strong influence on me, the valleys and mountains surrounding them, the indigenous Nahuatl region, the Zongolica, incredible vegetation, fruit. The city sport was hiking in the mountains, but so many set out on their excursions only for sport, they would climb up and down the mountains and not see the people."

Her father was one of the most accomplished mountaineers of the region, moonlighting as a guide for tourists. Born in 1912 on a hacienda, he lived his early childhood during the Mexican Revolution of 1910–1920. His earliest memories were of riding on a horse, held by someone, of revolutionaries coming to ask for food at their house; of lying on the floor with his mother as bullets pierced the walls around them.

Her maternal grandfather was forced to leave his native Hidalgo state. He had problems with Porfirio Díaz, his father had been murdered, and he worked as a journalist critical of Díaz. He was imprisoned. John Kenneth Turner visited him in jail and wrote a paragraph about him in his famous book about Mexico before the Revolution, *Barbarous Mexico*. He went from Puebla to Orizaba, sold soap that he made at home, rented out stables to people bringing their animals down from the mountains.

Her mother was a homemaker, very Catholic and dedicated to her family; her father was an atheist. They met climbing a volcano.

She and her sisters went to an all-girls public school, grew up naïve and mischievous; you would never catch them doing homework, yet they made straight A's. She liked history best, the tales of Greek myths and conflicts, the battle of Thermopylae.

But she did not fully realize as a child the social diversity of Mexico or even her home state.

"What I did notice was poverty," she said. "When you go out hiking in the mountains, you leave the city behind. I was just a child. One time night fell and we got lost. I was 9. We had not reached the peak, and my father said, 'Well, tough luck, we'll just have to camp out here.' We just had a plastic tarp that we held over us. We were on the edge of a *milpa*, and a woman approached us and invited us to sleep in her house. They invited us to eat with them. And then I noticed that the opposite happened when these people went to the city; they slept outside on the sidewalks; no one invited them to sleep in their houses or to eat with them, not even to have a cup of coffee or a piece of bread—that I did notice. In those years people would knock on doors and ask for a taco. My parents would give them something to eat, not for any political reason, just the human side; we were poor too."

She remembers the line in front of the town pawnshop: the line to pawn was always long, the line to redeem items very short.

"I liked so many things as a child," she said, "but I always thought about social movements." She first read about Miguel Hidalgo and the Mexican War of Independence and thought, "Why didn't we live in that era?"

"It took many years for me to realize that we live in a similar era. Perhaps this was always my vocation; that's why I am here," she said, looking up and out through the window to the high walls and coils of razor wire that surround the Mexico State Prison of Ecatepec.

She completed middle school and technical high school in Orizaba and then moved with her two sisters to Puerto de Veracruz to continue studying. They all stayed together in a pension. She worked in a small office supply store from nine in the morning until midnight. She then went to the small town of Úrsulo Galván to study agricultural science. No politics or social studies. She lacked one semester when she left.

One of her teachers had participated in the massive student protests in Mexico City in 1968. Back in Veracruz he coordinated a committee for political prisoners. He had to send a message to a mother of a political prisoner in Orizaba, and he asked her if she could deliver the message. She did, together with one of her sisters. The mother talked to the sisters about the social conditions in their region. The mother invited them to visit her son in prison. There she saw four young women her own age in prison for protesting, "and I thought, 'it can't be that they are prisoners'—that is when I realized, when it really hit me, that there are political prisoners." Her sister in Jalapa invited her to attend marches to demand liberty for political prisoners and an end to disappearances and torture. That is when she began to participate fully in activism, in a local campaign to free a few young political prisoners. In 1980, the prisoners were released and they felt as if they had won.

"Learning about young political prisoners impacted me politically," but her youthful activism had "nothing to do with armed struggle," she said.

By then a single mother with a baby daughter to care for, she began working at the CONASUPO store—the government grocery chain—in the Zongolica Mountains.[3] The municipality of Tehuipango, known as the Zongolica region, is the most marginalized and destitute part of Veracruz.

In Tehuipango, the people claimed the store as their own and used it to combat the local cacique, who routinely overcharged for basic goods at his store. The cacique did not appreciate the competition and had one store employee killed in an ambush, shot to death in the CONASUPO truck. "We used to walk at night, eight hours, to avoid ambushes," she said.

In the region, timber companies were cutting intensely; it seemed as if they would cut down the whole forest, and the people worried about how their kids would survive off the land with all the trees gone. She borrowed movies about peoples' struggles in Central America, Cuba, and Colombia from a local priest and showed them at night during community assemblies. "These were people bent over, bowed down," she said. "I asked myself, 'When will they rise up?' After watching the movies they decided to block the timber trucks on the road." The driver pulled a pistol, but he was outnumbered and the rocks had already started raining down; he put his gun away. They took the truck to the priest. The organization TINAM, which stands for the "union of all the poor peoples" in Nahuatl, sprang from that action.

"Now there was no stopping them," she said. "They had held so much back for years, 500 years, so that now they demanded roads, fertilizers, markets for their products." They organized committees in different villages, and the organization spread into various municipalities. The governor put them on his "red danger" list. Someone leaked a study written by the Veracruz secretary of state, Ignacio Morales, saying that he feared the Zongolica and Huayaco-cotla regions would further radicalize. Morales proposed two options: repress or solve the issues in order to calm things down. They did try at first to address one issue by building a road, but the people wanted more.

"They identified me as one of the leaders of the organization," she said. "They grabbed me in the doorway to my house, they threw me in a car, the Orizaba police. But they thought that I was my sister. I was disappeared for five days. You know you are disappeared, but you don't know for how long or what is going to happen, that is already torture. They did a bit of theater, saying that they were going to seek my arrest warrant for assault and throw me in jail, but if I would speak to the governor's adviser then they would let me go."

She agreed, but went to call a meeting first with the TINAM members; they all agreed to send a delegation go talk with the governor, Agustín Acosta Lagunes. The governor said to them, "It is all fine and good what you are doing, but why not join the party?" The party? "The PRI," he said. They refused. The governor lent them a truck to return to the Zongolica Mountains. On the highway they heard a strange sound, stopped, and realized that the front right wheel had only one bolt holding it in place. They removed one bolt from each of the other three wheels to supplement the front wheel.

Over the following months they were constantly watched and followed. "I could not go to my house anymore, because the police would be waiting in the doorway," she said. "The situation was unbearable. The life of the pursued is more difficult than the life of the prisoner. The prisoner says, 'Well, I am here now . . .' but the pursued is afraid, he or she does not want to be apprehended and thus lives in dread. There is a good chance that I would be dead by now, and think about it, for working at a crummy little government store but fighting against the local caciques."

The police attacked and beat up her sister during a march. The government spread the rumor that the TINAM activists were not even Mexican, but from Nicaragua; the government asked their father for their birth certificates. "I could not keep living like that," she said, "so I left with my daughter, fleeing the state government. I stopped seeing my family. Once you are burned, you have to break off contact. I changed my name; I bought new birth certificates for me and my daughter." Her daughter (who, now 25, received political asylum in Canada) was then 4 years old. Going underground became like a game with her daughter. She would say, "Remember when *that* happened," referring to her five-day disappearance. "Well, so *that* does not happen again, we are going to change our names."

Her name is Gloria Arenas Agis; she became Isabel Salgado Vicario.

"If they had not repressed me in Orizaba, I would never have left. Repression, the Veracruz state government, that is what led me to the armed movement; sometimes the bravest people are the ones who stay in the social movements."

"I arrived in Acapulco for the first time without knowing anyone or anything about the place," Gloria said. "I had been in Mexico City for a short time, but I really did not want to live in Mexico City. I am from the provinces, and I am going back to the provinces, but where? I asked myself. I wanted to go someplace where I was not known, where I could live unseen, unnoticed. Acapulco at that time was known across the country as a tourist paradise, but I also knew that Guerrero was a state with a deep history of social struggle. But at first, my struggle there was not political but for survival. I was not about to join any movements there; I thought that if I were to join a march they would grab me. In the meeting with the governor of Veracruz, there was a police officer from Guerrero present. I couldn't get involved with social movements. [Eventually] I sought out contact with the armed movements; it took years."

Her bus descended into Acapulco, passing through the outlying shantytown neighborhoods before sighting the lights and pomp of hotel-strung Papagayo Beach. At the bus station in Acapulco she went straight to buy a newspaper and looked for ads for rooms for rent. She got a room for herself and her daughter and immediately started looking for work, a constant search that would dominate her first years there. She worked in hotels, and a typewriter repair shop, a sweatshop, with a construction crew, selling homemade fruit punch on the beach, and finally selling bread and later chicken in the poor outlying districts.

At one point she got a job working for Pepsi, selling soft drinks in the small, rundown neighborhoods on the edge of the city. "I liked this job because we traveled throughout the entire municipality of Acapulco," she said. "We'd ride in the back of the Pepsi truck, holding on with both hands through bumpy back roads, and then arrive in a village, grab buckets filled with Pepsi and 7-Up, and walk the streets convincing people to buy the soft drinks. Confronting the reality of Acapulco this way made a huge impression on me. You have the idea of the Acapulco of tourists and grand hotels, and then you come upon houses made of mud walls and tin or plastic roofs, or no walls at all, only a tin roof supported by sticks embedded in the ground and an old mattress on the dirt. I saw houses in Acapulco as humble as any I had seen in the Zongolica Mountains of Veracruz.

"I had sometimes a rather naïve perspective," she continued. "I saw many advertisements for waitresses, for example, waitresses in hotels and on yachts. I imagined waitresses carrying food and drinks to customers. . . . One yacht manager at an interview told me that I'd have to take off my clothes first, before the interview, so he could see if I fit the requirements. Of course, I left. I came up against so much sexual harassment and aggression. But I would just leave that job and look for another. It was such a common thing. The union leader at one hotel, for example—and this was a job that really was considered a 'good job,' at a big hotel, stable and with good pay—told me, 'First you'll have to report to the union leader.' And of course, 'report' meant sleep with him.

"I ended up looking for the jobs that I mentioned, like selling chicken. I would wake up at five in the morning and buy twelve or thirteen chickens. I would cut half of them into the different pieces and leave the other half whole. My first investments were a knife, a cutting board, and a basin to carry them. I would then head up into the barrios to sell. I was pretty good at shouting out products and prices—*pregonar*, we call it— people would come out to see what I had and buy. Many women worked in jobs like these. They all had children to take care of and did not want to submit themselves to the sexual harassment of bosses. Selling chicken, by noon I would be done. This job gave me a lot of time. I always looked for jobs that would allow me to spend the most time possible with my daughter. I would take her to child care or leave her with neighbors when going out to work, but hating to leave her alone like that. I only had enough money to pay the rent and keep food on the table, not really enough to buy new clothes even. I always worked; even once I was inside the organization I never stopped working."

She would attend some protests and rallies in Guerrero, but did not join any social movement organization as a member, only attending certain events in solidarity. Once there was a march from Acapulco to Chilpancingo. She took her daughter and met the march at a small town before arriving in Chilpancingo, to accompany the marchers on the last leg. She got along great with the other women in the march. In Chilpancingo, at the end of the rally, a local union leader approached her to strike up small talk. She recognized him, had seen his photograph and read about him in the newspaper. They all would have to spend the night in Chilpancingo, and the union leader quickly made it known that his interest was sexual.

"Just like the bosses in Acapulco! He started off with a

manipulative discourse about the struggle. I took my daughter and went to stay at a house with a number of the other women in the march. I never held the idea of women as victims, nor felt self-pity, ah, poor me, for the harassment. But yes, I have confronted a society that views women as objects. But in this way precisely, I met and built trust with other women."

Seeing intense marginalization and repression in Acapulco, she began to question her isolated life.

"I asked myself, 'Gloria are you going to give up, are you going to hide, or are you going to do something?' But what should I do? What could I do? I could not go back; whatever I did, it would have to be with an armed group. People had told me about Lucio Cabañas, and I thought, 'I have to find someone.' "

It took "some years" to make the first contacts with the organization.

"To make the first contact that would lead me to an actual direct contact took a lot of work. I was looking for a contact, but of course there is no agency with a big sign saying, 'Here!' that one can go to. I traveled for work, walking the barrios and the small outlying villages, and I built friendships with people. Until I finally made a contact with the PROCUP-PDLP [the guerrilla organization formed sometime in the early 1980s by surviving members of the Guerrero-based Party of the Poor and the Mexico City–based Union of the People]."

"Jacobo was not my first contact. I met him some time later, once I had already been inside the organization. The organization sent me to Jacobo as the man responsible for the state of Guerrero. They sent me to meet him with a password. I did not know what he looked like, nor did he know what I looked like. A man would ask me, 'Where can one buy antique coins?' I had to answer with something totally absurd. If someone asks you where to buy antique coins, the normal thing, of course, is that you would respond with directions, telling that person where to go. So I had to respond with a password that was totally absurd. So Jacobo arrived at the meeting place and asked me, 'Where can one buy antique coins?' And I looked at him and was so relieved, so overjoyed that I was finally making deep contact, finally getting more involved, that I couldn't answer. I just looked at him, and he was getting uncomfortable, until I thought, 'Damn! I am blowing it!' And I said the password."

"I entered into the urban part of the organization. And for a long time my job was the rear guard. From the beginning, that was my job. This is something worthy of criticism in the movement that as a woman, especially with children . . . they have you participate at first as rear guard. For example, you keep a house where other compañeros will come to stay, but you create the appearance that the house belongs to a normal family. This was a common way to incorporate women's participation, and if the organization asks this of you, you do it. There are organizations where pregnant women were forced to leave, but I never saw this in our organization.

"If you, as a woman, were able to get past the rear-guard stage then no other obstacles or impediments stood in the way of your participation in the organization, concerning both political and military responsibilities. My participation began to involve both urban and rural activities and I was assigned to Guerrero. The organization followed the same idea as Lucio of forming a guerrilla nucleus to promote armed struggle in the countryside. What is truly amazing is that they have been successful. There are villages and towns where people have suffered the worst repression, assassinations, disappearances, torture, and yet they get involved. I thought that they would be too afraid to participate, but no. After the massacres and destruction of Lucio's movement, people escaped, fled, took time to reorganize, and then, little by little, returned to the same area.

"There is a myth that the guerrilla plans every movement down to the last detail, and that everything turns out perfectly. When I was in the rear guard I had to deliver arms from Mexico City to Atoyac [Guerrero]. I had to pass through military roadblocks. I went with my daughter, with the guns hidden on my person. I was able to pass through all the roadblocks. I got to Atoyac and went into a restaurant bathroom to take the guns and bullets and stuff them all in a rucksack. I waited for three hours and the contact never came. I was nervous and afraid and angry. I had no idea what to do. I didn't know anyone to whom I could deliver the arms, and to return to Acapulco I would have to pass through the military roadblocks again, which would be extremely risky. In a fit of desperation, I grabbed the rucksack and headed for the bus. On the bus I fell asleep, with such frayed nerves, I just fell asleep in my seat at the back of the bus. One has this idea of the *guerrillero chignon* [badass guerrilla], but no. . . . I woke up to someone lightly stroking the back of my wrist; it was a soldier. When I opened my eyes and saw the soldier standing there, with my daughter sitting next to me, and the rucksack on the floor between our legs, I thought, 'This is it.' He asked me, 'Is this bag yours, *señora*?' I said, 'Yes.' And he didn't search it! He searched every other bag around us, but he didn't search ours! I promised myself that I would not do something so careless ever again.

"The press and the government sensationalized the guerrillas. One newspaper reported that a plane had been spotted flying low and dropping big crates to the ground: 'Surely these contained guns for the guerrilla,' they wrote. We would say to ourselves, 'If only!' But support comes from the local population. Without the support of the population, you can't do anything at all, nothing; any guerrilla movement, in any country, is lost without the support of the local population, and the state knows this well.

"We spent a long time in silence, working at the grassroots, organizing, building the organization. People aren't stupid; it is not the way the state says, that guerrillas deceive and manipulate people to join them. People have their reasons, and they are the ones pushing the organization forward.

"We spent a long time working very slowly. In 1988, the PRI divided and there was fraud. People were truly angered; in Guerrero many people had participated in Cárdenas's campaign. At first it was really only elderly people who took to the streets in protest of the fraud, marching in Chilpancingo, Acapulco, and Iguala. The marches were *puros viejitos* [filled with elderly people], and the riot police stormed in and attacked them with clubs, breaking their arms. Look at the news photographs from that time and you will see all these elderly people with both arms slumped by their sides: they were broken; the police had gone in and broken their arms with clubs. This angered the younger people, who then joined the marches and protests.

"This was something the state did that forced people to consider other options. People had decided to participate in the elections, but the state committed fraud and repressed the protests. People realized that elections weren't the way to go and they began to join the guerrilla.

"In 1990, Guerrero state held municipal elections. People once again held high expectations, and again the PRI committed fraud. Protesters occupied several municipalities and there were several confrontations when the police went in to raid and people fought back with rocks and sticks. But again, the state imposed repression. During this period between 1988 and 1991 the state again disappeared and murdered protesters in Guerrero, leading many people to question the viability of elections; this caused the armed movement, which had been growing very slowly, to grow now very quickly. This exposes the myth that armed movements are responsible for bringing repression: the state represses people who are trying to participate in open politics and forces those people into armed movements.

"The PRD was at that time well positioned as a victim, and many people joined the party. But as always, the party looks out for the interests of the party and pays no attention to the local needs of the people until election time rolls around. The PRD did not help people to address their very local needs, acquiring fertilizers, dealing with falling coffee prices. When people start to realize that the PRD paid no attention to them, then they began to form independent social organizations to fight for their local demands. Here, there were people participating in all three paths: social movements, armed movements, and electoral politics."

On January 14, 1994—two weeks after the Zapatista uprising in Chiapas—Benigno Guzmán founded the Campesino Organization of the Southern Sierra in the coastal mountain region north of Acapulco known as the Costa Grande.

"Our motive for creating this organization was basic need," Guzmán told me. "Every day the products from the countryside were worth less, and everything that came from the city cost more. We did not have access to health care at all. Here in Guerrero, people in the countryside die from simple infections, diarrhea, dry heaves, fevers, things that are no longer dangerous in other countries."

The Campesino Organization of the Southern Sierra was

created to be "an organization exclusively for campesinos, and made up of campesinos, because we knew what we needed," Guzmán said.

The organization began to organize marches and public protests to express their demands for government support to small farmers and health care in rural communities. The governor of Guerrero at the time was Rubén Figueroa Alcocer—son of Rubén Figueroa Figueroa, Guerrero's governor during the second phase of the Dirty War in the late seventies. Figueroa Alcocer accused the members of the campesino organization of being guerrilla fighters linked to the EZLN.

State police arrested several members of the organization, and several more were assassinated and disappeared. Instead of intimidating and pacifying the campesino organization, Guzmán and others planned bigger marches and protests, now demanding that the governor release their political prisoners and present the disappeared, alive.

On June 26, 1995, the Campesino Organization of the Southern Sierra sent out a press release announcing marches and protests in both Atoyac and Zihuatenejo. Two days later, as about fifty members of the organization were on their way to the protest in Atoyac, several hundred state police officers ambushed the campesinos' trucks as they came around a curve near the small village of Aguas Blancas. The police stopped the two trucks, ordered everyone in the first truck to lie face down on the street, and then opened fire on the passengers in the second truck, firing upon them for more than ten minutes, killing seventeen peasants and seriously wounding twenty-three more. Francisca Flores Rizo, a municipal worker from nearby Coyuca de Benítez, pointed out wounded members of the Campesino Organization of the Southern Sierra to state police; the police then shot them in the back of the head.[4]

The police themselves filmed the attack and released a doctored version of the video in an attempt to present the massacre as a confrontation with guerrilla fighters. The deception did not last long. Someone leaked an unedited version of the video to national television news reporter Ricardo Rocha, who aired the entire video on his evening news program. The Massacre of Aguas Blancas became international news.

After months of incompetence on the part of Guerrero state officials charged with investigating the massacre, president Ernesto Zedillo requested that the Supreme Court step in and conduct its own investigation. The Supreme Court's final report showed that the killings had indeed been planned and carried out by the highest levels of state government, directly implicating then governor Rubén Figueroa and Guerrero secretary of state José Rubén Robles Catalán. "It is well known that in order to maintain a lie, one has to keep lying," the report states. "It is important to highlight the degree of absurdity of the declarations of state government officials, in their immeasurable eagerness to cover up, deceive, and protect [themselves]."[5]

And yet neither the Supreme Court nor the president took any legal action against Figueroa or Robles Catalán. Both walked free.

A year later to the day, the survivors of the massacre and family members of those killed held a ceremony in Aguas Blancas to demand justice. During the ceremony about 100 men and women in military dress, their faces covered with handmade cloth masks, all wearing Cuban-style green caps and armed with AK-47 and AR-15 assault rifles, arrived unannounced. They climbed up on the stage and read their Aguas Blancas Manifesto. The people gathered there to commemorate the massacre stood in applause while shouting: *"Justicia, justicia, justicia."*[6] The men and women said that they came from the Popular Revolutionary Army, or EPR:

Today, June 28, a year after the massacre of Aguas Blancas carried out by the repressive troops of the oligarchy and the anti-popular government against seventeen defenseless campesinos from the mountains of Guerrero, the situation has not changed. The repression, persecution, imprisonment, murders, massacres, torture, and disappearances continue as government policies, a situation similar to that in 1967 and 1968 which led the commanders Lucio Cabañas Barrientos and Genaro Vázquez Rojas to take up arms against exploitation and oppression; this experience of social injustices and revolutionary energy once again inspires the struggle of the Mexican people.

In Mexico there is no rule of law. Our political Constitution, in reality, consists of words dead on the page; every day they violate basic rights, the people remain excluded from political and economic decision making, the executive branch concentrates power, subordinating the other branches of government and disregarding the sovereignty of the states.

Confronted with such institutionalized violence, armed struggle is a legitimate and necessary tool of the people in order to rebuild their sovereign will and reestablish the rule of law.[7]

"When the EPR appears publicly, a new stage begins," said Gloria. "The army increased the militarization of the region—which had never been demilitarized—and the people began to demand that we act. They said, 'We have our armed movement, we want to use it.' Once again the army had begun to detain, rape, and disappear people in the communities. This was 1996 and 1997.

"When we carried out the Aguas Blancas operation, a lot of people attended. We knew there was a military base very close by—from which, in fact, the first helicopters and army trucks were dispatched. The columns began to disperse; the army was beginning to leave the base and Hurricane Boris hit. The hurricane made it impossible for the army to pursue us, but it also made it hard going in the mountains. One tree fell down less than an inch from one *compañero*'s face."

On August 28, 1996, the EPR attacked soldiers and police in five different states across Mexico; nine soldiers and police, two rebels, and two civilians were killed in the attacks.[8] The government responded with intense militarization and repression in rural areas suspected of supporting or sympathizing with the guerrillas.[9] Small attacks and confrontations continued throughout 1996 and 1997.

"There were many skirmishes in Guerrero, many of which were not planned but were the result of surprise—on both parts—encounters in the mountains. The army had begun to send columns out into the mountains as if they were guerrillas. One night a guerrilla column came upon a road where soldiers were camped out and had to tiptoe around them to avoid a confrontation."

She told of two guerrillas walking, armed, in the mountains who stumbled upon an army column. Both sides fired on each other, the soldiers taking up positions and the guerrillas trying to back away while firing. At one point one soldier, a bit more gung-ho than the rest, took off running straight at the guerrillas and got right up close, only to freeze, his rifle ready, the two guerrillas training their rifles directly at him. Without saying a word, slowly, they began to back away from each other. The two guerrillas escaped.

Gloria told of a shootout in the mountains where two EPR members were shot point-blank. Some EPR guerrillas had escaped, but there were several more hiding in the underbrush; the army camped there, and the guerrillas hiding right underfoot could not move so much as an inch for two days.

Just as before, in the Dirty War of the 1970s, the army attacked towns and villages, calling people out of their homes, huddling everyone together on the basketball court or soccer field, separating the men and women, raping women, taking men off to the military base for torture. Many disappeared; some came back.

"The army sought to infiltrate the organization, to get people from the towns and villages to collaborate with them. They knew that they needed to create a network from inside, that outsiders would be immediately detected and avoided. Their method was to grab people from the communities, take them off to the military bases or camps, torture them, and then offer to release them if they agree to pass information to the army."

The soldiers even made recommendations as to how the prisoners should lie to their families about their disappearance and torture wounds, saying that they had gone off to Acapulco and gotten drunk with their buddies and then were beaten up by some ruffians. "This happened to many people," she said, "and some immediately returned to their communities and told us about what had happened to them; this put us on alert. Others went back to their communities and didn't say anything. We knew that some had agreed to become informants."

On June 6, 1998, a column of some twenty guerrilla fighters called an assembly meeting with indigenous farmers in the Ñu Savi region of Guerrero's Costa Chica (Little Coast).[10] Villagers from communities throughout the region attended a talk in the tiny, two-room schoolhouse in the village of El Charco. The purpose of the talk was to tell the villagers about a recent major change in their guerrilla organization and the need to continue with their struggle on the grassroots level. Those attending the meeting were not guerrilla fighters but simply subsistence farmers making their lives in the isolated villages of the Costa Chica Mountains. Their decision to sit and listen to the masked men and women with AK-47s should not strike one as odd. Robert Taber, in his 1965 classic study of guerrilla warfare, *The War of the Flea*, writes, "Country people whose only contact with the government comes in the form of napalm and rocket attacks can scarcely be expected to feel sympathetic to the government cause, whatever it may be. On the other hand, they have every reason to feel solidarity with the guerrillas, usually recruited from their own villages, who share their peril and their hardships."[11] While in the 1990s the Mexican government did not use napalm and rocket attacks in the Costa Chica, it did use plenty of bullets, which had a similar effect, if less devastating in scale, on the population. And so it was that on June 6, 1998, a few dozen farmers sat in a tiny village lost in the mountains to listen to the guerrilla fighters.

After the talk, those who had walked for eight to twelve hours through mountain paths to reach El Charco were offered a place to sleep the night: one of the rooms of the schoolhouse. The same offer was extended to the guerrillas and they accepted, sleeping apart in the other schoolroom, just behind the first, where villagers, one activist from the area, and two Mexico City college students teaching basic literacy in surrounding communities all slept.

Someone in the village, or who happened to be passing through from another community, got wind of the presence of the masked and armed guerrillas early on and took off for Ayutla de los Libres, an eight-to-ten-hour walk, to inform the army.

In the early predawn hours of June 7, 1998, hundreds of soldiers crept into El Charco and set up positions surrounding the school.

The schoolhouse sits in a kind of pit in the surrounding folds of the mountain; a basketball court stretches out from the school's entrance, small mud-and-wood houses dotting the mountains on either side. The dense mountain vegetation forms a wall of sorts just behind the school.

In the darkness the first screams of the soldiers rang out: "Come out, you motherfuckers! You are all going to die, sons-of-bitches!"[12]

No one left the schoolhouse; they were afraid.

Some time later, the soldiers opened fire, shooting through the windows into the schoolhouse. In the front room, filled with civilians, people began to scream in pain; others fell dead on the floor. The shooting lasted some ten minutes. There was a pause, during which the soldiers again screamed at them to leave the schoolhouse, then they opened fire for another ten minutes.

In the back room the guerrilla fighters immediately shouted out to the soldiers to hold their fire, that unarmed civilians were present in the schoolhouse, but their voices were impotent against the sound of gunfire. They gathered their weapons and backpacks and decided to try to escape in pairs into the mountains behind the school. They reasoned that if they were able to escape, the army might spare the villagers, but if they captured them all together, the soldiers would certainly torture and perhaps disappear the innocent.

The guerrilla fighters began their escape, charging out of the back of the schoolhouse in pairs, firing into the darkness around them.

Soldiers by then had climbed up on the roof, and they shot at the guerrillas from behind as they fled. The captain of the guerrilla column, known as Capitán José, was the first to fall. One of the young volunteer literacy teachers, Ricardo Zavala Tapia, also tried to escape and was shot dead. Another sixteen guerrillas escaped; the final pair of guerrillas who had provided cover for those who escaped were unable to break the wall of gunfire against them.

With the first rays of sunlight, five civilians lay dead inside the schoolhouse, Capitán José and Ricardo Zavala lay dead on the ground. The two remaining guerrillas decided to surrender. The surviving villagers and the other student, 21-year-old Erika Zamora, all made their way out. The soldiers screamed at them to lie facedown, their hands clasped behind their heads on the basketball court. One of the first civilians to step out of the schoolhouse with the breaking dawn was shot dead. Once the others were assembled on the basketball court, the soldiers descended. They shot the two guerrillas and one wounded civilian point-blank in the back of the head as they lay facedown on the asphalt.

The survivors were taken to a military base in helicopters and tortured. Efrén Cortés, a 28-year-old activist who had been invited to the meeting to discuss local agricultural issues, said: "The stripped me naked and blindfolded me, and they applied electric shocks to my genitals and my knees. . . . They threatened to castrate me and to rape me. They covered my head with a plastic bag that smelled of insecticide to suffocate me, and then they beat me all over my body and with their open palms on my ears."[13] Erika Zamora was stripped naked, thrown on the floor and given electric shocks until she lost consciousness. The soldiers forced both Erika and Efrén to sign testimonies written up for them by the soldiers incriminating them both as members of the EPR.

The soldiers did not yet know that the guerrillas present at El Charco were not members of the EPR. In Capitán José's backpack the army found a series of documents describing a major division within the EPR and the creation of a new, hitherto unknown guerrilla organization: the ERPI.

"I am going to tell you about how the ERPI came about. This is something that has not been discussed very much, and I am not sure why, since the documents fell [into army hands] at El Charco; perhaps because the story is not convenient for the state, but not because of us. I want to tell you about it because it is truly interesting."

Gloria continued: "Consider the armed movement versus armed groups. The latter maintain the idea of the vanguard, that they will rise up in arms and take power; for me all that is not going to work. I completely reject that method. And this is effectively the root of the division.

"The *compas* from the PDLP [Party of the Poor] who survived [the Dirty War of the 1970s] moved to Mexico City and became a more urban guerrilla group. The PDLP and the Unión del Pueblo [Union of the People] joined together and formed the PROCUP-PDLP, and the EPR arose from there. The EPR was not a union of so many different groups; that is a lie. Rather, people had left many groups and come to the PROCUP-PDLP. The political line of the EPR continues to be that of the vanguard. They start by building small groups in different states.

"We, as an organization in Guerrero, experienced something similar to what Subcomandante Marcos discusses in relation to the EZLN. One arrives as a vanguard to raise consciousness amongst the people, and the people are going to join *you*, you are the vanguard; you are going to lead the people and take power. This clashes with the indigenous communities and their traditions of communal democracy, and it also clashes with the social movements who have confronted assassinations and disappearances and *continue* fighting without bowing to fear. We had to change our ideas that social movements were inferior forms of struggle, that armed movements were superior forms of struggle; and we had to change our ideas that the armed movements would arrive on the scene to lead the social movements.

"In Guerrero, between 1990 and 1991 the state assassinated or disappeared over 100 people. And these people were all campesinos and indigenous people, all of them poor, none of them famous leaders. These people gave everything, including their lives, for their struggle. These people are highly politicized; they don't need others to politicize them. This caused us to change our practices. And the organization began to grow.

"We came up against another factor inside the EPR. The leaders decided to expand the leadership structure and include people from the different regions to discuss and take decisions together. No names, concrete information, or faces, but yes, shared work experience. The newly amplified committee met, and we began to learn of others' experiences in other regions. We also needed to analyze our own experience in order to be able to explain it to the others. We in Guerrero began this analysis and then began to realize that our practices were quite different than the others.

"Another factor that led to the division was the EZLN's eruption on the national political scene. When they put forth their ideas of '*mandar obedeciendo*' [command by obeying], and Marcos told of the first insurgents' experience, we in Guerrero thought, 'Wow, that sounds a lot like what we have been going through, not exactly the same, but really similar.'

"We lived through a very similar process before the EZLN rose up in 1994; this happened to the group in the state of Guerrero. We entered into Guerrero and bumped right into the fact that in the communities you can't show up to tell people what to do, but rather to obey what they want done. If you want to try and build something, you must go through a long community process. The EPR soldiers would go into communities wearing combat boots and uniforms and carrying backpacks. The people in the communities would comment, 'Lucio and his troops used *morrales* [simple rucksacks] and *huaraches* [handmade sandals].' So instead of forcing dogmas on people we started to listen, and we changed some of our practices. This was the first thing that lead to our division.

"A second thing: in Guerrero repression has always been very intense, more so than in other regions. And just where people should be afraid, they aren't afraid, instead they join the social movements. We had this idea that armed struggle was a superior form of struggle, and thus the nucleus of the armed group should lead the peaceful social movement. And the movement that we went to lead in the end became the movement that we listened to and learned from.

"In Guerrero we thus produced a very different analysis than those in the other regions. The EPR leaders stopped the expansion project; they were still on the same Marxist-Leninist protracted-war path. But we knew that we could not return down that path. When we tried to share our experience, the small opening for such discussion promptly closed. We did not want to split off, we had not even considered it, but the leadership's actions to isolate us and prevent a split made division inevitable.

"We tried for two years to get the whole organization to change."

Throughout 1996 and 1997, when the EPR clashed with the army repeatedly in Guerrero and the communities suffered under the increased militarization of the region, the Guerrero branch of the EPR was engaging in deep self-criticism and proposing massive changes to the national leadership, changes that stemmed from the guerrillas' experiences interacting with the communities and social movements in the state. The leadership refused to debate the proposals from Guerrero and ousted them from the brief experiment of an expanded national leadership structure. After internal debate and consultations in Guerrero, they decided to split off from the EPR and form the ERPI. On January 8, 1998, they officially notified the EPR leadership of their separation via a letter. The EPR issued a death sentence for Jacobo Silva, alias Comandante Antonio, by then Gloria's husband of several years.

"Perhaps there are some organizations that are able to split in a peaceful way," she said. "They sentenced Jacobo to death and initiated an operation to carry out the sentence. I don't tell you this to speak ill of them; I was a part of that organization and that *cuadrada* [boxed-in] way of thinking. So I don't tell you this even as a condemnation so much as a fact that we need to understand and learn from."

Jacobo and Gloria had to be careful on two fronts. "We lived in clandestinity inside of clandestinity; we had to hide from the government, which is relatively easy, but then also from our own *compañeros* as well. In my case, I had not ever seen their faces, but they had seen mine."

The pressure was too much, she said. Sometime in mid-1998 Gloria and Jacobo left Guerrero, going first to Toluca, in Mexico state, and later to San Luis Potosí. Gloria had been in San Luis Potosí for only twenty days when the Mexican federal preventive police detained her on October 22, 1999.

The death sentence has never been lifted; the government used that as a pretext for keeping Jacobo in Mexico's highest-security prison, in a hallway of jail cells that contain some of the nation's most notorious drug traffickers.

Their trial was a plagued with irregularities from the very beginning. The federal government claimed that police had detained both Jacobo and Gloria in Chilpancingo, Guerrero; in fact, as witnesses would later confirm, police detained Jacobo in Mexico City and Gloria later in San Luis Potosí. Jacobo and Gloria were charged with and convicted of homicide, rebellion, and property damage, receiving a sentence of over forty years in jail. Both pleaded guilty to the charge of rebellion but denied the charge of homicide. Human rights lawyer Pilar Noriega first represented Jacobo and Gloria. Noriega was later offered a position in the Mexico City Human Rights Commission and accepted; her close friend, the internationally renowned human rights lawyer Digna Ochoa, took over Jacobo and Gloria's case. Weeks later Digna was assassinated in her office.[14] Six years later, Jacobo and Gloria wrote their own appeal, making a simple constitutional argument: no one convicted of rebellion may be convicted simultaneously of homicide. Rebellion carried a five-year prison sentence when they were convicted. They won their appeal, the homicide charges were dropped, and they should have been released, but since their original conviction the prison term for rebellion had been increased to fourteen years, and this new sentence was applied illegally. They wrote and submitted another appeal in late July 2008.

In the last minute, with visiting hours almost over, I ask Gloria one final question: How do you understand revolt in contemporary Mexico?

"I do not think of revolt as a vanguard or protracted war like in El Salvador, Nicaragua, or Guatemala," she said. "I think of it as a process with long and deep roots, a path that has tried to move through various methods—electoral, social, and armed movements. In the present moment, the process is searching for still another path, different from all the previous paths taken. I don't think of revolt as exclusively armed or exclusively not armed; it could be a social movement, and that movement could adopt different forms of struggle depending on the circumstances, but not defined by dogma independently of experience.

"I think revolt has a lot to do with building—starting now and from the grassroots—what you want the future to hold. Many say that we need to take power, but I think that we need to *build* power from below, and starting now."

8.

EMPIRE AND REVOLT

And this seems like the heart of what contemporary imperialist practice is about. The American bourgeoisie has, in
short, rediscovered what the British bourgeoisie discovered
in the last three decades of the nineteenth century, that, as
Arendt has it, "the original sin of simple robbery" which
made possible the original accumulation of capital, "had
eventually to be repeated lest the motor of accumulation
suddenly die down." If this is so, then the "new imperialism" appears as nothing more than the revisiting of the old,
though in a different place and time.

—David Harvey, *The New Imperialism*

The only analysis is that they are screwing us, the people,
and we have to organize to respond to them. [*El único análisis es que nos están fregando al pueblo y que tenemos que
organizarnos para contestarles.*]

—Lucio Cabañas

THEFT, WHEN SUSTAINED over generations, spread over
immense territories, and equipped with an elaborate justifica-
tory apparatus that can turn plunder into justice, murder into
security, and broken lives into liberty, is called empire. And the
thieves, dispatched into overlapping temporal, spatial, and ideological departments, are called entrepreneurs and venture
capitalists; politicians, judges, generals, and police officers; aca-
demics, pundits, and theoreticians. Names are important; they
allocate tiny patches of compliance and revolt. If I call George

W. Bush "Mr. President," I grant him a minuscule plot of legitimacy that, combined with hundreds of millions of other such plots, may constitute a significant platform for robbery and killing. If I call him a thief—take the Central American Free Trade Agreement as one kind of robbery, Guantánamo as another—or an assassin—take the invasion and occupation of Iraq, pushed through a sham legal performance that no one now defends—then I place him on a minuscule plot of rebel territory where he carries no command and that, if combined with hundreds of millions of other such plots, may constitute a significant platform for challenging and stripping him of his power to rob and kill. Of course, George W. Bush is only one individual—a particularly destructive individual in the history of humanity, but just one—and the power of the name "empire" is precisely that it targets both individuals and their weighty construct of power. Hence the importance of ripping apart the shroud of legitimacy that names like "free trade," "president," "senator," and "democracy," still enjoy: in our existing world, these names hide responsibility for actions, when we are really talking about "cartel markets," "thieves," "assassins," and "imperialism."

Sounds harsh, perhaps, but not so harsh as the destroyed lives—people ravaged by hunger and torn apart by bullets, their families dismembered, entire communities uprooted and cast into a long, shattered, walking servitude and early death— that lie in the wake of imperial ambitions.

One of the principal hopes behind this book is to widen the range of public debate upon the ideological underpinnings of the relative wealth and privilege that pass as everyday life in many stretches of the United States, Mexico, and other countries. This book is a shout in the street that says that we who inhabit various positions of luxury in the contemporary capitalist world are all complicit in the damage done to people and places here and across the world. But this shout of joint complicity has an upside. As my friend Jesse once put it, if we are all complicit in the damage, then we all share responsibility in the solutions; that is, we are united, or can be united, in taking a stand, in revolt.

And that leads to one of the other hopes of this book: to inspire people with tales of resistance, defense of dignity, and revolt in Mexico—a land with an abundant wealth of revolt, owing in large part to its diversity of still unconquered indigenous cultures. I know that my words do not do justice to the complexity and depth of the movements I have only sketched and touched upon in this book; my hope is to spark curiosity, amazement, and the desire to learn more about these movements and others not discussed here, precisely with the design of acting upon such knowledge, of incorporating lessons learned. Social justice struggles in the United States as well as in Mexico will not, I believe, be effective if they are not antiimperialist.

Imperial domination existed, quite amply, before the European invasions of the sixteenth century, as with the Triple Alliance and the Inca empires, but the Europeans outdid them all. The incalculable scope of Spanish plunder in the lands now called the Americas is a turning point in the evolution of imperialism.[1] The extent of subjugation, the decimation of entire populations, the steroid-like fueling of European empires with the wealth extracted through slavery and destruction in the Americas, all conducted over vast territories and maintained for centuries, were unparalleled in any previous imperial reign. The language, religion, and class system imposed by the Spanish 500 years ago still endures today.

Spain's enrichment prompted internal European competition, a race to build empire with nearly the whole lot joining in—Britain, France, Portugal, Holland, Belgium, Russia—

speeding about the seas in search of new territories to raid, new populations to conquer and force into slavery. Soon the European-descended colonists in the so-called New World decided that one did not need large boats to build empires, that horses and guns were sufficient, and the wave of independence movements—preying upon the rage and hunger of the millions of destitute to actually do the fighting—swept the lands and set about building their own regional empires. Around this time the British Empire took the lead in the imperial dash based on their brutal exploits across Africa, the Middle East, the Caribbean, and India, building "an empire on which the sun never set."[2]

Imperialism was not a uniquely European practice, and Europe lost its hold on the Americas to a competing imperial force: the United States. The first half of the twentieth century saw the imperial worlds collide and tear at each other's throats. In the aftermath of World War II, the scene had changed. Germany was broken, Japan conquered, the British Empire falling apart, and the United States projecting forcefully outward to take its place. The U.S. strategy was to avoid direct military conquest when possible, preferring the less costly strategy of military and economic coercion; U.S. dominance would be justified as world defense against the evils of Soviet imperial designs.[3] Enter the Cold War. Before 1945, however, the United States amassed territory and power through a series of brutal conquests and invasions conceived as "manifest destiny" and later, through a series of military and economic invasions of Latin America, self-justified under the Monroe Doctrine.[4]

For most of Latin America's past 500 years, empire has meant armed robbery: theft at the barrel of a gun while surrounded by burned villages and destroyed bodies, the dispossessed then being marched off to work as slaves on the land taken by thieves. That was the Conquest, and that was the underbelly—that is, the dirty nonmetropolitan side—of nearly 500 years of imperialism: for every London there are many Daccas, for every British Museum and Smithsonian Institution there lie decimated communities and histories around the world. The imperialists gave the sustained practice of plunder another name, and with that name a theoretical scaffolding to erect the temple of their delight in the pleasures and riches of thievery. They called it capitalism. And, adding insult to injury, they proclaimed that with it they would liberate the very people they destroyed—as the earlier imperialists enslaved and killed in order to save the souls of barbarians. Today, the new barbarians are the ghetto dwellers, the landless, and the hungry, wrecked by centuries of violent assault.

But what is capitalism all about anyway? Isn't it just buying and selling things? How are we supposed to get by if we don't buy and sell things? A simple definition: "We are in a capitalist system only when the system gives priority to the *endless* accumulation of capital. . . . Endless accumulation is a quite simple concept: it means that people and firms are accumulating capital in order to accumulate still more capital, a process that is continual and endless."[5] This has been said many ways; perhaps one of the more distilled and accepted versions among the agnostics of capitalism in the United States is "profit before people," the idea that profit (or capital accumulation) is taken as sacred and given higher priority, both culturally and legally, in contemporary society than the well-being of people and the environment. But the agnostics tend to think the problem is one of degree, or scale, that capitalism can be softened, or "humanized," by using the state to erect limits to profit (capital accumulation). And this sounds the death knell for their resistance: the capitalist state, composed of the privileged beneficiaries of exploitation and conquest, is the principal protector of endless "economic growth," the endless accumulation of capital. Asking the state to limit or redirect profit in order to help the downtrodden is akin to sending a detective on the mob payroll to infiltrate the mob and arrange a bust—that is, it will not work.

Advocates of capitalism claim that free markets reflect free individual will, and the collection of free individual choices itself reflects the free will of a healthy social body. Perhaps such might be the case, were free markets to exist. They do not. The rules guiding international trade and even intra-national trade, referred to as markets, are intensely regulated, scripted, structured, and crafted by the state and corporate lobbyists, that is, by the moneyed political class at the helm of political decision making. "The totally free market functions as an ideology, a myth, and a constraining influence, but never as a day-to-day reality . . . a totally free market, were it ever to exist, would make impossible the endless accumulation of capital," writes U.S. sociologist and world-systems analyst Immanuel Wallerstein.[6] There are two fundamental facts airbrushed out of the picture presented by "free market" ideology: first, that so much of the existing capital (wealth, money, land, control over natural resources like oil and water) in the world has been passed down among the children of conquest, of original theft; and second, that the vast bulk of the capital of the downtrodden (work, the ability to produce with one's effort, one's body, one's mind) is tightly harnessed—that is, unfree—by the laws of the state: under NAFTA, businesses, their property and their money can travel back and forth across national borders with relative ease, while workers who try to do the same are dubbed illegal, are snatched off the streets and off factory floors, and are carted back over the borders they crossed. In the "free market" of NAFTA, the freedom is for the wealth and personnel of the capitalists—

the thieves—there is no corresponding freedom for the refugees of land theft and conquest whose only capital is their daily toil.[7]

Capitalism is the immense and widely celebrated ideological package used to rewrap theft as freedom, to recast imperialism as democracy.

Perhaps, one might say, the imperialisms of old were indeed little more than plunder, but is it not an exaggeration to say that economic policies like NAFTA are the same? They are not the same. They are different. Before, imperialists simply occupied lands and slashed the bellies and throats of those who complained. The end effect, however, is always dispossession, stealing lands, and creating landless labor forces (be they slaves or later, peons and migrant wage-earners). The new tactics require more steps, more personnel, and more finesse. Now, the imperialists pass a law or negotiate a treaty that cuts all government aid to peasant farmers, expropriates land, strips tariffs on subsidized foreign grains to such an extent that peasant farmers cannot sell their grains and are forced off their land. The end effect again is dispossession. English geographer and social theorist David Harvey calls this process "accumulation by dispossession," and provides a rigorous explanation of its workings.[8] Whether dispossession is accomplished first by an army or by a congress (and then enforced by an army or a police force) the impact is always violent; people are forced from their land, running from bullets or hunger, they are dispossessed.[9] In *The New Imperialism*, Harvey writes:

> Military interventions are the tip of the imperialist iceberg. Hegemonic state power is typically deployed to ensure and promote those external and international arrangements through which the asymmetries of exchange relations can so work as to benefit the

hegemonic power. It is through such means that tribute is extracted from the rest of the world. . . . The
primary vehicle for accumulation by dispossession . . .
has been the forcing open of markets throughout the
world by institutional pressures exercised through the
IMF and the WTO, backed by the power of the
United States.

Mexico has long been caught in the crosshairs of U.S.
imperialism. From the massive U.S. land theft during the War
of 1846–1848 to the also massive dispossessions caused by
U.S. corporations, at Porfirio Díaz's explicit invitation,
throughout the late 1800s and the early 1900s,[10] to the U.S.
invasion of Mexico at the port of Veracruz to protect U.S.
investments and properties in 1914,[11] to the forced restructuring of Mexico's economy in the late 1980s and early 1990s
disguised as economic bailouts and then a "free trade" agreement, the United States has wielded both the visible and the
invisible hand to exercise imperial control over Mexico's people, land, and economy.[12]

When Mexico's economy crashed in the early 1970s, it
coincided with the U.S. economy's crisis of overaccumulation
(the bizarre capitalist problem of having too much money and
not finding a new place to use it in order to make even more
money). Aid packages from the United States gave U.S. capitalists new places to invest and the leverage to force economic
restructuring on Mexico.[13] And "restructuring" meant priva-
tizing on a mass scale. President Miguel de la Madrid
privatized more than 900 of the 1,600 state-owned enterprises
between 1982 and 1988; Carlos Salinas sold off 300 of the
remaining state firms by 1994, including the telecommunications giant TelMex that was Carlos Slim's gateway to
becoming one of the world's wealthiest people (i.e., one of the

world's most successful thieves). De la Madrid's privatizations "brought [U.S.] capital into the economy on a scale not seen since the Porfiriato."[14] But this was only the opening act; the constitutional reforms carried out under Salinas and then the passing of NAFTA constitute one of the most devastating acts of accumulation by dispossession ever to strike Mexico. In the words of U.S. historian John Mason Hart, author of the exhaustive study *Empire and Revolution: The Americans in Mexico since the Civil War*, "NAFTA's advantages would have pleased J. P. Morgan. It offered U.S. financial elites a historic opportunity for a systematic restructuring of capital, labor, and resources in Mexico that can be compared to the introduction of railroads and industry in the nineteenth century."[15] NAFTA also enabled a few Mexican elites "to advance to world-class wealth while exercising even greater power in Mexico."[16] Mexican economist Juan Manuel Sandoval writes that "by betting everything on NAFTA, it is clear that the Mexican government tacitly accepted the rules of the game unilaterally imposed by the United States regarding migration and many other issues."[17]

In the daily life of Mexicans, U.S. imperialism stands constant in the background, like warships on the horizon. But to reduce state violence in Mexico to a puppet's moves on behalf of the looming giant is to profoundly misunderstand the nature both of the state and of contemporary imperialism. A tiny elite political class has benefited tremendously from implementing the mandates of U.S. economic imperialism in Mexico.[18] The number of billionaires and millionaires grows with the number of people dispossessed. The Mexican state exercises forms of internal imperialism that overlap entirely with the dictates of the United States. As English historian Alan Knight commented: "Informal control requires congenial collaborating elites."[19]

Would it not be a contradiction of sorts to have two congenial empires working together? If the United States is really an empire, would not that mean that all other states are either enemies in some way, or else lackeys? No, I think not. The design of empire has changed since the days when imperial might traveled over the seas to dispatch foot soldiers and cavalries on distant shores. Now the captains of empire travel in private jets, and their foot soldiers move unseen through wire transfers and satellite communications. Empire has decentered. Its locus of power is split between financial (former colonial) capitals across the world, it can move with speed and force unparalleled. Empire is no longer synonymous with the nation-state; it stands above and the nation-states serve its will. And while the United States is the strongest, most destructive of the multiple centers of imperial power, empire itself denies boundaries; it claims to be ahistorical and transcendental, beyond any particular ideology or web of cultural practices.[20] Empire and its "logic of rule" extend across the globe.[21] In the illusion of its strength lies its weakness.

MEXICO TODAY is the descendant of revolution betrayed, a betrayal that has been repeated now many times over, or perhaps, a betrayal that has been upheld and defended while always paraded as its opposite—and a revolution that has never slipped quietly into the past. When people shout during street protests, "*¡Zapata vive! ¡La lucha sigue!*"—"Zapata lives! The fight continues!"—they are both paying homage to their shared history and asserting the true destination of their defiance. The revolution that Zapata and millions waged at the turn of the twentieth century has yet to be consummated.

Mexican political theorist Arnaldo Córdova traces the formation of political power in twentieth-century Mexico to the betrayal of the revolution.[22] The first element of betrayal—

beyond the assassinations of Zapata and Villa—consisted in the apparently radical agrarian and labor social reforms built into the postrevolutionary constitution, reforms that in effect sought to contain further rebellions, to create an image of the state as a state of the people (*estado del pueblo*), to serve as a threat against the landowning elite of the Porfiriato, and to enable the leaders of the state to mobilize masses for electoral and nationalist ends.[23] "In practice," writes Córdova, "the social reforms were employed as instruments of State power."[24] The political class thus created a nationalist populism not to fight the oligarchy, writes Córdova, but to combat the independent and socially radical campesino movements led by Zapata and Villa: "Thus Mexican populism had counterrevolutionary roots."[25]

The second element of betrayal came with the creation of the PRI, and its apotheosis: the cult of the president. After watching the decay of the Díaz dictatorship and the political chaos of the 1920s, particularly the assassinations of presidents Venustiano Carranza and Álvaro Obregón, writes Córdova, the political class saw the need to secure its power in something stronger than the pure individual control of the president, the old-style caudillo.[26] Thus they built a constitutionally strong presidency with extraordinary powers and a deep and complex relationship to the masses and the rest of the state apparatus: "The president was no longer a person, but an institution."[27] Córdova calls this the "profound secret of the Mexican political system," that political power, masked as revolutionary, is based on domination and the manipulation of the masses. Córdova lists five elements of this secret: first, the political system appears to be an institutional alliance between various social organizations that hold the real power; second, the office of the president is invested with exceptional powers secured in the constitution; third, the president serves as the "supreme arbiter" to whom all the various social organizations submit their differences; fourth, the masses are indoctrinated with the "cult, not only of the president's personality, but of presidential power"; and fifth, the employment of traditional forms of personal relations and debts create dependence upon the president and cement control over the political personnel of any particular administration.[28]

Indeed, the president became an institution, an ingenious amalgamation of the powers of the Spanish Crown (in its absolute nature) and the Mexican *cacicazgo* (in its manipulation of extensive personal and social relationships). The state-party fusion created in the PRI (and maintained to this day, despite mutations imposed by the very real divisions and infighting amongst the various parties)[29] served the president much the way a royal court would serve a king. And the entire construct of the independent, postrevolutionary state in Mexico has served to continue the process of conquest within its own national borders, subjecting the indigenous, rural, and working classes to a sustained onslaught of violence while advancing the spread of capitalism and the amassing of fortunes in the hands of the few.[30]

Mexican sociologist Pablo González Casanova writes in his classic study *Democracy in Mexico*, "Inherited from the past, marginalization, plural society, and internal colonialism continue in Mexico today in new forms, despite so many years of revolution, reforms, industrialization, and development and still make up the characteristics of national politics and society."[31] Just over forty years have elapsed since González Casanova wrote these words, forty years during which the violence of internal colonialism has remained steady, if not increased. One year after the publication of *Democracy in Mexico*, the Mexican army opened fire on protesting students in Tlatelolco Plaza in Mexico City, killing hundreds. Massacres and disappearances, the economic abandonment of rural communities combined with the economic imperialism of NAFTA, death squads and torture—political practices that make up the laws of internal colonialism—have all continued or increased in the four decades since the appearance of *Democracy in Mexico*. Horribly, González Casanova's analysis still holds: while there have been significant changes in Mexican political society, the state continues the policies of internal colonialism, the policies of ongoing conquest. As Mexican philosopher Bolívar Echeverría writes, the Conquest "is an enterprise that has *not* finished."[32]

There will no doubt be resistance amongst outside observers and the non-oppressed in Mexico to the idea that the conquest continues, the idea that the Mexican government wages a politics of internal colonialism. The Tunisian writer Albert Memmi analyzed the various facets of the colonial psyche in his landmark 1957 work *The Colonizer and the Colonized*. One of the main psychological attributes of the colonizer is denial: either the denial of the illegitimacy of colonialism or the denial of the humanity of the colonized, or both. Memmi writes that "accepting the reality of being a colonizer means agreeing to be a nonlegitimate, privileged person, that is, a usurper."[33] This is not a viable option. Legitimacy is essential to the principle of democracy that holds up the modern state; governmental actions are portrayed as being just, in and of themselves, by virtue of their flowing from a democratic regime, a regime elected by the people and thus granted full legitimacy.[34] For this reason, Memmi writes, the defender of colonialism (especially within supposed democracies) "endeavors to falsify history, he rewrites laws, he would extinguish memories—anything to succeed in transforming his usurpation into legitimacy."[35]

Hence the importance of ideology—the intellectual tool

used to transform usurpation into legitimacy. How does such a process of transformation work? In his essay "On the Concept of Ideology" Mexican philosopher Luis Villoro offers a political definition of ideology that combines logical and sociological criteria to explain the peculiar and often ambiguous task of performing this transformation. Villoro writes:

> The shared beliefs of a social group are ideological if and only if:
>
> They are not sufficiently justified; that is, the statements used to express the beliefs are not founded in objectively sufficient reasons.
>
> The beliefs fulfill the social function of promoting the political power of this group; that is, the acceptance of the statements that express the beliefs favor the establishment or conservation of the power of this group.[36]

In Mexico, the Conquest continues and the internal colonialists disguise their usurpations with various ideologies such as those explored in these pages: the rule of law, poverty, migration, and the racism referred to above as Holmberg's Mistake, the ideology of the indigenous past. The continuation of conquest forces the continuation of revolt. As Memmi writes: "Revolt is the only way out of the colonial situation, and the colonized realizes it sooner or later. . . . The colonial situation by its own internal inevitability brings on revolt. For the colonial condition cannot be adjusted to; like an iron collar, it can only be broken."[37]

Conquest makes revolt both necessary and inevitable, and revolt illuminates the often disguised features of contemporary conquest. Bolívar Echeverría writes: "I see the outbreak of indigenous rebellion in Chiapas [on January 1, 1994] as evidencing this historical situation that is still our present, the fact that we still live in both a process of interrupted Conquest as well as of interrupted *mestizaje*."[38] Precisely the interrupted *mestizaje*, argues Echeverría, contains radical potential for opposing conquest and constructing a new society free of colonialism and capitalism.

For Echeverría *mestizaje* is the "natural form of existence of cultures" and involves a reciprocal exchange of customs used in constructing cultural identity.[39] *Mesitzaje* as reciprocity in the construction of cultural identities, he writes, involves the acknowledgment of the validity of alternative ways of doing things, for people in one culture incorporate customs from other cultures into both their practices and their identities. In a sense they call into question their own identity when confronted with other alternatives, but then rebuild their identity through the inclusion of certain aspects of different cultural practices.[40] This *mestizaje*, argues Echeverría, is the natural form of cultural development. It occurred in the initial wake of the Conquest in the Americas throughout the seventeenth century but was then truncated and suppressed by the continued Conquest—though still not vanquished.[41] *Mestizaje* in this sense is a radical cultural politics of reciprocity, not to be confused with the Mexican government's ideology of racial mixing, which meant only the elimination of the indigenous as such.[42]

The cultural logic of conquest seeks to destroy the radical potential of *mestizaje* by denying the humanity of the conquered and thus denying the validity of their cultural practices; conquest is the cultural development of imposition, apartheid, and elimination of difference, and such is the continuing political legacy across Latin America. Echeverría writes:

> The "bourgeois States" and the "liberal republics" throughout all of Latin America took up and continue

up into the present the historical line of the Spanish Crown, and *not* the line of *mestizaje*. Even though almost all of these States say that they affiliate themselves to the idea of "*mestizaje*," in reality theirs is the same politics of the ancient conquerors; that is, that of apartheid, that which only accepts others within the borders of their domains in the extent to which they stop being others, they self-annihilate and become "co-nationals." . . . The Latin American states . . . in so far as they are western, modern, and capitalist states, have a task that is fundamental, basic, and essential from which they cannot excuse themselves, and that is precisely the task to *conclude* the process of the Conquest, that is, to eliminate the sketch of a project of civilization implied by the indigenous, to substitute it, or "integrate" it . . . in a political life that springs from the homogenization of the citizenry, passing it through the common denominator of private property. The great dilemma that faces Latin American states when they confront the "indigenous question" stems from the fact that, as they exist now, these states possess an inherent *telos*, the *telos* that is to conclude the process of the Conquest.[43]

The continued conquest seeks to extinguish the process of *mestizaje* that would imply considering alternatives to capitalism; that would imply acknowledging the validity of alternative ways of doing things the way they were done before the conquest and are still done by indigenous peoples across Mexico in spite of the continuing conquest. Taken to its full conclusion, the telos, or ultimate end, of the conquest is nothing less than the eradication of the indigenous and their alternatives.

What, then, are the possibilities of resistance and revolt, of *mestizaje* and the end of conquest? One answer is to turn first to the oppressed, for, as Brazilian educator Paulo Freire wrote, "who better than the oppressed to understand the terrible significance of an oppressive society? Who suffers the effects of oppression more than the oppressed? Who can better understand the necessity of liberation?"[44] And thus in Mexico (and beyond) we should turn to the indigenous. As Subcomandante Marcos said during a gathering of the Other Campaign with Zapotec, Mixe, and Chinanteco indigenous peoples in Guelatao, Oaxaca, on February 8, 2006: "The advance of the capitalist system means the total—total—destruction of indigenous peoples. We are indigenous people, and we are ready to do anything—anything—so that we may continue to be so." And again, Echeverría: "For the indigenous to continue surviving, for them to maintain their mode of existence, the Latin American states must change. . . . The only possible way for these human beings who are the indigenous to continue existing as they are and as they want to be, is through the *radical self-transformation* of political modernity as such."[45]

Francisco López Bárcenas, the Ñu Savi lawyer and historian, concurs with Bolívar Echeverría when he writes that indigenous autonomy—proposed as a politics of emancipation from internal colonialism—requires the recasting of the state. State policies of internal colonialism, he writes, have become "a situation that neither the legal equality of citizens trumpeted by nineteenth-century liberalism, nor the indigenous policies (*políticas indigenistas*) carried out by various Latin American states during the twentieth century were able to resolve because they did not go to the root of the problem, which now appears to be the recognition of indigenous peoples as subjects of collective rights, but also the recasting of the states to correct their historic anomalies of considering themselves to be monocultural in multicultural societies."[46]

Indigenous autonomy within the state, López Bárcenas writes, requires that the state recognize indigenous peoples as subjects of collective rights—not individual rights—and that such rights would account for the indigenous peoples' demand for "self-affirmation, self-definition, self-delimitation, and internal and external self-disposition."[47] Rephrasing, indigenous autonomy means that the indigenous peoples decide where to draw the boundaries and what to do with their territory and all the resources within it (the federal government would hold no absolute powers of expropriation); how to organize their internal political affairs (for example to hold elections in open assemblies and to hold all land in collective); how to organize their internal social affairs (such as what to teach their children in their schools and how to treat the ill in their clinics); and how to regulate their interactions with external communities and individuals, that is, what projects, technologies, and collaborations to accept and participate in.

Critics say that such autonomy consists of isolationism, or futile, ahistorical utopian dreams. These critics miss the essential point of autonomy: the elimination of imposition. "Now whatever we do, be it good or bad," said the EZLN's Lieutenant Colonel Moisés at a gathering on Zapatista autonomy in Oventik on July 21, 2007, "it is what we the Zapatistas have decided; it is no longer what the *patrón* [boss] orders." At the end of his philosophical study of the conquest of the Americas, Bulgarian philosopher Tzvetan Todorov writes, "It is possible to establish an ethical criterion to judge the form of influences: the essential thing, I should say, is to know whether they are *imposed* or *proposed*. . . . No one asked the Indians if they wanted the wheel, or looms, or forges; they were obliged to accept them. Here is where the violence resides, and it does not depend upon the possible utility of these objects."[48]

In fact, this principle—propose, not impose—is the one of the guiding principles of governance *inside* Zapatista autonomous territory. As we saw earlier, many of the indigenous rebels in Chiapas who are building their autonomy in spite of the Mexican government's hostilities articulated this principle in gatherings with outside visitors in 2007. These statements are well worth quoting a second time: "The people make the decisions. We only propose, we don't impose," said Jesús from the good government council of La Realidad. "The authority should serve and not serve itself, propose, not impose," said Roel, also from La Realidad. This basic principle—to propose, not impose—is inherent to the concept of *mestizaje* developed by Bolívar Echeverría: it implies recognizing the humanity of the other, the validity of their cultural alternatives, and their autonomy of decision.

Indigenous autonomy rejects imposition not only from the outside in, but also within internal forms governance. Here indigenous autonomy offers hope to a politics of radical *mestizaje*; people are taking the initial and profoundly risky steps of creating autonomous territories where imposition is not tolerated but proposals are encouraged. This opens a space for solidarity, but not a solidarity where charity disguises imposition, rather a solidarity where the outsider comes to learn, to question his or her own cultural identity (which will invariably contain elements of the oppressive capitalist system in which most outsiders were raised) when confronted with the alternative of indigenous autonomy and then redefine that identity through self-transformation. Paulo Freire writes: "Solidarity requires that one enter into the situation of those with whom one is in solidarity; it is a radical posture."[49] In the context of internal colonialism and capitalist oppression in Mexico, such solidarity with the indigenous implies taking sides, choosing against empire, and embracing the politics of radical *mestizaje*. It implies recognizing the validity of indigenous alternatives and using them to question one's own cultural identity—to question and then reconstruct.

In 2005, with the Sixth Declaration of the Lacandón Jungle, the EZLN announced the political program that would come to be called the Other Campaign. The Zapatistas announced: "A new step forward in the indigenous struggle is only possible if the indigenous join together with workers, campesinos, students, teachers, employees: the workers of the city and the countryside."[50] Indigenous autonomy, the continued existence of indigenous peoples, as López Bárcenas and Echeverría both argue, requires the recasting of the state, and such a recasting will include "the workers of the city and the countryside" and be explicitly anticapitalist. The EZLN's Other Campaign calls for building an anticapitalist movement outside the traditional political party structures that are inseparably wed to the state precisely for this reason: the new politics must be built from outside—as they say, "from below and from the left." The capitalist state and its policies of internal colonialism demand the ultimate destruction of the indigenous; a true politics of radical *mestizaje* will draw from and include multiple alternatives that have sprung from and survived within the capitalist state (the printing press and radio technology, for example, both forcefully employed by indigenous struggles in Mexico); hence the Zapatista vision of "one world in which many worlds fit."

Perhaps one of the most significant contributions of the Other Campaign to date has been the focus on shifting class consciousness away from potentially divisive political identities and toward the bridging class of *los de abajo*—the underdogs, the excluded. The Other Campaign called on all those cut out of the benefits, all those exploited and violated by capitalism and political repression in Mexico to join together, to hold onto and defend their particular political or social identities—indigenous, woman, homosexual, transsexual, worker, intellectual, anarchist, student—while forming a unified organization of *los de abajo*. The class antagonism expressed by the Other Campaign is at root the antagonism between included and excluded, between the political class and *los de abajo*. This recasting of class consciousness could be extremely powerful and emancipatory: it builds bridges and connects people based on their shared political identity—the excluded—while calling for a radical equality of inclusion and respect for diverse political identities.

Slovenian philosopher Slavoj Žižek writes that "it is the antagonism between the Excluded and the Included which is the zero-level antagonism, coloring the entire terrain of struggle . . . it is only the reference to those Excluded, to those who dwell in the blanks of the space of the state, that enables true universality."[51] Beyond the antagonism of the included and the excluded, Žižek writes, all other class antagonisms "lose their subversive edge: ecology turns into a 'problem of sustainable development'" such that "political action and consumption become fully merged."[52] Thus the Other Campaign's strict rejection of capitalism and political parties—the political class, the included—and the campaign's equally strong union of disparate political identities into *los de abajo*—the excluded—creates the possibility of political equality built within *mestizaje*, equality built on the simultaneous maintenance of and respect for difference and the shared experience of exclusion and struggle for liberation. The Other Campaign articulates this radical equality of class consciousness in *los de abajo*, and is still in the process of building the national alliances and organizational structures necessary to actualize such consciousness into revolt.

The APPO movement benefited from the Other Campaign's presence and meetings throughout Oaxaca and came closer to actualizing the class consciousness of *los de abajo*. During the months of the civil disobedience offensive in 2006, especially during the *defensive* move of organizing nightly barricades throughout Oaxaca City, people from incredibly diverse political identities—indigenous, worker, teacher, anarchist, woman, even middle class—joined together in the actual activity of revolt. Not all participants overcame the old divisions in the Left (for example, the anarchists against the Stalinists), and these divisions resurfaced after the federal police violently lifted the last protester camps.

The true legacy of the Oaxaca uprising is the lived experience of such radical equality during shared struggle. Here also the solidarity of the not-excluded with the excluded took on Freire's "radical posture." One evening at the barricades protecting the APPO-occupied radio station known as La Ley (The Law), a well-dressed middle-class couple approached the barricade with trepidation, asking to speak with the people gathered there. There were insistent rumors that night that the police would conduct another raid in their "death convoy," as they had in late August. The middle-class couple gave the barricade guards instructions to their house, saying that in the case of a raid, the back door would be open. The husband added: "I have prepared piles of rocks on the roof" for throwing down at the police. The people at the barricade responded with nods and the words "*Gracias, compañeros.*"

The argument here is not that indigenous autonomy is the *only* possible strategy of revolt, but rather that any nonimperialist revolt in Mexico must *include* the struggles of indigenous autonomy and, as well, that such struggles constitute the most radical sites of revolt in Mexico today, offering the excluded classes, *los de abajo*, a model of struggle that can help break open new sites of autonomy and revolt *beyond* those sanctioned by the state. Here again, indigenous autonomy struggles open the possibility for a politics of radical *mestizaje*, the non-indigenous *de abajo*, by incorporating elements of the struggles for indigenous autonomy in their own spheres of revolt, step out of the domain of the state's authority—out of the trap of "compliant defiance," to use U.S. anthropologist Matthew Guttman's phrase[53]—and engage in the cultural practice of *mestizaje* by incorporating and thus acknowledging the validity of the indigenous alternatives. Herein lies the insurgent message from the EZLN to those who would stand in solidarity: "Be a Zapatista where you are."

Echeverría writes that the "bewilderment and inactivity of the Left results from its fidelity to the political world of the modern nation-state."[54] This is the world of electoral politics, lobbyists, think tanks, nongovernmental organizations, and even marches and street protests, which all make demands of the state and thus continue to perpetuate its very dominance. Indigenous autonomy and a politics of *mestizaje* that springs from the experience and influence of such struggles demand opening new sites of struggle, new sites of political participation beyond the state, that diminish its dominance. The Zapatista autonomous municipalities, the autonomous municipality of San Juan Copala, and, for a brief time, the occupied streets, plazas, and television and radio stations in Oaxaca all opened such independent sites of political action. There is much to be learned here. Again Echeverría writes: "What should be done in our time is to rescue the spontaneous proposal of political activity that is not carried out in obedience with the dogma of modern capitalism, as an exercise of what capital permits and promotes, but rather precisely against it."[55]

This is not a call to a simple unleashing of outrage, it is a call to reflection and action based on the radical concept of *mestizaje*, a profound questioning of one's own cultural identity and political practices while engaging the sovereign practices of indigenous autonomy. Direct participation in revolt does not require (but does not dogmatically exclude) shooting guns, throwing rocks, building barricades, filling Molotov cocktails with gasoline, or blowing up dams. Educating the community about the movement's demands and the social inequities they spring from is just as rebellious as setting tires on fire in the intersection. Revolt needs the mundane as urgently as it needs the heroic. The man who hands out tamales at the barricades is no less or more of a rebel than the woman who takes over the television station and broadcasts live or the artist who spray-paints stencil art born of the revolt on cathedral walls. In Oaxaca, during the two months of nightly barricade construction throughout the movement-occupied city (August 21–October 28, 2006), hundreds of families spent hours preparing coffee, sandwiches, tamales, and *atole* for the volunteers who stood watch at the barricades. Recall the 8-year-old girl accompanying her parents who served me coffee and bread at 3:00 a.m. as I interviewed six indigenous teachers at a barricade protecting a movement-occupied radio station. "Aren't you tired?" she asked. And the risks of her activity were (are) mortal: plainclothes soldiers shot and killed Alejandro García at a barricade on October 14, 2006, while he was handing out food and drink with his wife and children.

Revolt begins long before barricades appear in the street. Revolt begins with conviction, the joining of resolve and hope, of anger and imagination, the simultaneous belief that one *must* and one *can* live to undo systems of oppression. As Paulo Freire writes: "In order for the oppressed to be able to wage the struggle for their liberation, they must perceive the reality of oppression not as a closed world from which there is no exit, but as a limiting situation which they can transform."[56]

There may always be murder, theft, dishonesty, and abuse

amongst people, but when murder, theft, dishonesty, and abuse become the defining traits of a social system, as they have in Mexico, people have the inherent right to revolt. Understanding how the system survives through oppression is a prerequisite to undermining the ideologies that conceal oppression.

THEY WANTED TO NAME their daughter Doni Zänä, which means "flower of the night" in Ñañú, an indigenous language spoken by over 100,000 people in the state of Hidalgo, just north of Mexico City. César Cruz and Marisela Rivas sell flowers during the Mexican Day of the Dead festivals, and their daughter was born on November first, Day of the Dead. "That's where we got the idea of giving her the name that means flower of the night," César Cruz told a reporter from *La Jornada*.[57]

César and Marisela went to the civil registry office in Tepeji del Río, but the registrar refused to accept the name Doni Zänä. They went to nearby Tula de Allende and received the same response. They went to the Hidalgo state registry and again were turned away. Each time the registry officials told them that the name Doni Zänä "does not register in the computer system."[58]

José Antonio Salomón, the director of the Hidalgo State Family Registry, told *La Jornada* that the name Doni Zänä was just "a whim that could bring negative consequences" for the daughter.[59]

The 2003 federal General Law on the Linguistic Rights of the Indigenous People recognized Ñañú—and all other indigenous languages in Mexico—to be official national languages and to "share the same validity" as Spanish wherever they are spoken.[60] Even though the law guarantees the parents' rights, the registry officials claimed that, "unfortunately the [computer] systems did not contemplate" such rights.[61]

José Antonio Salomón recommended that they register the name as Doni Zana, but César and Marisela refused: written without the underlined "o" and the umlauts over the a's, the name would mean "the rock that bites" in Ñañú. And so the response from the municipal and state registries, as well as from the National Commission for the Development of Indigenous Peoples and the Hidalgo State Human Rights Commission was this: give her another name.

This was not their first negative experience with the civil registry. When they went to register their 8-year-old daughter Yohoki, the official told them that no foreign or rock-star names were allowed. "I told them that this was a Ñañú name, not Chinese or Japanese," said César Cruz, "and that in our language it means to be reborn, or to renovate, or to create between two. Where is the foreignness? Their ignorance leads them to intolerance and racism."[62]

César and Marisela took their fight to the press. The answer from the state officials remained the same: choose another name. The Hidalgo state secretary of government (the number-two post in the state executive branch), Francisco Olvera Ruiz, called César to his office and scolded him to find another name. The Hidalgo state office of the Mexican foreign relations secretary said that they would not be able to issue a passport with the name Doni Zänä.

But César and Marisela refused to give up and refused to accept that the name they had chosen for their daughter was a "whim."

"This is about defending our culture, our language, our race, which apparently the authorities would like to disappear," César told *La Jornada*.

César and Marisela had to fight for two and a half years to register their daughter's name, Doni Zänä, in their own native language.[63]

Sometimes revolt can be something so simple, and often unnoticed, as the fight for a name. This book focuses on stories of revolt from Southern Mexico—Chiapas, Oaxaca and Guerrero—but revolt, both indigenous and nonindigenous, occurs every day across Mexico. The Yaqui indigenous people fought the Spanish nonstop, fought the newly independent Mexican state right up to the Revolution, and have resisted the economic imperialism of the post-revolutionary state up to the present.[64] In the mountains and valleys where the four states of Nayarit, Jalisco, Durango, and Zacatecas meet in western Mexico, the Wixaritari (often called the Huicholes in Spanish and English) have resisted territorial, cultural, linguistic, and religious imperialism for five centuries without a day's rest.[65] As I write these words the Wixaritari have established a permanent assembly on their lands to block a proposed federal highway, saying clearly, "We, the Wixaritari, do not want this progress; we want a respectful relationship with the mother Earth, who is alive."[66]

While covering the Other Campaign in the city of Campeche, I met 66-year-old Emiliano Centurrón. He had never held a microphone before when, to tell his story to a gathering during the Other Campaign, he stood between a crowd of 200 people and Subcomandante Marcos. A subsistence farmer who never went to school, Centurrón cofounded a beekeepers' cooperative in the 1960s and spent the next twenty years working and reinvesting with other small farmers. By the late 1970s Campeche Honey had a processing plant with seventy tanks capable of producing millions of gallons of honey a year. In 1977, the state government offered to loan the co-op $700,000 to purchase storage facilities and cargo trucks. By 1981 the co-op had paid off the principal and was chipping away at the interest when the state government took control of the co-op by force, sold the land and equipment, and cashed in the investments and pensions of 1,200 worker-owners, a sum of around $15 million. Centurrón then spearheaded a twenty-year effort to fight for the stolen life savings. He traveled to Mexico City. He pressured the state treasurer to conduct an audit of the co-op's financial record—which he had meticulously preserved—and thus proved that the state government had cooked the books to take over and sell the co-op. But the government refused to settle. Centurrón turned down blank checks and offers of positions in local government in exchange for dropping the fight. He turned down a settlement offer of paying $300 to each worker-owner. He never gave up.

"I have always preferred to live by my own work, not on the backs of others," Centurrón said. "Those who live in the governor's mansion live on the earnings of the people. For me those sons-of-bitches are not governmental authorities."

Such is the spirit of revolt among Mexico's unconquered.

MEXICO REMAINS UNCONQUERED because after centuries of evolving regimes whose power has always been drawn from violence, the dominating elites have yet to eviscerate the social hunger for a form of governance that rises from humility. The migrants refuse simply to be disposable labor; they take to the streets and derail U.S. legislation. The protesting school-teachers refuse to let children go to school without shoes, and they refuse to take a beating in the street; they come together, turn around, and return the beating, chasing the police out of town. The indigenous refuse to be contained in a colonial discourse that rewrites their own past, a discourse that rationalizes continued violence, racism, and dispossession; they rise up both in arms and in words and subvert the entire premise of the legitimacy of the state. After more than 500 years, Mexico has yet to be fully conquered. New autonomous territories are established, rebels network and connect across the country. New ways of relating to one another free of domination and class control evolve and spread. History is alive, revolt is alive, both maintained through the visceral need to imagine.

Mexico is important to the world—urgent to the United States—for its furious labor in the imagination of utopia—this utopia that rises from the brute will to survive, to at all costs overcome the violence that bears down upon one.[67] The "coordinates of the possible"[68] in Mexico have constantly shut out millions of people, mostly based on divisions of race, sex, and class. Mexicans have tried, time and time again, to push against the coordinates of the possible with nonviolent protest: marches, sit-ins, strikes, and electoral campaigns. And yet, each time, these tactics have led only to the state's response of absolute violence: massacres of marching students in 1968 and 1971; electoral fraud in 1988; massacres of protesting farmers in 1995; the 1997 massacre at Acteal; mass beatings and rape of protesters in Atenco in 2006; and coordinated disappearances, torture, and extrajudicial killings of protesters in Oaxaca in 2006 and 2007. After most of these acts of state repression, new or regrouped guerrilla movements appeared on the scene in Mexico, attacking military camps and, in 2007, national gas pipelines.[69] These acts of armed insurgency are perhaps last-ditch efforts to act *within* the realm of the possible. The utopian, quixotic imaginings of revolt are other: the Zapatista uprising; the reach of the Other Campaign predicated on listening; the women's takeover of the Oaxaca state television station and the mass, popular takeovers of *every radio station in Oaxaca City* within hours of the armed para-police attacks on the occupied television station; a guerrilla *compañera* who ignores aged revolutionary dogmas in order to build peoples' power from below—such acts are the stuff of concrete, urgent, political utopia. And this is what I mean by the word "revolt," both an urgent reimagining and a course of action set through the exploded boundaries of what was thought to be possible.[70]

"Why empire and revolt?" one might ask. "Don't you exaggerate? Why not talk of authoritarian politics and social movements?" Social movements largely operate within the coordinates of the possible, through marches, campaigns, strikes, sit-ins, and the like. Social movements tend to thrive in relatively tolerant, or better yet, flexible states.[71] Under authoritarian regimes, themselves guardians of imperial design, such movements are either co-opted, vanquished through violence, or repressed to the point of forcing them to reimagine the possible, forcing them to deeper revolt.[72]

The decentered empire of capital—composed of states and corporations run by people with names and addresses—depends upon maintaining the fantasy of individual freedom to in turn mask the illegitimacy of its plunder. The field of legitimacy is the first contested territory in revolt. The fantasy of freedom is itself composed of a web of ideological artifacts, and in the case of Mexico these include the "rule of law," poverty, the "search for a better life," and the indigenous past. Many of Mexico's rebels have broken these ideological artifacts apart and stepped beyond the rubble; they have broken the grip of colonial control and the ordained inevitability of their own destitution; they have abandoned the coordinates of the possible and entered the contested territory of legitimacy, and there imagined something different, something other; they have begun the reinvention of utopia and defended their imaginings in the streets. Conquest is not inevitable, injustice is not the lamentable requirement for some so that empire may advance its transcendent mission. This is what the Zapatista rebellion, the Oaxaca uprising, and the profusion of everyday revolt in Mexico tell us: we can counter the attempts of official violence to control us, we can build another realm of possibilities, we can build something else, and the building will begin with recasting everything we thought possible, it will spread to our collective imagination, and from there, woven with the breath of humility and the unbending resolve to fight injustice, we can win. And the underdogs and rebels of Mexico—*los de abajo*—are teaching us what this winning can begin to look like, from the Zapatista good government councils and their "propose, not impose"; to the spontaneous, collective occupation of the media in Oaxaca; to the visionary advice of a guerrilla *compañera*: "Many say that we need to take power, but I think that we need to *build* power from below, and starting now."

ACKNOWLEDGMENTS

EVERY BOOK IS, to some degree, a collective endeavor, and perhaps it is necessary to write one to understand how deep and vital is the community that helps create what appears under an individual's lonely name. Many people have contributed to and helped with this book in myriad ways. What rings true in these pages stems from this community; what falls short is my failing alone.

With deepest gratitude, respect, and solidarity:

Los de abajo: The people of Mexico in the streets and in the fields fighting for their dignity, and thus fighting to rescue human dignity itself from its perverse distortion into denial and complacency.

Global Exchange for the Media Fellowship (2006–2008) that enabled me to report in Mexico throughout 2006—experiences that formed the basis for this book—and enabled me to dedicate time to further research, reporting, and writing throughout 2007 and 2008. Above and beyond the fellowship, GX Human Rights director Ted Lewis has been a source of knowledge, inspiration, and friendship since we met in 1999.

City Lights editor Greg Ruggiero for his vision, belief, encouragement, work, intelligence, and passion, which are woven throughout the text: *va un fuerte abrazo, compa*. It is a brilliant honor to work with Greg, Elaine, Robert, Stacey, Sarah, Maia, and all the amazing people at City Lights Books, a veritable temple to critical thought, social action, and beautiful writing which I enter in awe, with my head deeply bowed.

The community of independent and alternative media fighting to bring in-depth reporting and analysis to the building of a movement, for opening their pages and airwaves to the voices of resistance and revolt in Mexico: Justin Podur and the community at Z Communications who created space for reporting from the Other Campaign when few cared to listen; John Ross, who first suggested to Global Exchange that it send someone along with the Other Campaign (the idea that evolved into a fellowship to cover the campaign for the alternative press) and who has been a source of knowledge and inspiration concerning the Zapatistas ever since I stumbled upon his book *Rebellion from the Roots* in 1996; Al Giordano for often pointing me in the right direction and for consistently publishing what no one else will dare to, and also Nancy Davies and the Narco News team for covering the Oaxaca uprising from day one; filmmaker Jill Freidberg for her excellent reporting, company, and solidarity on the ground in Oaxaca; Mario Viveros y la banda de Canal Seis de Julio; *La Garafona* and its talented crew, Juan, Ramses, Samuel y Hugo, for several thousand miles, fresh coffee, and good conversation; the *Left Turn* collective; Brian Cook and *In These Times*; KPFA and the *Flashpoints* team; KPFK; *Democracy Now!*; WBAI; John Tarleton and *The Indypendent*; *Yes! Magazine*; *New Politics*; Ben Dangle and UpsideDownWorld.com; and *WIN Magazine*.

Small sections of chapters 2, 4, and 6 first appeared, in slightly different form, in *Left Turn*, *Z Magazine*, Znet, and *In These Times*.

El abusado, Diego Osorno, amigo y compañero, con quien compartí muchos de los largos caminos contados aqui.

Ed Allaire and Janet Swaffar, two teachers who believed in teaching college kids how to read and write, no matter how badly it hurt. And after the thesis was in and the letters started arriving, thanks, Ed, for never giving up.

Andy Couturier for his unrelenting, fierce, and joyful love of writing.

My parents for raising me with one foot in the countryside.

Susan for having the strength to hear criticism of what seemed natural, and upon discovering the violence hidden there, for working to change, and for support and faith.

Sheridan for those late-night trips to secondhand bookstores and the long talks at the Back Porch—I miss those.

Catherine and Taylor Marie for unwavering smiles and goodness, with a big jump-hug.

Taylor for our endless journeys to Mecca and the discussions, debate, learning, and laughter they bring; may our journeys be many.

Mis queridísimos amigos y compas, con todo corazón: Vicente, Ada, Mario, Nieves, la memoria de Miguel Mansilla Guevara, Letty, Julio, Amelia, Chaska, Walter, la familia Benhumea, Obtilia y Andrea, Gloria, Eugenia, Maribel y Juan Angulo, Abel y Tlachinollan, Paola, Elizabeth, Ernesto, Hayley, Erb, Drew, Will Lynn, Abel y Gonzalo, Carlos y Enrique, Amyv, Rodrigo, José, Irene, Chris Michael, El Sonrisas, Foxy, Uncle Bergie, Popstar, Val, Cyn, Kirsten, Kevin, Mr. P, Manuel a.k.a. Manolo, Rick, Jacquie, Big Noise, Sabi, Jacopo, Silvia, Los Tíos, Sameera, Damara, Jesse, Juliette, Anna, Deborah, Carleen, Eleuterio, Juanjo, Timo y Luz, Amate Books, Los Cuiles, Café Nuevo Mundo, Amy T, Holly, Susan, Jonathan, Naoko and Kai-kun, Chesley, Hiroko and Yuko, Harumi and Masami, Sandra, Paola, Marta, Miriam, Alisha, Conner, Wenonah, Joe Z, Lin Due and friends at *Terrain*.

Taylor, Ted, Jill, Jonathan, Hector, Andy, Erb, Poppy, and anonymous readers for commenting on early drafts.

Susanna for believing and trusting always.

Diana, con amor: tu puño alzado me acompaña siempre.

NOTES

PROLOGUE: A NATION DIVIDED

1. Details and facts for this sketch of Rubén Jaramillo are taken entirely from Laura Castellanos, *México armado*, 2007, pp. 23–62; Fritz Glockner, *Memoria roja*, 2007, pp. 19–81; and Marco Bellingeri, *Del agrarismo armado a la guerra de los pobres*, 2003, pp. 17–68.

2. Laura Castellanos, *México armado*, 2007, p. 25.

3. Ibid.

4. The description of the assassination is from Carlos Fuentes' article at the time in *Siempre!* magazine, quoted in Laura Castellanos, *México armado*, 2007, pp. 25–26.

5. Fritz Glockner, *Memoria roja*, 2007, p. 77.

6. Bolívar Echeverría, *Vuelta de siglo*, 2006, p. 242, emphasis in original. This and all other translations from the Spanish are my own unless otherwise noted.

7. Diego Osorno. "Acabamos con los pinches nacos." *Milenio.* July 4, 2006.

8. Stephanie Mehta. "The Richest Man in the World." *Fortune.* August 20, 2007, pp. 23–29. Monetary figures are given in U.S. dollars unless otherwise noted.

9. Helen Coster, "Slim's Chance," *Forbes.com*, March 26, 2007, available at www.forbes.com/forbes/2007/0326/134_print.html and Stephanie Mehta, "Carlos Slim: The Richest Man in the World," *Fortune*, August 20, 2007, p. 24.

10. "Las 39 familias más ricas de México," *El Universal*, July 1, 2008.

11. Erik Olin Wright, "Foundations of a Neo-Marxist Class Analysis," in Wright (ed.), *Approaches to Class Analysis*, 2005.

12. See Pierre Bourdieu on forms of symbolic capital: Bourdieu, *Outline of a Theory of Practice*, 1977 and Bourdieu, *Distinction*, 1984.

13. Wright, op. cit.

14. Said, *Culture and Imperialism*, p. 9.

15. See chapter 2.

16. See Al Giordano, "Mexico's Presidential Swindle," 2006.

17. Benedict Anderson, *Imagined Communities*, 2006, and Roger Bartra, *La jaula de la melancolía*, 1987.

18. Slavoj Žižek, *The Sublime Object of Ideology*, 1989, p. 33. "Ideology is not a dreamlike illusion that we build to escape insupportable reality; in its basic dimension it is a fantasy-construction which serves as a support for our 'reality' itself: an 'illusion' which structures our effective, real social relations and thereby masks some insupportable, real, impossible kernel. . . . The function of ideology is not to offer us a point of escape from our reality, but to offer us the social reality itself as an escape from some traumatic, real kernel" (ibid., p. 45).

1. THE HISTORICAL CONTINUITY OF CONQUEST AND REVOLT

1. Alan Riding, *Distant Neighbors*, p. 22.
2. The Triple Alliance was formed by the Aztec, Texcoco, and Tlacopan kings to defeat the Tepanec Empire.
3. Ross Hassig, *Mexico and the Spanish Conquest*, pp. 20–21 and Enrique Semo and Enrique Nalda, *México, un pueblo en la historia*, pp. 72–72.
4. Hassig, pp. 23–24 and Semo and Nalda, pp. 97–107.
5. Hassig, p. 25 and Alan Knight, *Mexico: From the Beginning to the Spanish Conquest*, p. 141.
6. Semo and Nalda, p. 109.
7. Knight, pp. 141–142 and Hassig, pp. 25–26.
8. Knight, pp. 143–145; Hassig, pp. 26–27 and Semo and Nalda, pp. 118–120.
9. Semo and Nalda, pp. 122–123 and Knight, p. 177.
10. Hassig, pp. 27, 34–35.
11. Hassig, p. 38.
12. Knight, pp. 148–151.
13. Knight, pp. 152–155.
14. The English, Spanish and French executed roughly twice the number of people, each, as the Aztecs, Charles C. Mann, *1491*, pp. 133–134.
15. Knight, pp. 152–161.
16. Knight, p. 154. Knight writes: "Aztec gods served as allies, succoured by sacrifice, who contested the inexorable destructive forces—an Aztec anticipation of the astrophysicist's entropy, according to one imaginative analysis—which ceaselessly threatened man and the universe."
17. Semo and Nalda, pp. 127–128.
18. Semo and Nalda, p. 122 and Knight, p. 174.
19. Knight, pp. 190–191.
20. Ibid.
21. Tzuetan Todorov, *The Conquest of America*, p. 11.
22. Ibid., p. 133.
23. James D. Cockcroft, *Mexico's Hope*, pp. 19, 21.
24. Ibid., p. 20.
25. Todorov, op. cit., pp. 34–50 and 129–130. Todorov writes: "Cortés goes into ecstasies about the Aztec productions but does not acknowledge their makers

as human individuals to be set on the same level as himself" (ibid., p. 129). Montezuma famously mistook the Spaniards for gods, also failing to acknowledge their humanity, though this was quite different from the Spaniards' treatment of the indigenous as animals, or worse. Moreover, the Indians' misapprehension of the Spaniards' nature did not last long (while racism against the Indians continues). In the words of a Mayan chronicle of the conquest: "Those who die are those who do not understand; those who live will understand it" (ibid., p. 77).

26. "When Cortés must express his opinion on Indian slavery (as he does in a memorandum addressed to Charles V), he envisages the problem only from one point of view, that of the profitability of the enterprise; it is never a question of what the Indians, for their part, might want (not being subjects, they have no desires)" (ibid., p. 130).

27. Ibid., p. 137.

28. Ibid., p. 139.

29. Friedrich Katz, *Revuelta, rebelión, y revolución*, 2004; Cockcroft, pp. 35–40; Brian R. Hamnett, *A Concise History of Mexico*, pp. 104–106; and Leticia Reina, *Las rebeliones campesinas en Mexico*, 1996.

30. Hamnett, *A Concise History of Mexico*, pp. 83–84.

31. Cockcroft, pp. 39–40.

32. Anna Macías, *Against all Odds*, pp. 4–5.

33. Jean Franco, *Plotting Women*, 1989.

34. Cockcroft, pp. 12 and 34.

35. The following brief summary of Mexican economic history is paraphrased from Semo, *Historia mexicana*, 28–69. All translations are my own. See also, Semo, *Historia del capitalismo en México*, González Casanova, *La Democracia en México*, and Cockcroft, chapters 1–4.

36. "Producing mainly cotton and woolen textiles . . . the *obrajes* concentrated laborers in sweatshop conditions. . . . The tendency in most places was toward the concentration of production under one roof (manufacturing) and toward centralized control by *obraje* owners of the merchant bourgeoisie, often one and the same. . . . The typical owner of an *obraje* was a Spanish settler (or his descendants) who had other economic interests, usually as a merchant. . . ." Cockcroft, p. 30.

37. Semo, *Historia mexicana*, 29. The original Spanish uses the present tense.

38. Ibid., p. 51.

39. Cockcroft, p. 55.

40. Semo, *Historia mexicana*, pp.161–199.

41. See the discussions in chapters 4 and 8 for more analysis of United States imperialism in Mexico.

42. Friedrich Katz, *La servidumbre agraria en Mexico*, p. 49.

43. Severo Iglesias, *Juárez*, 2006.

44. "It fell to Juárez to create the first strong image of the presidency as an *institution* of power that was truly above the fray, and his strategy was to present

himself as a complex embodiment of the meeting between the nation and the law." Claudio Lomnitz, *Deep Mexico, Silent Mexico*, p. 95.

45. Riding, p. 39.

46. "Under PRI rule there had always been murderous violence at the bottom of the system, in the farming villages and the city slums, but not at the top. The PRI's commitment to national 'social peace' was one of the few that the system consistently kept" (Julia Preston and Samuel Dillin, *Opening Mexico*, p. 231). The concept of stability is argued from the reference point of the State, and precisely where it entails the repression of resistance, it sanctions and legitimizes that violence in the same stroke. In the above quote the writers, both former *New York Times* correspondents in Mexico, fall into the daze of equating "social peace" with the norm of "murderous violence at the bottom." Shall we look any further for a clearer example of class bias in the U.S. media? Political stability, itself a euphemism today for unhindered cartel markets and political monopoly, plays the role of forced conversion that during early colonial times involved Christians announcing the benevolent actions required to save the savage's soul—massacre, rape, land theft, forced labor. Now state officials proclaim forced conversion to the ideology of the "rule of law," which is only another involuntary liberation predicated on massacre, rape, land theft, and forced labor.

47. Porfirio Díaz built the imposing stone statue of Cuauhtémoc—emblem of indigenous resistance to Spanish colonialism—in Mexico City while he promoted the raiding of indigenous lands, dispossessing millions and forcing them into debt peonage. There is no contradiction here: the past too is colonized territory. With their statues of Aztec warriors the "moderns" say, "Your past is our past; we share this as we share our national identity—you cannot overcome us, or do away with us, because we are you, things are as they should be, our shared past is our shared present, our shared future—we are forever locked in the position of conqueror and conquered." Through this colonization of the past the "moderns" open and control the territory of shared national identity. The ideology of nationalism in Mexico is a tool of colonialism.

48. Beatriz Urías Horcasitas, *Historias secretas del racismo en México*, p. 15.

49. Eric Wolf, *Peasant Wars of the Twentieth Century*, p. 14.

50. Alan Knight, "Racism, Revolution, and *Indigenismo*," pp. 78–80.

51. As historian John Womack puts it: "No important politicking had gone on in Mexico for over thirty years without Díaz involving himself in it," (Womack, *Zapata*, 11). Díaz's slogan was, "poca política y mucha administración." A hundred years later this ideology would take root in institutions like the World Bank bent on carrying out economic colonialism under the guise of poverty alleviation. See Arturo Escobar, *Encountering Development*, 1995, and James Ferguson, *The Anti-Politics Machine*, 1994.

52. Cockcroft, p. 86; Hamnett, p. 177; and Womack, p. 15. For a short and gripping account of the impact of railroad construction in the U.S. West, see Marc Reisner, *A Dangerous Place*, 2003.

53. Dan La Botz, *Democracy in Mexico*, p. 45, and Hamnett, p. 182.

54. Katz, *La servidumbre agraria en México*, pp. 9 and 13 and Adolfo Gilly, *La revolución interrumpida*, p. 9.

55. Ibid. A similar pattern of raiding indigenous lands, writing fanciful and colonial laws, pushing capitalist development, and forcing the absurd concentration of land ownership took place in California during this time. See Robert Fellmeth, *Politics of Land*, 1972, and Donald J. Pisani, *Water, Land, and Law in the West*, 1996.

56. Womack, p. 18.

57. Ibid.

58. Ibid., p. 49.

59. From *Regeneración*, September 3 and October 8, 1910, cited in Cockcroft, p. 96. See also ibid., pp. 91–92.

60. Ibid., pp. 4–6 and 62–66.

61. Roger Bartra writes: ". . . the Revolution was an explosion of myths, the most important of which was that of the Revolution itself. The revolutionary myths were not, as in other nations, built on the biographies of heroes and tyrants, but rather over the idea of a fusion between the masses and the State, between the *Mexican* people and the *revolutionary* government. . . . National culture is identified with political power to such an extent that whomsoever would wish to break the rules of authoritarianism will be immediately accussed of renouncing—or, worse: betraying the national culture" (*La juala de la melancolía*, p. 227, emphasis in original).

62. Womack, p. 55 and La Botz, *Democracy in Mexico*, p. 46.

63. Womack, pp. 10–11 and 54–55.

64. Hamnett, pp. 199–200.

65. La Botz, *Democracy in Mexico*, 47.

66. Womack, pp. 67–89.

67. Ibid., p. 96 and, more generally, chapters 3 and 4. Of Madero and his clique, Womack writes: "Few revolutions have been planned, carried out, and won by men so uniformly obsessed with the continuity of legal order as the high Maderistas of 1910–1911. There seems to have been nothing they cared more about than preserving regular forms and routines. Díaz's regime, like his character, fascinated them. . . ." (ibid., p. 90).

68. From the Plan de Ayala, translated in Womack, ibid., p. 402.

69. John Mason Hart, *Revolutionary Mexico*, pp. 364–365.

70. Hamnett, pp. 203–207.

71. Tutino, *From Insurrection to Revolution in Mexico*, 338–339.

72. Hart, pp. 366–367.

73. Ibid., p. 367.

74. Ibid., p. 368.

75. John Tutino, pp. 338–340. Article 27 was later gutted by Carlos Salinas to meet requirements of U.S. negotiators for the North American Free Trade Agreement.

76. Cockcroft, p. 106.

77. Womack, pp. 322–330.
78. Cockcroft, pp. 106–107.
79. Gilly and Gilly, et al. *Interpretaciones de la Revolución Mexicana*, pp. 50–51.
80. Cockcroft, pp. 114–120, Hamnett, pp. 218–226, and Tutino, pp. 343–346.
81. Cockcroft, pp. 118–119.
82. Arnaldo Córdova, *La política de masas y el futuro de la izquierda en México*, pp. 10–13. Two probing studies on Cárdenas and his legacy are Córdova, *La política de masas del cardenismo*, 1974 and Gilly, *El cardenismo, una utopia mexicana*, 1994.
83. Cockcroft, pp. 122–125.
84. Ibid., pp. 128–133 and Hamnett, p. 232.
85. La Botz, *Democracy in Mexico*, pp. 58–59.
86. See Alan Knight, "Historical Continuities in Social Movements," pp. 78–102 in Joe Foweraker and Ann L. Craig, eds., *Popular Movements and Political Change in Mexico*, 1990.
87. Luis González de Alba, *Los días y los años*, 1971, and Elena Poniatowska, *La noche de Tlatelolco*, 1997.
88. Only three years after the massacre, on June 10, 1971, police, soldiers, and government-trained thugs attacked and again massacred students during a peaceful march in Mexico City. See the recent documentary and exposé on government involvement in the massacre by Canal 6 de Julio, *Halcones*, 2006.
89. One of the best accounts of the Cabañas guerrilla movement is Carlos Montemayor's amazing historical novel *Guerra en el Paraíso*, 1991. Also, see the recent documentary by Gerardo Tort, *La guerrilla y la esperanza: Lucio Cabañas*, 2007.
90. A number of books exploring the Dirty War and armed movements have been published in Mexico recently, see: Laura Castellanos, *México armado*, 2007; Fritz Glockner, *Memoria roja*, 2007; Marco Bellingeri, *Del agrarismo armado a la guerra de los pobres*, 2003; and Solano et al., *Movimientos armados en México*, 2006.
91. Vivienne Bennett, "The Evolution of Urban Popular Movements in Mexico Between 1968 and 1988," in Arturo Escobar and Sonia E. Álvarez, *The Making of Social Movements in Latin America*, 1992.
92. La Botz, *Mask of Democracy*, 1992, and Maria Elena Cook, *Organizing Dissent*, 1990.
93. Marta Lamas, *Feminismo*, 2006, pp. 13–22.
94. Preston and Dillon, pp. 97–98.
95. Ibid., p. 103.
96. Ibid., pp. 106–107.
97. Carlos Monsiváis, *"No sin nosotros"*, 2005.
98. La Botz, *Democracy in Mexico*, pp. 83–94.
99. A gripping account of the 1988 electoral fraud in English is Preston and Dillon, pp. 149–180.
100. La Botz, *Democracy in Mexico*, p. 16.

2. THE RULE OF LAW

1. Photograph by Carlos Tomás Cabrera published on page 9 of *Proceso*, No. 1595, May 27, 2007. The Spanish original is: "Por hacer una llamada anonima a las autoridades me paso esto: y ellos mismos me pusieron" (*sic*).

2. On Saturday, May 26, 2007, a group of men in a Jeep Cherokee delivered a refrigerator to the front door of the newspaper *Tabasco Hoy*. In the refrigerator the newspaper's security guards found the head of Terencio Sastré Hidalgo, a farmer who had called the authorities. "Dejan en *Tabasco Hoy* cabeza de delegado ejidal; directivos del diario exigen seguridad." *La Jornada*, May 27, 2007, p. 7.

3. Photographs of the severed heads in Acapulco were widely published. The Acapulco-based newspaper *El Sur* ran two photographs by Gonzalo Pérez on pages 1 and 3 on April 21, 2006. The Spanish original is: "Para que aprendan a respetar."

4. Ricardo Ravelo, *Herencia maldita*, p. 22.

5. Roberto López, "De un vistazo," *Milenio*. July 2, 2007, p. 39.

6. Vicente Hernández. "Reconoce PFP 2,794 ejecuciones." *Milenio*. January 12, 2008, p. 25.

7. Maria Cecila Toro, "The Political Repercussions of Drug Trafficking in Mexico," pp. 131–145. The United States not only provides the market for illegal drugs that come from or through Mexico, but it also supplies the drug cartels with their incredible array of automatic weapons. See Louis E. V. Nevaer, "American Guns Help Fuel Mexico's Drug Trade Killings," *San Francisco Chronicle*. July 15, 2007, p. D4.

8. Ricardo Ravelo, *Los Capos*, pp. 85–94.

9. Carlos Monsiváis, *Viento rojo*, pp. 139–140.

10. Official involvement in the illegal drug industry is not limited to Mexico; the United States has its own dark history there. Charles Bowden's *Down by the River: Drugs, Money, Murder, and Family* shows how the U.S. Department of Justice stonewalls investigations that might reach too high into Mexican government involvement in the drug trade (for example, pp. 152 and 198–199). See also Gary Webb, *Dark Alliance: The CIA, the Contras, and the Crack Cocaine Explosion*, 1998.

11. Ricardo Ravelo, *Herencia maldita*, 2007. Several *New York Times* correspondents won the Pulitzer Prize for International Reporting in 1998 for a series of articles on government involvement with drug mafias in Mexico. The articles are archived on the Pulitzer Web site: http://www.pulitzer.org. Two of the correspondents, Julia Preston and Samuel Dillon, provide an overview of drug trafficking and government involvement in *Opening Mexico*, pp. 323–352.

12. Ricardo Ravelo, "Se llaman *Los Zetas* y aquí están." *Proceso* No. 1595, May 27, 2007.

13. Ibid., p. 9 and George W. Grayson. "Los Zetas: A Ruthless Army Spawned by a Cartel." *The News*, May 26, 2008, p. 4.

14. Ricardo Ravelo, *Herencia maldita*, p. 20.

15. Manuel Roig-Franzia, "Mexican Drug Cartels Move North," *Washington Post*, September 20, 2007, p. A14.

16. Bowden, *Down by the River*, p. 3. The same study found that the U.S. economy would shrink by 19 to 22 percent without the drug business.

17. "Fox Facts: Mexico's Drug Trade," Fox News, March 14, 2007. Available at www.foxnews.com/story/0,2933,258702,00.html.

18. Alex Sanchez, "Mexico's Drug War: A Society at Risk—Soldiers versus Narco Soldiers." Washington: The Council on Hemispheric Affairs, May 22, 2007.

19. Charles Bowden writes, "The key thing about the War on Drugs is that the war never occurs, there are simply skirmishes dictated from time to time by political needs within the United States and Mexico. The second thing is that drugs threaten power more than people. The money, whatever its amounts, goes to feed the basic hungers we call capitalism. The violence, whatever its oscillations, mainly kills people in the business, either drug merchants or the police who feed off them. The only matter seriously altered is power, because the new source of money creates new men with money." *Down by the River*, 2004, p. 136.

20. Ravelo, *Los Capos*, 2004, and Ravelo, *Herencia maldita*, 2007.

21. Julia Preston. "Mexico's Jailed Anti-Drug Chief Had Complete Briefings in U.S." *The New York Times*, February 19, 1997; Preston and Dillon; and, for a profile of Carrillo Fuentes, Bowden, *Down by the River*, 2004. Rebollo is now in prison.

22. Alma Guillermoprieto, *Looking for History*, p. 182.

23. Ibid., p. 183.

24. Ibid., pp. 182–183.

25. Luis Estrada. *La ley de Herodes*. Bandidos Films, 1999. For information about the film: www.laleydeherodes.com. Watch this film; it is genius.

26. The original quote in Spanish: "Con el librito y la pistola, a ejercer la autoridad."

27. Some names have been changed by request of those interviewed for their security.

28. A personal aside: while covering the unarmed uprising in Oaxaca from July through December 2006, I was stopped and questioned several times by federal police. They seemed eager to catch a foreigner playing journalist without the proper visa. I had the proper visa. One time, after the massive November 25 smackdown, federal preventive police (PFP) stopped me at a checkpoint. It was me and my camera facing about fifty cops with machine guns on the corner of a narrow colonial street. A commander stepped forward and asked me what I do. I thought I would play tough and remind him that only immigration authorities had the right to ask such questions to foreigners. The commander pointed to his PFP baseball cap and said: "I am a federal police officer, I can ask you whatever the hell I feel like asking you." I said, "Ah, okay, I'm a journalist" and handed over my visa.

29. I do not mean to make light of the risky and important work of documentation conducted by human rights organizations. Such work is essential, but not enough on its own.

30. Human Rights Watch. "Mexico," in *World Report 2007*. New York: Human Rights Watch, 2007. Available at: hrw.org/englishwr2k7/docs/2007/01/11/mexico14885.htm.

31. Amnesty International. "Mexico: Unfair trials: unsafe convictions." March, 23, 2003.

32. Amnesty International. *Mexico: Laws without justice: Human rights violations and impunity in the public security and criminal justice system*. Washington D.C.: Amnesty International, 2007.

33. Ibid.

34. The historian Edward Peters (*Torture, 1999*) provides a compelling argument linking the resurgence of torture in the twentieth century to the internal imperial practices in modern states.

35. See Peters, *Torture*, 1999 edition, citations from pp. 137–138. For studies on the uses of torture in Algeria see Rita Mann, *Torture*, 1989, and Jean-Paul Sartre, *Colonialism and Neocolonialism*, 2006 edition; on Brazil and Uruguay see Lawrence Weschler, *A Miracle, a Universe*, 1990; on Chile and other Southern Cone countries see Ronald D. Crelinsten and Alex P. Schmid, *The Politics of Pain*, 1993; on Argentina see Marguerite Feitlowitz, *A Lexicon of Terror*, 1998; on Israel see Stanley Cohen, "Talking About Torture in Israel," *Tikkun*, 1991, 6(6): 23–30, 89–90; and for the United States see Mark Danner, *Torture and Truth*, 2004.

36. Herbert C. Kelman, "The Policy Context of Torture," 2005, pp. 125–126.

37. Ibid, pp. 128–129, emphasis in original.

38. Elaine Scarry, *The Body in Pain*, 1985, p. 27.

39. Ibid, pp. 28 and 35.

40. "It is not primarily the victim's information, but the victim, that torture needs to win—or reduce to powerlessness" (Peters, *Torture*, p. 164). "In compelling confession, the torturers compel the prisoner to record and objectify the fact that intense pain is world-destroying. It is for this reason that while the content of the prisoner's answer is only sometimes important to the regime, the form of the answer, the fact of his answering, is always crucial" (Scarry, *The Body in Pain*, 29).

41. The United Nations Convention Against Torture went into effect in Mexico on June 26, 1987, and thus became a formal part of Mexican law. See Elma del Carmen Trejo García, *Tratados internacionales vigentes en México: relación en Legislaturas y/o períodos Legislativos en que fueron aprobados*. Mexico City: Servicio de Investigación y Análisis Subdirección de Política Exterior, February 2007, p. 274.

42. Analyses of this aspect of the Mexican legal system abound. For example, see Human Rights Watch, *Lost in Transition*, 2006. Available at hrw.org/reports/2006/mexico0506/5.htm#_Toc134005759.

43. Ibid., footnote 307.

44. Ibid., footnote 268.

45. Michele Heisler MD, MPA and Alejandro Moreno, MD, MPH; Sonya DeMonner, MPH; Allen Keller, MD; Vincent Iacopino, MD, PhD, "Assessment of Torture and Ill Treatment of Detainees in Mexico Attitudes and Experiences of Forensic Physicians." *The Journal of the American Medical Association*, Vol. 289 No. 16, 2135–2143, April 23, 2003.

46. National Human Rights Commission (CNDH), General Recommendation 10, November 2005.

47. U.S. Department of State, "Mexico: Country Reports on Human Rights Practices, 2006." Available at www.state.gov/g/drl/rls/hrrpt/2006/78898.htm.

48. "Fitzjames Stephen observed that during the preparation of the Indian code of Criminal Procedure in 1872, there was some discussion about the Indian Police's habit of torturing prisoners: during the discussion a colonial civil servant remarked: 'There is a great deal of laziness in it. It is far pleasanter to sit comfortably in the shade rubbing red pepper into a poor devil's eyes than to go about in the sun hunting up evidence.'" (Quoted in Peters, *Torture*, p. 136.) Notice how the worn racist stereotype of the lazy native finds its way even into a colonialists' explanation of the practice of torture!

49. This, again, is the tale told in the brilliant film *La ley de Herodes*, where Vargas is himself molded by the preexisting relations of authority into becoming an authoritarian tyrant who, in order to survive, must surpass his predecessors in the scale and intensity of his brutality, including the use of torture to extract false confessions.

50. This section is based on personal experience and extensive interviews with participants, witnesses, and other reporters. See Comisión Civil Internacional de Observación por los Derechos Humanos, *Informe preliminary sobre los hechos de Atenco, México, 2006*.

51. Information for the preceding four paragraphs is drawn from: Manuel Roig-Franzia, "In Juarez, Expiring Justice," *Washington Post*: May 14, 2007, A10; Emanuella Grinberg, "In Juárez murders, progress but few answers," *CNN Court TV*: April 9, 2004; Evelyn Nieves, "To Work and Die in Juarez," *Mother Jones*: May/June 2002; Max Blumenthal, "Day of the Dead," *Salon.com*: December 4, 2002; Laurie Freeman, "Still Waiting for Justice: Shortcomings in Mexico's efforts to End Impunity for Murders of Girls and Women in Ciudad Juárez and Chihuahua," May 2006; and Luis Ignacio Velásquez, "Oaxaca primer lugar en feminicidios," *Noticias de Oaxaca*: June 1, 2007. See also Rodriguez et al., *The Daughters of Juárez*, 2007.

52. Laurie Freeman, "Still Waiting for Justice: Shortcomings in Mexico's efforts to End Impunity for Murders of Girls and Women in Ciudad Juárez and Chihuahua," *Washington Office on Latin America*, May 2006.

53. Freeman, ibid., and Evelyn Nieves, "To Work and Die in Juarez," *Mother Jones*, May/June 2002

54. Amnesty International, *Intolerable Killings*, 2003, and CEDAW, *Report on Mexico*, 2005.

55. Rubén Villalpando, "Hallan otra mujer asesinada en Ciudad Juárez," *La Jornada*, May 27, 2007, p. 18.

3. THE GULF

1. Much excellent work has been written on the construction of the ideology of development economics and the structure of plunder. See Eduardo Galeano, *Las venas abiertas de América Latina*; Arturo Escobar, *Encountering Development*; and Rahnema "Poverty," in Wolfgang Sachs, *The Development Dictionary*; on the creation of the World Bank and its ideological foundations, see Bruce Rich, *Mortgaging the Earth*.

2. Jeffrey D. Sachs, *The End of Poverty*, pp. i, 1 and 2.

3. I refrain from using the author's name in the text to avoid personalizing my analysis of the ideology of poverty in his book, and also because I treat his text as representative of an economics-based worldview that, I believe, underlies contemporary economic imperialism.

4. This idea is also at the heart of Marx's theory: "In actual history, it is a notorious fact that conquest, enslavement, robbery, murder, in short, force, play the greatest part" in the development of the institution of private property and the accumulation of wealth (Marx, *Capital*, p. 874).

5. Frantz Fanon, *The Wretched of the Earth*, p. 53.

6. Galeano, pp. 16–17, emphasis in original.

7. Semo, *Historia mexicana: Economía y lucha de clases*, pp. 29–30.

8. Indeed, even Adam Smith got this much right. Noam Chomsky quotes Smith: "But it was possible for an honest eye to see what had taken place. 'The discovery of America . . . certainly made a most essential' contribution to the 'state of Europe,' Smith wrote, 'opening up a new and inexhaustible market' that led to vast expansion of 'productive powers' and 'real revenue and wealth.'" Chomsky, *Year 501*, p. 4.

9. Ward Churchill, *A Little Matter of Genocide*, 1998.

10. A slight rephrasing of the following quote from Edward Said: ". . . in so globalizing a world-view as that of imperialism, there could be no neutrality: one was either on the side of empire or against it. . . ." from *Culture and Imperialism*, p. 279.

11. Semo, *Historia mexicana: Economía y lucha de clases*, p. 37.

12. Ibid., p. 51.

13. Cockcroft, p. 44.

14. For a description (first published in 1965) of the dynamic of internal colonialism in Mexico, see Gonzalez-Casanova, pp. 103–108.

15. Cockcroft, p. 81.

16. González-Casanova, p. 92.

17. Judith Adler Hellman, *Mexican Lives*, p. 1, see also Cockcroft, p. 156.

18. Hellman, p. 2.

19. Ibid., pp. 7–9.

20. Hamnett, p. 269.
21. Apologies to W. H. Auden (*Collected Poems*, p. 247).
22. Riding, p. 378.
23. David Luhnow, "The Secrets of the World's Richest Man," *Wall Street Journal*, August 4, 2007, p. A1.
24. Preston and Dillon, p. 249.
25. Between 1993 and 2002, about 2 million farmers left their land: Jeff Faux, *Global Class War*, p. 134. Between 1994 and 2000, the poverty rate rose from about 45 to over 50 percent: Faux, p. 139. By 2005, 3.3 million children were forced to work: Zósimo Camacho, "Clasificación de la pobreza extrema." *Contralínea*, 5, no. 75 (March 2007), p. 25.
26. The information in this paragraph comes from Luhnow; Helen Coster, "Slim's Chance," *Forbes.com*, March 3, 2007, available at www.forbes.com/forbes/2007/0326/134_print.html; and Stephanie N. Mehta, "Carlos Slim, the richest man in the world," *Fortune*, August 6, 2007, available at money.cnn.com/2007/08/03/news/international/carlosslim.fortune/index.htm.
27. Luhnow.
28. Ibid.
29. Consejo Nacional de Población, *Índices de marginación, 2005*, p. 56.
30. The following section is composed both from personal experience in Guerrero and Chiapas states and, in its majority, from information and interviews published in an outstanding series of articles on contemporary "poverty" in Mexico published by the investigative journalism magazine *Contralínea*, 5, nos. 75–83, published between March and August 2007. All of the articles are also available online at: www.contralinea.com.mx. The writers of the series are Ana Lilia Pérez, Nancy Flores, Nydia Egremy, Paulina Monroy, and Zósimo Camacho. The photographers: David Cilia, Julio César Hernández, and Rubén Darío Betancourt.
31. When Cilia and Camacho arrived, after a five-hour walk, at the villages they asked: "Are there families here with relatives who are ill?" The people responded: "Every family has sick people." Camacho asked: "When was the last time you ate meat?" A group of men and boys looked at each other, hesitant, and then burst out laughing: they could not remember.
32. For those who think that I am going overboard with all this talk of contemporary imperialism, it is worth pointing out that many U.S. politicians and political theorists *themselves* use the word imperialism or various substitutes to outline their policy proscriptions. William Easterly, former World Bank economist and now economics professor at New York University, provides a good overview and introductory bibliography (in the endnotes) to these "postmodern imperialists" in chapter 8 of his book *The White Man's Burden*. Here is a taste: "Harvard historian Niall Ferguson, whose work on every topic but this one I greatly admire, says that 'there is such a thing as liberal imperialism and that on balance it was a good thing. . . . In many cases of economic 'backwardness' a liberal empire can do better than a nation-state" (p. 271). Stephen

Krasner, appointed "to be head of policy planning at the State Department on February 4, 2005" (p. 270), wrote in *Foreign Affairs* a year before his appointment: "Left to their own devices, collapsed and badly governed states will not fix themselves because they have limited administrative capacity, not least with regard to maintaining internal security. Occupying powers cannot escape choices about what new governance structures will be created and sustained. To reduce international threats and improve the prospects for individuals in such polities, alternative institutional arrangements supported by external actors, such as de facto trusteeships and shared sovereignty, should be added to the list of policy options" (p. 270).

4. THE HEIST

1. While I exclusively discuss Mexico, the argument here would only be made stronger and more urgent by bringing Central American and even many South American countries into the discussion. For a devastating report (and powerful photographs) on the trials of Central American workers economically evicted from their homes as they travel through Mexico, see Sonia Nazario, *Enrique's Journey*, 2007.
2. For recent reports on the experience of crossing the U.S.-Mexico border see Joseph Nevins, *Dying to Live*, 2008; Rubén Martínez, *Crossing Over*, 2001; and John Annerino, *Dead in Their Tracks*, 1999.
3. "The Border Patrol captured 695,841 people nationwide in the first three quarters of fiscal year 2007, down from 907,445 for the same period the previous fiscal year. . . ." edition.cnn.com/2007/US/07/06/border.arrests/index .html.
4. The state of Guanajuato expels more people than any other: over 43,000 leave the state every year for the United States. The numbers all come from the Mexican *Consejo Nacional de Población* (CONAPO). See: www.conapo.gob.mx/ mig-int/series/070104.xls. There are an estimated 9,752,600 refugees and asylum seekers in Africa. See www.unhcr.org/basics.html.
5. Raúl Delgado Wise, "Migration and Imperialism," p. 40.
6. Raúl Delgado Wise, migration expert at the University of Zacatecas, writes that "migration constitutes a loss of valuable economic resources and the export of potential wealth." Ibid., p. 40.
7. Hamnett, *A Concise History of Mexico*, p. 150.
8. John Mason Hart, *Empire and Revolution*.
9. Ibid., pp. 432–442.
10. Robert E. Scott and David Ratner, "NAFTA's Cautionary Tale"; Gómez Cruz and Rindermann, "NAFTA's Impact on Mexican Agriculture"; Picard, "NAFTA in Mexico: Promises, Myths, and Realities"; Faux, *The Global Class War*; and Juan Manuel Sandoval, "Mexican Labor Migration and the North American Free Trade Agreement."

11. See Papademetriou, "The Shifting Expectations of Free Trade and Migration," e.g., pp. 40 and 44.
12. Delgado Wise, p. 33.
13. Sandoval, pp. 23 and 25.
14. This section is based on interviews and reporting carried out in Zacatecas during January and February 2008. For in-depth further reading, see: Justin Akers Chacón and Mike Davis, *No One is Illegal*, 2006; Gilbert G. González, *Guest Workers or Colonized Labor?*, 2006; Victor Ronquillo, *Migrantes de la pobreza*, 2007; Rafael Fernández de Castro and Rodolfo García Zamora, Roberta Clariod Rangel and Ana Vila Freyer, eds. *Las políticas migratorias en los estados de México. Una evaluación.* Mexico City: Miguel Ángel Porrúa, 2007; and Stephen Castles and Raúl Delgado Wise, *Migración y desarrollo*, 2007. See also the Autonomous University of Zacatecas-based Migration and Development group's excellent electronic archive in Spanish and English available online at www.migracionydesarrollo.org.
15. This section is based on interviews and reporting conducted in Nogales, Altar, and Sasabe in Sonora, Mexico, on October 16–19, 2007.
16. See Oscar Martínez, "Un pueblo en el camino a la frontera" *Gatopardo*, No. 84 (October 2007), pp. 36–49. Also, on Altar, see Eileen Traux, "Altar, la nueva ruta de los migrantes," *La Opinión Digital*, June 19, 2006.
17. Oscar Martínez, p. 45.
18. Ibid.

5. THE OAXACA UPRISING

1. This chapter is drawn from over six months of on-the-ground reporting in Oaxaca from July through December 2006, and again in March, June, and August 2007. Nancy Davies covered the Oaxaca uprising from day one for NarcoNews.com, and her reporting has been published by Narco News Books in *The People Decide: Oaxaca's Popular Assembly*, 2007. For Spanish-language books on the events, see the book by Oaxaca-based sociologist and expert on Section 22 Victor Raúl Martínez Vásquez, *Autoritarismo, movimiento popular, y crisis política*, 2007; also national correspondent for *Milenio* Diego Osorno's *Oaxaca Sitiada*, 2007; the International Civil Commission for Human Rights Observation's *Informe sobre los hechos de Oaxaca*, 2007; and the edited collection of essays and articles, Carlos Beas Torres, *La Batalla por Oaxaca*, 2007.
2. Martínez Vásquez, pp. 16–19.
3. On the history of the teachers' movement see Cook, *Organizing Dissent*, 1996, and the documentary films by Jill Freidberg of Corrugate Films: *Granito de Arena*, 2004, and *A Little Bit of So Much Truth*, 2007.
4. See Diego Osorno's *Oaxaca Sitiada*, 2007, for a well-reported inside scoop on Ruiz's threat.

5. Diego Osorno reports on the composition of Ulises Ruiz's death squads in "Ulises Ruiz creó su propia brigada blanca," *Milenio*, May 1, 2008.

6. RECLAIMING INDIGENOUS AUTONOMY

1. There is an amazing wealth of writing by and about the Zapatista Army of National Liberation available in dozens of languages. A recent select bibliography of articles and books is over 300 pages long (Gordillo y Ortiz, 2006). The Zapatistas' own writings have been translated into English and are readily available on the Internet (flag.blackened.net/revolt/mexico/ezlnco.html) and in collections (Marcos, *Shadows of Tender Fury*, 1995; *Our Word is Our Weapon, The Other Campaign*, 2006; and *The Speed of Dreams*, 2007); they have also been collected in a five-volume series published in Mexico by Ediciones Era and are available on a CD ROM published by *Rebeldía* magazine, titled *EZLN: 20 y 10, El fuego y la palabra*. Most of these writings were first published in Mexico in *La Jornada* and *Proceso* and are available in their archives. Excellent compilations of chronicles and essays are available in English (*First World, Ha Ha Ha!*, 1995, and *The Zapatista Reader*, 2002). John Ross has chronicled the Zapatista uprising nonstop since 1994 (*Rebellion from the Roots*, 1995; *The War Against Oblivion*, 2001; and *¡Zapatistas!*, 2006). *La Jornada* and the web magazine *Narco News* (www.narconews.com) reported the Other Campaign from day one. The retelling of the Zapatista uprising in this chapter draws from these works and from speeches made by Subcomandante Marcos during the first leg of the Other Campaign (January 1–May 3, 2006).

2. Communiqué from January 11, 1994, reprinted in *Shadows of Tender Fury*, pp. 62–64.

3. Blanche Petrich y Henríquez Elio, "Entrevista al Sub comandante Marcos," *La Jornada*, February 7, 1994.

4. "First Declaration of the Lacandón Jungle," reprinted in *Shadows of Tender Fury*, pp. 51–54. Note that, in contrast, the U.S. government has never invited the International Red Cross to observe and regulate combat or declared itself subject to the Geneva Convention, much less abided by the laws of war in waging its recent invasions abroad, nor has the Mexican Army in its decades of counterinsurgency, so-called "low-intensity warfare," in southern Mexico.

5. Originally reported in the London *Guardian* on January 5, 1994, quoted in Tello, 1995–2006, p. 19.

6. "Drug Control: Counter-narcotics efforts in Mexico," Government Accounting Office Report, June 15, 1996, n. 5. Available online at www.gao.gov/archive/1996/ns96163.pdf. Quoted in Nick Henck, 2007, p. 218.

7. From the testimony of an army captain sent to Chiapas who later sought political asylum in the United States after giving testimony. Quoted in Henck, p. 424, n. 27.

8. Communiqué dated January 18, 1994, reprinted in Marcos, *Shadows of Tender Fury*, pp. 80–82.

9. Quoted in Mann, *1491*, p. 9.

10. Ibid.

11. Ibid, p. 10.

12. Ibid.

13. One commentator on Holmberg's book wrote that Holmberg had, "discovered, described, and introduced into history a new and in many respects extraordinary Paleolithic experience." (Quoted in Mann, *1491*, p. 413, n. 8.)

14. Semo, *Historia mexicana*, p. 37.

15. Knight, *Racism, Revolution, and* Indigenismo: *Mexico, 1910–1940*, p. 72.

16. Ibid., p. 78.

17. Ibid., pp. 78–79.

18. Katz, *La servidumbre agraria en México*, p. 12.

19. Knight, *Racism*, p. 79.

20. See ibid., pp. 80–86. For a recent study on racism in post-Revolutionary Mexico, see Beatriz Urías Horcasitas, *Historias Secretas del Racismo en México (1920–1950)*, 2007.

21. Knight, *Racism*, pp. 85–86. Knight quotes Luis Cabrera.

22. González-Casanova, *La Democracia en México*, 1967, p. 104.

23. "Pueblos indios americanos mantienen rezagos de hace 40 años, señala estudio." *La Jornada*, May 15, 2007, p. 15.

24. John-Andrew McNeish and Robyn Eversole, "Introduction: Indigenous Peoples and Poverty," in Eversole, et al., *Indigenous Peoples and Poverty*, p. 2. McNeish and Eversole write, "Around the world, in vastly different cultures and settings, indigenous peoples are nearly always disadvantaged relative to their nonindigenous counterparts. Their material standard of living is lower; their risk of disease and early death is higher. Their . . . political participation and voice are more constrained, and the lifestyles and livelihoods they would choose are very often out of reach. . . . In most countries indigenous peoples have less access to education than other groups, and they are very often subjected to curricula designed for other cultural groups which ignore their own history, knowledge and values. Indigenous peoples also tend to have less access to national health systems and appropriate medical care, and may suffer nutritional problems when denied access to their traditional lands" (ibid., pp. 2–3).

25. For the estimated population of the Americas in 1491, see Mann, *1491*, pp. 68–106. For the number 100-plus million, Mann, p. 104.

26. Knight, *Racism*, p. 75: "The attribution of Indian identity began, of course, with the Conquest."

27. Francisco López Bárcenas, *Autonomías indígenas en América Latina*, 2007, p. 15.

28. Ibid.

29. The opposite also happens: the state uses indigenous identity to further domination. A recent study by Carmen Martínez Novo, *Who Defines Indigenous?*,

2006, explores the pitfalls of such imposed identities on Oaxacan migrant communities in Northern Mexico.

30. John-Andrew McNeish and Robyn Eversole, "Introduction: Indigenous Peoples and Poverty," in Eversole, et al., *Indigenous peoples and poverty*, p. 5.

31. J. Martínez Cobo, "Study of the problem of discrimination against indigenous populations," UN Sub-commission on the Prevention of Discrimination and the Protection of Minorities, UN Doc. E/CN.4/Sub.2/1986/7, quoted in McNeish and Eversole, "Introduction: Indigenous Peoples and Poverty," p. 5. No definition is complete, nor should be. And the act of defining from the outside—I am not an indigenous person—may be considered an imperial act by those meant to be folded into the definition. Thus I do not propose the above, or any, definition of indigenous peoples. I do however, believe that interesting reflections may be drawn from the above definition, reflections that do not seek to point at another definition, but to lead to greater understanding of how some peoples have been held with a boot on their necks for centuries, and how they are lifting that boot, and how they can help others lift the boots that also pin them down.

32. Comisión Nacional para el Desarrollo de los Pueblos Indígenas, www.cdi.gov.mx/index.php?id_seccion=90.

33. Consejo Nacional de Población, *Índices de marginación 2005*, quoted in Zósimo Camacho, "Clasificación de la pobreza extrema," *Contralínea*, Number 75, March 15–31, 2007, p. 25.

34. Yenise Tinoco, "La pobreza tiene cara indígena," *Contralínea*, Number 76, April 1–15, 2007, p. 27.

35. López Bárcenas, *Autonomías indígenas en América Latina*, p. 13.

36. Ibid., p. 25.

37. Ibid., p. 18.

38. Ibid., pp. 41–45.

39. Ibid., pp. 60–61.

40. "First Declaration of the Lacandón Jungle," reprinted in *Shadows of Tender Fury*, pp. 51–54.

41. John Ross writes: "The Ley Cocopa [the bill version of the San Andrés Accords] had literally been drawn and quartered. Gone were the autonomy provisions—'autonomy' would now be defined and implemented not by the indigenous peoples themselves but by 31 state congresses, the most corrupt legislative level on the republic's political map. . . . Indian communities were not autonomous but submissive to the state according to the PAN-PRI rewrite of the Indian Rights Law—the essence of the change of a single word from 'entities of public right' to 'entities of public interest'" (Ross, 2006, p. 89).

42. They say so explicitly in the *Sexta*. See Marcos, *The Other Campaign*, pp. 91 and 93.

43. Laura Castellanos, *Corte de Caja*, 2008, p. 46.

44. This brief history of the Triqui region is drawn from my interview with Francisco López Bárcenas and from his forthcoming book, *San Juan Copala: Dominación política y resistencia popular.*
45. Martínez Vásquez, *Autoritarismo, movimiento popular, y crisis política,* 2007, p. 104, and Osorno, *Oaxaca sitiada,* 2007, p. 97.

7. THE GUERRILLA

1. This portrait of Gloria Arenas Agis is based on three seven-hour interviews conducted inside the Mexico State Prison of Ecatepec in Santa María Chiconautla, Mexico state, on January 13, March 17, and July 13, 2008. Before beginning the interviews we agreed that I would not ask for names, specific dates or specific locations; she alone would decide when to provide such details. Though Gloria Arenas has been either disappeared or in jail since October 22, 1999, and has publicly declared that upon release she will participate openly in social movements, the guerrilla organization she belonged to and helped found, the Insurgent Peoples' Revolutionary Army (Ejército Revolucionario del Pueblo Insurgente, ERPI), continues to exist and to operate in Mexico. The ERPI website, which includes several documents in English, is: www.enlace-erpi.org. Bill Weinberg's book *Homage to Chiapas* (New York: Verso, 2002, chapter 14) contains background information on the ERPI, a discussion of their concept of "popular power" as well as an interview with ERPI members. The Mexico City–based documentary film studio Canal 6 de Julio released a filmed interview with ERPI members: *Habla el ERPI.* Mexico City: Canal 6 de Julio, no date.
2. Interview with Jacobo's sister Elizabeth in Mexico City on July 18, 2008.
3. CONASUPO, the National Popular Subsistence Company, was a pre-NAFTA state agricultural company. See, for example: Antonio Yúnez-Naude, "The Dismantling of CONASUPO, a Mexican State Trader in Agriculture," *World Economy,* 26 (January 2003), pp. 97–122.
4. The massacre of Aguas Blancas has been well documented. See Maribel Gutiérrez, *Violencia en Guerrero,* pp. 119–131 and Minnesota Advocates for Human Rights, "Massacre in Mexico: Killings and Cover-up in the State of Guerrero," December 1995.
5. Suprema Corte de Justicia de la Nación. "Acuerdo del Tribunal Pleno de la Suprema Corte de Justicia de la Nación correspondiente al día veintitrés de abril de mil novecientos noventa y seis," Expediente 3/96, April 23, 1996, pp. 107–108.
6. Maribel Gutiérrez, *Violencia en Guerrero,* pp. 221–224.
7. Cited in ibid., pp. 222.
8. Salvador Corr, "Una noche de terror: Las fuerzas del EPR destruyeron el mito de la pantomima." *Proceso,* September 1, 1996.
9. One famous example of sweeping military repression in search of guerrillas outside of Guerrero took place in the tiny mountain village of San Agustín

Loxicha in Oaxaca state. Soldiers arrested more than 125 people, tortured forty-four of them, and held many incommunicado; some are still in prison over twelve years later. Bill Weinberg describes the climate of repression following the mass detentions in *Homage to Chiapas*, pp. 284–286.

10. The story of El Charco is told in Maribel Gutiérrez, *Violencia en Guerrero*, pp. 291–304. Addition information comes from my interviews with Gloria Arenas Agis as well as survivors of the massacre.

11. Robert Taber, *The War of the Flea*, 2002, p. 91.

12. Maribel Gutiérrez, *Violencia en Guerrero*, p. 300.

13. Ibid., p. 301.

14. On October 19, 2001 Digna Ochoa was found dead in her office. Eight years later not only has no one been punished for the crime, but the Mexico City government investigators actually turned the blame back on Digna herself, saying, against all credible evidence, that Digna killed herself. Such insidious impunity in the case of Digna's murder dealt a mortal blow to the Mexican national human rights community. Not only was Digna killed and nothing done about it, but this took place under the watch of the new "democratic" president and the new "progressive" mayor of Mexico City. Digna was investigating the army's use of torture to extract false confessions from two campesino ecologists (later released by Fox after Digna's murder and awarded the Goldman Environmental Award) and had just accepted the ERPI case, where again, both Jacobo and Gloria had been held incommunicado and tortured. Digna's killing left a clear message: regardless of who is in what political office, the army is still untouchable. Mexico's national human rights organizations divided and largely dissolved in the wake of Digna's murder. See Linda Diebel's excellent investigation, *Betrayed: The Assassination of Digna Ochoa*, 2007, and Canal 6 de Julio's documentary *Digna*, 2007. I met Digna Ochoa in November 1999 and came to know her a little and respect her greatly when I traveled to Mexico City through Global Exchange as a volunteer human rights accompanier assigned to Digna after she had suffered a kidnapping and simulated assassination. During the early dawn hours of October 29, 1999—just days after Jacobo and Gloria's detention—men in unmarked military dress subdued and interrogated Digna in her own apartment; they accused her of having contacts with guerrillas, specifically mentioning "Antonio" and "Aurora" of the ERPI. They left her tied to a chair with her gas oven turned on; she was able to escape. (See Diebel, *Betrayed*, 2007; for a news account at the time, see: Bertha Fernández, "Sufre otro atentado el Centro Pro," *El Universal*, October 30, 1999, p. 10.)

8. EMPIRE AND REVOLT

1. A few excellent books on this subject: Galeano, *Las venas abiertas de América Latina*; Todorov, *The Conquest of the Americas*; and Noam Chomsky, *Year 501*.

2. Harvey, *The New Imperialism*, p. 1.

3. For a succinct and extremely perceptive discussion of the formation of U.S. imperialism, see chapter 2, "How America's Power Grew," in Harvey, pp. 26–86. For example: "From the late nineteenth century onwards, the US gradually learned to mask the explicitness of territorial gains and occupations under the mask of a spaceless universalization of its own values, buried within a rhetoric that was ultimately to culminate . . . in what came to be known as 'globalization'" (ibid., p. 47).

4. Dee Brown, *Bury My Heart at Wounded Knee*, 1971; Churchill; and Greg Grandin, *Empire's Workshop*, 2006.

5. Immanuel Wallerstein, *World-Systems Analysis*, p. 24.

6. Ibid., p. 25.

7. Much has been written about this. For the basics see, the Sexta and pretty much everything by Marcos and the Zapatistas; Immanuel Wallerstein; and Robin Hahnel, *Panic Rules!* If you have a few extra months, Marx, *Capital*, is an excellent place to start, but so are Galeano, Roy, Chomsky, and the Zapatistas.

8. Harvey, pp. 137–182. The technical definition in a few words: "What accumulation by dispossession does is to release a set of assets (including labor power) at very low (and in some instances zero) cost. Over-accumulated capital can seize hold of such assets and immediately turn them into profitable use" (ibid., p. 141).

9. Harvey notes: "Liquidation can come by a variety of means. The economic power to dominate . . . can be used with equally destructive effect as physical force" (ibid., p. 39). Fanon writes: "Artillery shelling and a scorched earth policy have been replaced by an economic dependency" (*The Wretched of the Earth*, p. 27).

10. For an in-depth discussion of this period see Hart, *Empire and Revolution*, pp. 73–267.

11. "In January 1914 the cabinet secretly agreed to prepare the U.S. Armed Forces for an armed invasion of Mexico in order to protect American interests in strategic materials such as oil, rubber, copper, and zinc, and, as a corollary, to protect political stability. . . . On April 21, . . . the American fleet struck at Veracruz itself. . . . The Mexican army withdrew. . . . The Mexican civilian populace resisted, mounting a stout defense, and the attack on Veracruz turned into a tragedy. The American warships bombarded the city for hours, and their upgraded guns took a terrible toll on the populace" (Hart, *Empire and Revolution*, pp. 307 and 308).

12. In the introduction to his exhaustive study on the United States and Americans in Mexico, John Mason Hart writes: "Seeing the opportunities for wealth and power that their southern neighbor offered, U.S. elites sought to extend their interests into Mexico by employing the strategies that were so successful for them in the American West" (ibid., p.2)

13. On overaccumulation of capital see Harvey, pp. 138–143. On U.S. manipulation of Mexican debt crisis, see Hart, *Empire and Revolution*, pp. 432–458.

14. Hart, ibid., p. 434.

15. Ibid., p. 439.
16. Ibid., p. 439.
17. Sandoval, "Mexican Labor Migration," p. 20.
18. The Mexican political class drives the internal colonialism in Mexico, though at different points in the country they have done so with more or less interference or guidance from the United States. (See González-Casanova, *La democracia en México*, pp. 89–90, emphasis in original.)
19. Cited in Hart, *Empire and Revolution*, p. 432. Harvey writes that "what the critics [of U.S. imperialism who focus on military interventions] all too often fail to acknowledge is that coercion and liquidation of the enemy is only a partial, and sometimes counterproductive, basis of U.S. power. Consent and cooperation are just as important" (Harvey, p. 39).
20. "The concept of Empire is characterized fundamentally by a lack of boundaries: Empire's rule has no limits. . . . [T]he concept of Empire presents itself not as a historical regime originating in conquest, but rather as an order that effectively suspends history and thereby fixes the existing state of affairs for eternity. . . . It not only regulates human interactions but also seeks directly to rule over human nature. . . . [A]lthough the practice of Empire is continually bathed in blood, the concept of Empire is always dedicated to peace—a perpetual and universal peace outside of history" (Michael Hardt and Antonio Negri, *Empire*, pp. xiv–xv).
21. Ibid., p. xii.
22. Córdova, *La formación del poder político en México*, 1972.
23. Ibid., p. 22.
24. Ibid., p. 21.
25. Ibid., p. 32.
26. Ibid., p. 53.
27. Ibid., p. 57.
28. Ibid., p. 57.
29. Rodolfo García Zamora, an economist and sociologist at the University of Zacatecas, and author of the book *Migración, remesas, y desarrollo local*, told me during an interview in February 2008 that there is still only one political party in Mexico. His description of this party is one of the most eloquent expressions of the contemporary state of the Mexican political parties I have yet heard: "There is only one political party in Mexico: the PRI. There is the PRI of the dinosaurs, and there is the PRI with hepatitis, the guilty-feeling dinosaurs contaminated a bit with the Communist Party, that is, the PRD. And then there is the blue PRI, which is just as inept, as corrupt, and as nepotistic as the old PRI; here I am speaking of the PAN."
30. Córdova, pp. 41 and 62.
31. González Casanova, *La democracia en México*, 1967, pp. 89–90.
32. Bolívar Echeverría, *Vuelta de siglo*, 2006, p. 242, emphasis in original.
33. Albert Memmi, *The Colonizer and the Colonized*, p. 52.
34. On legitimacy as a feature of the principle of democracy see Enrique Dussel, *20 tesis de política*, pp. 76–80.

35. Memmi, p. 52.
36. Luis Villoro, *El concepto de ideología*, 2007, p. 27.
37. Memmi, p. 127–128.
38. Bolívar Echeverría, p. 245.
39. Ibid., p. 204.
40. Ibid.
41. Ibid., pp. 208–209 and 245–247.
42. On the inherent racism of the Mexican government's concept of *mestizaje*, see Knight, *Racism*, pp. 85–86 and López Bárcenas, *Autonomías indígenas en América Latina*, 2007, p. 23.
43. Bolívar Echeverría, pp. 245–246, emphasis in original.
44. Paulo Freire, *Pedagogy of the Oppressed*, 1993, p. 27.
45. Bolívar Echeverría, pp. 246–247, emphasis in original.
46. López Bárcenas, *Autonomías indígenas en América Latina*, 2007, p. 60.
47. Ibid., p. 26.
48. Todorov, p. 179, emphasis in original.
49. Freire, p. 31.
50. Marcos, *The Other Campaign*, p. 93.
51. Slavoj Žižek, *In Defense of Lost Causes*, 2008, pp. 428 and 430.
52. Ibid., p. 430.
53. Matthew Guttman, *The Romance of Democracy*, 2002.
54. Bolívar Echeverría, p. 268.
55. Ibid., pp. 268–269.
56. Freire, p. 31.
57. César, Marisela, and Doni Zänä's story is drawn from Carlos Camacho, "Pareja ñañú lucha contra el gobierno de Hidalgo en defensa de su cultura." *La Jornada*, May 10, 2007.
58. Ibid.
59. Ibid.
60. Ley General de Derechos Lingüísticos de los Pueblos Indígenas, Article 4, available online at www.diputados.gob.mx/LeyesBiblio/pdf/257.pdf.
61. Carlos Camacho, "Pareja ñañú lucha contra el gobierno de Hidalgo en defensa de su cultura." *La Jornada*, May 10, 2007.
62. Ibid.
63. Carlos Camacho, "Luego de dos años, logran registro de niña ñañú en Hidalgo," *La Jornada*, June 11, 2008.
64. See, for example, Evelyn Hu-DeHart, "Rebelión campesina en el noroeste: Los indios Yaquis de Sonora, 1740–1976" in Friedrich Katz, ed. *Revuelta, rebelión, y revolución*, 2004, pp. 135–163.
65. See Fernando Benítez, *Los indios de México Vol. II, Los Huicholes*, 2002.
66. Juan Cosío Candelario, quoted in Magdalena Gómez. "Wixáritari: derechos en serio," *La Jornada*, 26 February 2008.
67. Consider the following paradox of political imagination as described by philosopher Slavoj Žižek: "Think about the strangeness of today's situation. Thirty, forty years ago we were still debating about what the future will be—

communist, fascist, capitalist and so on. Today nobody debates this issue; we all silently accept that global capitalism is here to stay. On the other hand, we are obsessed with cosmic catastrophes—the whole life on earth disintegrating because of some virus, because of an asteroid hitting the earth and so on. So the paradox is that it is much easier to imagine the end of all life on earth than a more modest radical change in capitalism, which means that we should reinvent utopia, but in what sense? There are two false meanings of utopia: one is this old notion of imagining an ideal society which we know will never be realized; the other is the capitalist utopia in the sense of new and perverse desires that you are not only allowed to but even solicited to realize. The real utopia is when the situation is so without a way to solve it within the coordinates of the possible that out of the pure urge of survival you have to invent a new space. Utopia is not a kind of free imagination. Utopia is a matter of innermost urgency; you are forced to imagine it as the only way out" (from a talk in Buenos Aires shown in the film *Zizek!* by Astra Taylor). I use "utopia" in this sense.

68. Žižek, shown in the film *Zizek!* by Astra Taylor.

69. Carlos Montemayor, author of the historical novel *War in Paradise* (*Guerra en El Paraiso*) about Lucio Cabañas and the Dirty War, argues that armed movements continue to appear in Mexico as a result of the government's refusal to analyze and understand the social roots of guerrilla conflicts: the "social violence" of the regime. "The official perspective characterizes guerrilla movements within a pre-established strategy of combat," Montemayor wrote in *La guerrilla recurrente*, "not from an analysis that would lead to understanding them as social processes. . . . This perspective puts forth a constant reductionism that confuses and eliminates the social characteristics indispensable to understanding armed movements politically and thus develop a meaningful solution. The government's reasoning does not follow from a social understanding of the nature of the conflict, but from the need to reduce as much as possible the social dimension and its political and moral motivations. As the government reduces to a minimum the facts of social causes, it favors the exclusive application of police or military responses," (Montemayor, *La guerrilla recurrente* 2007, p. 23). Philosopher Slavoj Žižek distinguishes between "subjective" and "objective" forms of violence; where the former is easy to spot (one person knifes another), the latter is invisible (people who live in destitution and discrimination). He writes: "The catch is that subjective and objective violence cannot be perceived from the same standpoint: subjective violence is experienced as such against the background of a nonviolent zero level. . . . However, objective violence is precisely the violence inherent to this 'normal' state of things" (Slavoj Žižek, *Violence*, 2008, p. 2). One form of objective violence is what Žižek calls systemic violence: "We're talking here of the violence inherent in a system: not only direct physical violence, but also the more subtle forms of coercion that sustain relations of domination and exploitation, including the threat of violence" (Slavoj Žižek, *Violence*, 2008, p. 8). Montemayor's notion of social

violence is a systemic violence in this sense, typically invisible to those who do not suffer it.

70. In Spanish I would use *"rebelión,"* not *"revuelta."*

71. "The rise and fall of social movements mark the expansion and contraction of democratic opportunities" (Tilly, *Social Movements, 1768–2004,* 2004, p. 3).

72. Most U.S. mainstream press coverage of Mexican popular movements and revolts is plagued with such a degree of obvious disdain, class bias, colossal misreporting of basic facts, and near total absence of simple curiosity as to the motivations and intentions of the participants that it merits its own book-length analysis. Still, the plague fits a consistent pattern: the failure of political imagination. Reporters and editors will call protests "riots" (without actually going to witness the events themselves), government repression "restoring order" (mass rape in Atenco, para-police killings in Oaxaca), and any popular or opposition grouping of peoples generic "leftists" without ever even so much as asking them what they think or what they hope to achieve. They do this because they themselves cannot see beyond capitalism; the urgent reinvention of utopia in Mexican revolts is filtered through the lens of capitalist imagining, stripped of social and political content so that the rebels become generic "rioting leftists." I wrote briefly about this in "Who's Not Listening: The Los Angeles Times and the Failure of Political Imagination," Znet, February 13, 2006. For blow-by-blow accounts of class bias and misreporting in U.S. press coverage in Mexico, see the web journal Narco News, www.narconews.com.

BIBLIOGRAPHY

Amnesty International. *Intolerable Killings: 10 years of Abductions and Murders of Women in Ciudad Juárez and Chihuahua.* London: Amnesty International, 2003.

———. *Mexico: Laws without Justice: Human Rights Violations and Impunity in the Public Security and Criminal Justice System.* Washington D.C.: Amnesty International, 2007.

———."Mexico: Unfair Trials: Unsafe Convictions." Washington D.C.: Amnesty International, March, 23, 2003.

Anderson, Benedict. *Imagined Communities: Reflections on the Origins and Spread of Nationalism.* Revised edition. London: Verso, 2006.

Annerino, John. *Dead in Their Tracks: Crossing America's Desert Borderlands.* New York: Four Walls Eight Windows, 1999.

Auden, W. H. *Collected Poems.* New York: Vintage International, 1991.

Bartra, Roger. *La jaula de la melancolía: Identidad y metamorfosis del mexicano.* México: Grijalbo, 1987.

Beas Torres, Carlos, et al. *La Batalla por Oaxaca.* Oaxaca: Ediciones Yope Power, 2007.

Bellingeri, Marco. *Del agrarismo armado a la guerra de los pobres: Ensayos de guerrilla rural en el México contemporáneo, 1940–1974.* México: Casa Juan Pablos, 2003.

Benítez, Fernando. *Los indios de México, vol. II Los Huicholes.* México: Era, 2002.

Bonfil Batalla, Guillermo. "Historias que no son todavía historia," in Carlos Pereyra et al. *Historia ¿Para qué?* México: Siglo XXI, 1980.

Bourdieu, Pierre. *Outline of a Theory of Practice*. Cambridge: Cambridge University Press, 1977.

———. *Distinction: A Social Critique of the Judgment of Taste*. Cambridge, MA: Harvard University Press, 1984.

Bowden, Charles. *Down by the River: Drugs, Money, Murder, and Family*. New York: Simon and Schuster, 2004.

Brown, Dee. *Bury My Heart at Wounded Knee: An Indian History of the American West*. New York: Henry Holt, 1971.

Castellanos, Laura. *México armado: 1943–1981*. México: Era, 2007.

———. *Corte de caja: Entrevista al Subcomandante Marcos*. Mexico City: Bunker and Alterno, 2008.

Castles, Stephen and Raúl Delgado Wise, eds. *Migración y desarrollo: perspectivas desde el sur*. Zacatecas: Universidad Autónomo de Zacatecas, 2007.

Chacón, Justin Akers and Mike Davis. *No One is Illegal: Fighting Racism and State Violence on the U.S.–Mexico Border*. Chicago: Haymarket Books, 2006.

Chomsky, Aviva. *"They Take Our Jobs" and 20 Other Myths about Immigration*. Boston: Beacon Press, 2007.

Chomsky, Noam. *Year 501: The Conquest Continues*. Boston: South End Press, 1993.

Churchill, Ward. *A Little Matter of Genocide: Holocaust Denial in the Americas 1492 to the Present*. San Francisco: City Lights, 1998.

Cockcroft, James D. *Mexico's Hope: An Encounter with Politics and History*. New York: Monthly Review Press, 1998.

Cook, Maria Lorena. *Organizing Dissent: Unions, the State, and the Democratic Teachers Movement in Mexico*. University Park, PA: Penn State Press, 1996.

Comisión Civil Internacional de Observación por los Derechos Humanos. *Informe preliminary sobre los hechos de Atenco, México.* Bilbao: Comisión Civil Internacional de Observación por los Derechos Humanos, 2006.

————. *Informe sobre los hechos de Oaxaca.* Bilbao: Comisión Civil Internacional de Observación por los Derechos Humanos, 2007.

Consejo Nacional de Población. *Índices de marginación, 2005.* México: Consejo Nacional de Población, November 2006.

Córdova, Arnaldo. *La formación del poder político en México.* México: Era, 1972.

————. *La política de masas del cardenismo.* México: Era, 1974.

————. *La política de masas y el futuro de la izquierda en México.* México: Era, 1979.

Crelinsten, Ronald D. and Alex P. Schmid, eds. *The Politics of Pain: Torturers and Their Masters.* Boulder, Colorado: Westview Press, 1994.

Danner, Mark. *Torture and Truth: America, Abu Ghraib, and the War on Terror.* New York: New York Review of Books, 2004

Davies, Nancy. *The People Decide: Oaxaca's Popular Assembly.* Mexico City: Narco News Books, 2007.

De Castro, Rafael Fernández, et al. *Las políticas migratorias en los estados de México: Una evaluación.* Zacatecas: Universidad Autónomo de Zacatecas, 2007.

De Jesus, Carolina María. *Child of the Dark.* New York: Mentor, 1962.

Delgado Wise, Raúl. "Migration and Imperialism: The Mexican Workforce in the Context of NAFTA." *Latin American Perspectives.* Issue 147, Vol. 33 No. 2 (March 2006), pp. 33–45.

Diebel, Linda. *Betrayed: The Assassination of Digna Ochoa.* New York: Carroll & Graf, 2007.

Dussel, Enrique. *20 tesis de política.* México: Siglo XXI, 2006.

Easterly, William. *The White Man's Burden: Why the West's Efforts to Aid the Rest Have Done So Much Ill and So Little Good.* New York: Penguin Books, 2006.

Echeverría, Bolívar. *Vuelta de siglo.* México: Era, 2006.

Escobar, Arturo. *Encountering Development: The Making and Unmaking of the Third World.* Princeton: Princeton University Press, 1995.

Escobar, Arturo and Sonia E. Alvarez, eds. *The Making of Social Movements in Latin America: Identity, Strategy, and Democracy.* Boulder: Westview Press, 1992.

Eversole, Robyn and John-Andrew McNeish and Alberto D. Cimadamore, eds. *Indigenous Peoples and Poverty: An International Perspective.* London: Zed Books, 2005.

Fanon, Frantz. *The Wretched of the Earth.* New York: Grove, 2004.

Faux, Jeff. *The Global Class War.* Hoboken, New Jersey: John Wiley and Sons, 2006.

Feitlowitz, Marguerite. *A Lexicon of Terror: Argentina and the Legacies of Torture.* Oxford: Oxford University Press, 1998.

Fellmeth, Robert. *Politics of Land.* New York: Grossman, 1972.

Ferguson, James. *The Anti-Politics Machine: "Development," Depoliticization, and Bureaucratic Power in Lesotho.* Minneapolis: University of Minnesota Press,1994.

Foweraker, Joe and Ann L. Craig, eds. *Popular Movements and Political Change in Mexico.* Boulder: Lynne Rienner Publishers, 1990.

Franco, Jean. *Plotting Women: Gender and Representation in Mexico.* New York: Columbia University Press, 1989.

Freire, Paulo. *Pedagogy of the Oppressed.* New York: Continuum, 1993.

Galeano, Eduardo. *Las venas abiertas de América Latina.* México: Siglo XXI, 2004.

Gilly, Adolfo. *La revolución interrumpida: México, 1910–1920: una guerra campesina por la tierra y el poder.* México: Ediciones "El Caballito," 1975.

———. *El cardenismo, una utopia mexicana*. México: Cal y Arena, 1994.

———, et al. *Interpretaciones de la Revolución Mexicana*. México: Nueva Imagen, 1988.

Giordano, Al. "Mexico's Presidential Swindle." *New Left Review*. Vol. 41 September–October 2006, pp. 5–27.

Glockner, Fritz. *Memoria roja: Historia de la guerrilla en México (1943–1968)*. México: Ediciones B, 2007.

González Casanova, Pablo. *La democracia en México*. México: Era, 1967.

González de Alba, Luis. *Los días y los años*. México: Era, 1971.

Gonzalez, Gilbert G. *Guest Workers or Colonized Labor? Mexican Labor Migration to the United States*. Boulder, Colorado: Paradigm Publishers, 2006.

Gordillo y Ortiz, Octavio. *EZLN: Una aproximación bibliografica*. México: Editorial Praxis, 2006.

Grandin, Greg. *Empire's Workshop: Latin America, the United States, and the Rise of New Imperialism*. New York: Metropolitan Books, 2006.

Guillermoprieto, Alma. *Looking for History: Dispatches from Latin America*. New York: Vintage Books, 2001.

Gutiérrez, Maribel. *Violencia en Guerrero*. México: La Jornada Ediciones, 1998.

Guttman, Matthew C. *The Romance of Democracy: Compliant Defiance in Contemporary Mexico*. Berkeley: University of California Press, 2002.

Hahnel, Robin. *Panic Rules! Everything You Need to Know about the Global Economy*. Cambridge, Massachusetts: South End Press, 1999.

Hamnett, Brian R. *A Concise History of Mexico*. Second edition. Cambridge: Cambridge University Press, 2006.

Hardt, Michael and Antonio Negri. *Empire*. Cambridge, Massachusetts: Harvard University Press, 2000.

Hart, John Mason. *Revolutionary Mexico: The Coming and Process of the Mexican Revolution.* Berkeley: University of California Press, Tenth Anniversary Edition, 1997.

――――. *Empire and Revolution: The Americans in Mexico since the Civil War.* Berkeley: University of California Press, 2002.

Harvey, David. *The New Imperialism.* Oxford: Oxford University Press, 2005.

Hassig, Ross. *Mexico and the Spanish Conquest.* Second edition. Norman: University of Oklahoma Press, 2006.

Hayden, Tom, ed. *The Zapatista Reader.* New York: Nation Books, 2001.

Hellman, Judith Adler. *Mexican Lives.* New York: New Press, 1994.

Henck, Nick. *Subcommander Marcos: The Man and the Mask.* Durham: Duke University Press, 2007.

Human Rights Watch. *World Report 2007.* New York: Seven Stories Press, 2007.

Iglesias, Severo. *Juárez: Sociedad civil y nación.* Morelia, Michoacán: Morevallado Editores, 2006.

Kapuscinski, Ryszard. *The Emperor: Downfall of an Autocrat.* New York: Vintage International, 1989.

Katz, Friedrich. *La servidumbre agraria en México en la época porfiriana.* México: Era, 1980.

――――, ed. *Revuelta, rebelión, y revolución: La lucha rural en México del siglo XVI al siglo XX.* México: Era, 2004.

Katzenberger, Elaine, ed. *First World, Ha, Ha, Ha!* San Francisco: City Lights, 2001.

Kelman, Herbert C. "The Policy Context of Torture: A Social-psychological Analysis." *International Review of the Red Cross.* Volume 87, Number 857, March 2005, pp. 123–134.

Knight, Alan. "Racism, Revolution, and *Indigenismo*: Mexico, 1910–1940." In *The Idea of Race in Latin America, 1870–1940*, edited by Richard Graham. Austin: University of Texas Press, 1990.

———. *Mexico: From the Beginning to the Conquest*. Cambridge: Cambridge University Press, 2002.

La Botz, Dan. *Democracy in Mexico: Peasant Rebellion and Political Reform*. Boston: South End Press, 1995.

———. *Mask of Democracy: Labor Suppression in Mexico Today*. Boston: South End Press, 1992.

Lamas, Marta. *Feminismo: Transmisiones y retransmisiones*. México: Taurus, 2006.

Lomnitz, Claudio. *Exits from the Labyrinth: Culture and Ideology in the Mexican National Space*. Berkeley: University of California Press, 1992.

———. *Deep Mexico, Silent Mexico: An Anthropology of Nationalism*. Minneapolis: University of Minnesota Press, 2001.

López Bárcenas, Francisco. *Autonomías Indígenas en América Latina*. México: mc editores, 2007.

Macías, Anna. *Against All Odds: The Feminist Movement in Mexico to 1940*. Westport, Connecticut: Greenwood Press, 1982.

Mann, Charles C. *1491: New Revelations of the Americas Before Columbus*. New York: Vintage Books, 2006.

Mann, Rita. *Torture: The Role of Ideology in the French Algerian War*. New York: 1989.

Marcos, Subcomandante, and the Zapatistas. *Shadows of Tender Fury: The Letters and Communiqués of Subcomandante Marcos and the Zapatista Army of National Liberation*. New York: Monthly Review Press, 1995.

———. *Our Word Is Our Weapon: Selected Writings of Subcomandante Insurgente Marcos*. New York: Seven Stories Press, 2002.

———. *The Other Campaign*. San Francisco: City Lights, 2006.

———. *The Speed of Dreams*. San Francisco: City Lights, 2007.

Martinez Novo, Carmen. *Who Defines Indigenous? Identities, Development, Intellectuals, and the State in Northern Mexico*. New Brunswick, New Jersey: Rutgers University Press, 2006.

Martínez, Rubén. *Crossing Over: A Mexican Family on the Migrant Trail*. New York: Picador, 2001.

Martínez Vásquez, Víctor Raúl. *Autoritarismo, movimiento popular, y crisis política: Oaxaca 2006*. Oaxaca, México: Universidad Autónoma "Benito Juárez" de Oaxaca, 2007.

Marx, Karl. *Capital*, Volume I. London: Penguin Books, 1976.

Memmi, Albert. *The Colonizer and the Colonized*. Boston: Beacon Press, 1967.

Monsiváis, Carlos. *"No sin nosotros" Los días del terremoto 1985–2005*. Mexico City: Era, 2005.

Monsiváis, Carlos, et al. *Viento rojo: Diez historias del narco en México*. México: Plaza Janés, 2004.

Montemayor, Carlos. *Guerra en el paraíso*. México: Editorial Planeta: 2002.

———. *La guerrilla recurrente*. México: Debate, 2007.

Moore, Barrington. *Injustice: The Social Bases of Obedience and Revolt*. White Plains, New York: M. E. Sharpe, 1978.

Nazario, Sonia. *Enrique's Journey*. New York: Random House, 2007.

Nevins, Joseph. *Dying to Live: A Story of U.S. Immigration in an Age of Global Apartheid*. San Francisco: City Lights Books, 2008.

Olcott, Jocelyn. *Revolutionary Women in Postrevolutionary Mexico*. Durham: Duke University Press, 2005.

Osorno, Diego Enrique. *Oaxaca sitiada: La primera insurrección del siglo XXI*. México: Grijalbo, 2007.

Peters, Edward. *Torture*. Philadelphia: University of Pennsylvania Press, 1999.

Pisani, Donald J. *Water, Land, and Law in the West: The Limits of Public Policy, 1850–1920*. Lawrence: University of Kansas Press, 1996.

Poniatowska, Elena. *La noche de Tlatelolco*. México: Era, 1997.

Preston, Julia, and Samuel Dillon. *Opening Mexico: The Making of a Democracy*. New York: Farrar, Straus, and Giroux, 2004.

Ravelo, Ricardo. *Los capos: Las narco-rutas de México*. México: Plaza Janés, 2005.

———. *Herencia maldita: El reto de Calderón y el Nuevo mapa del narcotráfico*. México: Grijalbo, 2007.

Reina, Leticia. *Las rebeliones campesinas en México (1819–1906)*. México: Siglo XXI, 1996.

Reisner, Marc. *A Dangerous Place: California's Unsettling Fate*. New York: Penguin, 2003.

Rich, Bruce. *Mortgaging the Earth: The World Bank, Environmental Impoverishment, and the Crisis of Development*. Boston: Beacon Press, 1995

Riding, Alan. *Distant Neighbors: A Portrait of the Mexicans*. New York: Vintage Books, 2000.

Rodriguez, Teresa, Diana Montané, and Lisa Pulitzer. *The Daughters of Juárez: A True Story of Serial Murder South of the Border*. New York: Atria Books, 2007.

Ronquillo, Victor. *Migrantes de la pobreza*. Mexico City: Grupo Editorial Norma, 2007.

Ross, John. *¡Zapatistas! Making Another World Possible: Chronicles of Resistance 2000–2006*. New York: Nation Books, 2006.

———. *The War Against Oblivion: Zapatista Chronicles 1994–2000*. Monroe, Maine: Common Courage Press, 2000.

Roy, Arundhati. *Public Power in the Age of Empire*. New York: Seven Stories Press, 2004.

———. *An Ordinary Person's Guide to Empire*. Cambridge, Massachusetts: South End Press, 2004.

Sachs, Jeffrey D. *The End of Poverty: Economic Possibilities for Our Time.* New York: Penguin, 2005.

Sachs, Wolfgang, ed. *The Development Dictionary: A Guide to Knowledge as Power.* London: Zed Books, 1992.

Said, Edward W. *Culture and Imperialism.* New York: Vintage Books, 1994.

Sanchez, Alex. "Mexico's Drug War: A Society at Risk—Soldiers versus Narco Soldiers." Washington: Council on Hemispheric Affairs, May 22, 2007.

Sandoval, Juan Manuel. "Mexican Labor Migration and the North American Free Trade Agreement (NAFTA): 1994-2006." Paper presented at the "Push and Pull: Immigration and Free Trade" national speaking tour organized by Global Exchange, April 15 through May 2, 2007, available online at: www.globalexchange.org/getInvolved/speakers/SandovalNAFTA.pdf.

Sartre, Jean-Paul. *Colonialism and Neocolonialism.* London: Routledge, 2006.

Scarry, Elaine. *The Body in Pain: The Making and Unmaking of the World.* Oxford: Oxford University Press, 1985.

Scott, Robert E. and David Ratner. "NAFTA's Cautionary Tale." *Economic Policy Institute.* Issue Brief: No. 214, July 20, 2005.

Semo, Enrique. *Historia del capitalismo en México.* México: Era, 1973.

———. *Historia mexicana: Economía y lucha de clases.* México: Era, 1978.

Semo, Enrique, and Enrique Nalda. *México, un pueblo en la historia. Volumen 1 De la aparición del hombre al dominio colonial.* Mexico City: Alianza Editorial, 1989.

Solano, Verónica Oikión, and Marta Eugenia García Ugarte, eds. *Movimientos armados en México, siglo XX.* 3 vols. Zamora, Michoacán and México: El Colegio de Michoacán and Centro de Investigaciones y Estudios Superiores en Antropología Social, 2006.

Stephen, Lynn. *Zapotec Women: Gender Class and Ethnicity in Globalized Oaxaca.* Chapel Hill: Duke University Press, 2005.

Taber, Robert. *The War of the Flea*. Washington, D.C.: Potomac Books, 2002.

Tello Díaz, Carlos. *La rebelión de las Cañadas: Origen y ascenso del EZLN*. México: Editorial Planeta Mexicana, 2006.

Tilly, Charles. *Social Movements, 1768–2004*. Boulder, Colorado: Paradigm Publishers, 2004.

Todorov, Tzvetan. *The Conquest of America: The Question of the Other*. New York: HarperPerennial, 1984.

Toro, Maria Cecilia. "The political repercussions of drug trafficking in Mexico," pp. 131–145 in Elizabeth Joyce and Carlos Malamud, eds. *Latin America and the Multinational Drug Trade*. London: Institute of Latin American Studies, 1998.

Tutino, John. *From Insurrection to Revolution in Mexico: Social Bases of Agrarian Violence, 1750-1940*. Princeton: Princeton University Press, 1989.

United Nations Committee on the Elimination of Discrimination against Women (CEDAW). *Report on Mexico produced by the Committee on the Elimination of Violence against Women under article 8 of the Optional Protocol to the Convention, and reply from the Government of Mexico*. CEDAW/C/2005/OP.8/MEXICO, 27 January 2005.

Urías Horcasitas, Beatriz. *Historias secretas del racismo en México (1920–1950)*. México: Tusquets Editores Mexico, 2007.

Villoro, Luis. *El concepto de ideología y otros ensayos*. México: Fondo de Cultura Económica, 2007.

Wallerstein, Immanuel. *World-Systems Analysis: An Introduction*. Durham: Duke University Press, 2004.

Webb, Gary. *Dark Alliance: The CIA, the Contras, and the Crack Cocaine Explosion*. New York: Seven Stories Press, 1998.

Weinberg, Bill. *Homage to Chiapas: The New Indigenous Struggles in Mexico*. New York: Verso, 2002.

Weschler, Lawrence. *A Miracle, a Universe: Settling Accounts with Torturers*. New York: 1990.

Wolf, Eric. *Peasant Wars of the Twentieth Century*. New York: Harper and Row, 1969.

Womack, John, Jr. *Zapata and the Mexican Revolution*. New York: Vintage Books, 1968.

Wright, Erik Olin, ed. *Approaches to Class Analysis*. Cambridge: Cambridge University Press, 2005.

Zamora, Rodolfo Garcia. *Migración, remesas, y desarrollo local*. Zacatecas: Universidad Autonoma de Zacatecas, 2003.

Žižek, Slavoj. *The Sublime Object of Ideology*. New York: Verso, 1989.

———. *In Defense of Lost Causes*. New York: Verso, 2008.

———. *Violence: Six Sideways Reflections*. London: Profile Books, 2008.

FILMS

Compromiso cumplido. Oaxaca: Mal de Ojo TV, 2007.

Digna. Mexico City: Canal 6 de Julio, 2007.

Granito de arena. Seattle: Corrgute Films, 2004.

La guerrilla y la esperanza: Lucio Cabañas. Mexico City: Gerardo Tort, 2007.

Habla el ERPI. Mexico City: Canal 6 de Julio, no date.

Halcones. Mexico City: Canal 6 de Julio, 2007.

La ley de Herodes. Mexico City: Luis Estrada, 1999.

Un poquito de tanta verdad. Seattle: Corrugate Films, 2007.

Romper el cerco. Mexico City: Canal 6 de Julio and Promedios, 2006.

Zapatistas. New York: Big Noise Films, 1998.

Zizek! New York: Zeitgeist Films, 2006.

INDEX

"Passim" (literally "scattered")
indicates intermittent discussion
of a topic over a cluster of pages.

AFI, 64, 159–60
Abascal, Carlos, 161
Acámbaro, 106–07
Acapulco, 244–47 passim
Acosta Lagunes, Agustín, 243
Acosta, Nahúm, 54
Acteal, Chiapas, 207
ad campaigns, 15–17 passim
advertorials, 156–57
African slaves, 30
Agencia Federal de Investigación.
　　See AFI
Aguas Blancas, Guerrero, 252–55
　　passim
Aguilar, Manuel, 172
Albino Ortiz, Jorge, 226–28
　　passim
Alemán, Miguel, 3
Altar, Sonora, 136–38
Alvarado Martínez, Fortino, 226
Amate Books, 169–70
Amnesty International, 66–68, 83
Antonio, Comandante. See Silva
　　Nogales, Jacobo

APPO, 147–87 passim, 226, 287–88
Araoz, Manuel, 36
Archduke Ferdinand Maximilian.
　　See Maximilian I
Arenas Agis, Gloria, 231–265
Arendt, Hannah, 267
army. See Mexican Army
Asamblea Popular de los Pueblos
　　de Oaxaca. See APPO
assassinations, 14, 38, 46, 166,
　　252, 261
　　of Carranza, 41, 277
　　of Digna Ochoa, 264
　　of Guerrero, 32
　　of Iturbide, 33
　　of Jaramillo, 5
　　of Madero, 40
　　of Obregón, 42, 277
　　of protester in Oaxaca, 160–
　　　61, 226
　　of Triqui coffee growers, 225
　　of Villa, 41–42
　　of women radio hosts, 223,
　　　228–30 passim
　　of Zapata, 41
Augustín I, 32–33
Aurora, Coronel. See Arenas Agis,
　　Gloria

authority, 57–60 passim
autonomous municipalities, 226–27, 289
Autonomous State University of Oaxaca, 174–79
autonomy, 202–04 passim, 210–11, 221–22, 283–85 passim, 319n41
Ávila Camacho, Manuel, 2
Aztecs, 22–26, 304n25, 306n47

Barbarous Mexico (Turner), 239
Barrera, Abel, 100–101
Barricade Radio, 179
barricades, 162–79 passim, 290
   middle-class solidarity and, 288
Barrios, Roberto, 4
Bartra, Roger, 307n61
Batalla, Guilermo Bonfil, 21
Bautista Merino, Teresa, 222–23, 228–30 passim
beekeepers, 293–94
beheadings, 51–52, 309n2
   in films, 59
Benhumea, Ángel, 74–78 passim
Benhumea, Ollín Alexis, 74–78
Benítez, Joaquín, 168
billionaires, 7, 96–99 passim, 275
Body in Pain, The (Scarry), 69–70
Bolivia, 196
Bolón Ajaw, Chiapas, 213, 215

border crossing, 109–11, 119, 132–38
   anti-immigrant Right and, 120
Bowden, Charles, 310n19
boycotts, 218
branding of slaves, 27–28
Bush, George W., 267–68

CGOCM, 43
CNC, 44, 48
CNTE, 145–47 passim
   Section 22, 140, 146
CORTV, 150, 155
Cabañas Barriento, Lucio, 46, 247–49 passim, 254, 262, 267
cacerolas, 154
caciques, 10, 27, 43, 73
   Chiapas, 191
   Oaxaca, 144
   Veracruz, 241
Café de la Selva, 217, 218
Calderón, Felipe, 7, 14–16 passim, 166
   drug violence and, 52–53
   National Development Plan, 83
   Zapatistas and, 216, 220
Calles, Plutarco Elías, 42
campaign ads, 15–17 passim
Campeche Honey, 293–94
Campesino Organization of the Southern Sierra, 251–52
Caña, Lisbeth, 180–81

CAPISE, 214–16 passim
capitalism, 31–32, 44, 85–103
   passim, 271–75
   indigenous peoples and, 201–
      03, 283
   Zapatistas on, 208–09
caracoles, 211–12
Carácuaro, Michoacán, 61–63
Carasco, Diodoro, 224
Cárdenas, Cuautémoc, 48–49, 250
Cárdenas, Lázaro, 1–3 passim,
   43–45 passim, 48, 95
Carranza, Venustiano, 40–41, 277
Carrillo Fuentes, Amado, 56
castas, 30
Castellanos Domínguez, Absalón,
   191, 218
Castillo López, Jesús, 3
Catholic Church, 26, 27, 43, 224
   Constitution of 1917 and, 41
   See also Cristero Rebellion
classism in media, 325n72
Cuauhtémoc statue, 306n47
Center for Political Analysis and
   Social and Economic Inves-
   tigation. See CAPISE
Centurrón, Emiliano, 293–94
Cerrito de Agua, Zacatecas, 123–
   24
Chapingo University, 75
Chiapas, 101–102, 189–230
chickens, 106–07, 246
Chihuahua, 82, 102
child labor, 97, 101

children
   on migration, 113–15
Chilpancingo, Guerrero, 246
Chomsky, Aviva, 105
científicos, 35
Cilia, Alberto, 183–84
Cilia, David, 102–103
Ciudad Juárez, 80–83
class. See social class
class war, 6–7, 18
Coca-Cola, 141, 176
Cochoapa El Grande, 8, 100
coffee industry, 101, 225
Colmenares, José Jiménez, 160–
   61, 226
colonialism, 13, 35, 86–89 passim
   indigenous peoples and, 201,
      203–04
   "internal colonialism," 278–
      79, 283, 285
   Spanish, 94
Colonizer and the Colonized, The
   (Memmi), 279
Colosio, Luis, 57
Columbus, Christopher, 26
combis, 78
community radio stations, 150–
   52 passim, 222
CONAPO, 99
CONASUPO, 241
Confederación General de
   Obreros y Campesinos de
   México. See CGOCM

Confederación Nacional Campesina. *See* CNC
Confederation of Mexican Workers (CTM), 43, 48
conquest, 5–6, 11–13 passim, 17, 22, 270–71, 280–82 passim
Consortium for Critical Development Studies, 126
Constitution of 1917, 41
cooperatives, 2, 293–94
Coordinadora Nacional de Trabajadores de la Educación. *See* CNTE
Córdova, Arnaldo, 276–78 passim
corn, 107
Coronel Aurora. *See* Arenas Agis, Gloria
corruption, 54
    border crossing and, 133
    prison staff and, 235–37
    unions and, 145
    See also political corruption
Cortés, Efren, 259
Cortés, Hernan, 22, 26, 304n25, 305n26
Costa Chica, Guerrero, 256–57
coyotes (smugglers), 109, 132–37
criminal justice system, 64–71
criollo class, 31, 32, 197–98
Cristero Rebellion, 42
Cruz, Alejandro, 145
Cruz, César, 291, 292
Cruz, Luis Alberto, 162
Cue, Gabino, 145

Day of the Dead, 174, 291
De Jesús, Carolina María, 85
De la Madrid, Miguel, 48, 121, 274, 275
death squads, 14, 162, 163, 166, 226
decapitation. *See* beheadings
Del Valle, Ignacio, 74
Delgado Wise, Raúl, 122, 126–27, 129
Democratic Revolutionary Party. *See* PRD
Democracy in Mexico (González Casanova), 278
demonstrations. *See* protests and demonstrations
deportation, 133, 134
Díaz, Porfirio, 8, 34–39 passim, 95, 198, 239, 274, 306n51
    statue of Cuauhtémoc and, 306n47
Dios Castro Lozano, Juan de, 229
Dirty War, 252, 256, 260
disappeared people, 46, 49, 161, 180, 183–84, 242–43, 261
    Guerrero, 251, 252, 254
doctors, 124, 175–76
drug cartels, 14, 52–55 passim
drug trafficking, 51–56 passim
    migrants and, 134, 137
drug violence, 51–53

EPR, 253–56, 259–63 passim

EZLN, 37–38, 49, 189–230 passim, 261, 284–89 passim. *See also* Other Campaign

earthquakes, 47

Easterly, William, 314n32

Echeverría, Bolívar, 5, 279–89 passim

economy, 31–32, 85–103, 274–75

drugs and, 54–55

migration and, 105–138

See also capitalism; drug trafficking; inequality; poverty; remittances

Ejercito Popular Revolucionario. *See* EPR

Ejercito Revolucionario del Pueblo Insurgente. *See* ERPI

ejidos, 44, 49. *See also* Union of Ejidos of the Selva

El Cargadero, Zacatecas, 129–30

El Charco, Guerrero, 256–60 passim

elections, 3, 13, 15–16, 39–40

1988, 48–49, 96, 250

1990, 250–51

2000, 144

2006, 148

fraud and, 3, 16, 49, 145, 166, 184, 250

Zapatistas and, 210

See also campaign ads; voting

Emperor Augustín I. *See* Augustín I

Emperor Maximilian I. *See* Maximilian I

empire and empires, 22–26 passim, 93, 267–70 passim, 276, 296

Eduardo Galeano on, 90

Spanish, 91

Triple Alliance, 31

U.S., 86

encomienda system, 91, 94–95

End of Poverty, The (Sachs), 87–90

ERPI, 234, 260, 263, 320n1

Estrada, Luis, 59

Excelsior, 181

executions, 25, 51–54 passim. *See also* beheadings

exploitation, 10

FPR, 147

Fanon, Frantz, 90, 322n9

farmers, 1–2, 39, 49, 96, 97

farming, 106–07, 118

Federal Agency of Investigation. *See* AFI

Federal Attorney General. *See* PGR

Federal Election Tribunal. *See* IFE

Federal Electricity Commission, 44

Federal Preventive Police. *See* PFP

Félix Gallardo, Miguel Ángel, 53

feminist movements, 46

Figueroa Alcocer, Rubén, 252, 253

Figueroa Figueroa, Rubén, 252
Flores Magon, Enrique, 37
Flores Magon, Ricardo Flores, 1, 37
Flores Rizo, Francisca, 252
flower vendors, 73
Forbes, 96, 97
foreign investment, 35, 95
Fox, Vicente, 13–15 passim, 98, 100, 144, 152
    Oaxaca and, 166, 171, 173, 174
    Zapatistas and, 207, 214–15
France, 33
fraud, 3, 16, 49, 145, 166, 184, 250
Frente Popular Revolucionario. *See* FPR
"free market," 272
Freire, Paulo, 283, 285, 290
Friedburg, Jill, 157, 158

General Confederation of Workers and Peasants of Mexico. *See* CGOCM
Gilly, Adolfo, 42
González Casanova, Pablo, 199, 278, 279
González Luna, Efraín, 44
good government councils, 205–11 passim, 219, 285
Guadalupe, Guanajuato, 106–119
Guelaguetza, 149–50
Guerrero, 244–64 passim
Guerrero, Vicente, 32
guerrillas, 32, 41, 46, 231–265 passim, 325n69. *See also* women guerrillas
Gullermoprieto, Alma, 57
Gutiérrez, Eugenia, 215–16
Gutiérrez Rebollo, Jesús, 54, 56
Guttman, Matthew, 289
Guzmán, Benigno, 251–52

Galeano, Eduardo, 85, 90
Gama, Felipe, 182–83
García, Carlos, 234
García Hernández, Alejandro, 168, 290
García, Mario, 129–31
García Medino, Macario, 227
García Zamorra, Rodolfo, 127–28, 323n29

Halil, Johnatan, 168
Hamilton, Lee, 68
Hardt, Michael, 322n20
Hart, John Mason, 275, 322n11–12
Harvey, David, 167, 267, 273–74, 321n3, 322n8–9, 322n19
health care, 100–101, 124–25
Hernández López, Roberto, 173
Hernández Navarro, Luis, 184

Hernández, Pánfilo, 168, 170
Herod's Law, 59
highway construction, 219, 293
historiography, 21, 87–94
Holmberg, Allan R., 196–97
honey producers, 293–94
hospitals, 47, 100, 182–83
Huerta, Victoriano, 40
Huicholes. *See* Wixaritari
human rights organizations, 64–67
Human Rights Watch, 64–66, 70
human sacrifice, 25
hunger, 85, 97, 103, 118
Hurricane Boris, 255

IFE, 15, 16
IMF, 48, 96
Ibarra, Rodrigo, 106–107
ideology, 18, 279–80, 304n18
illiteracy, 102
imperialism, 13, 88–93 passim,
    122, 267–276 passim,
    314n32, 322n20
U.S., 86, 274
income, 96
Independent United Triqui
    Movement for Struggle. *See*
    MULTI
"Indian" (label), 200
indigenous peoples, 6–11 passim,
    18, 21–35 passim, 283,
    318n24, 318n31

Bolivia, 196
colonialism and, 201, 203–04
economic conditions, 101–102
languages, 203, 205, 222, 291
law and, 319n41
names, 291–92
Oaxaca, 144, 223–24
population, 26–27, 203
resistance and rebellion, 28–
    29
Chiapas, 189–230
Oaxaca, 223–24
self-definition, 200–01
Spaniards and, 94–95, 305n25
Indymedia, 171
inequality, 7–9, 85–103
Institutional Revolutionary Party.
    See PRI
Instituto Federal Electoral. *See* IFE
Insurgent Peoples' Revolutionary
    Army. *See* ERPI
International Bank for Recon-
    struction and Development,
    86
International Monetary Fund. *See*
    IMF
investors, 7, 98
Iturbide, Agustín de, 32–33
Itzcóatl, 24

Jaramillo, Rubén, 1–5
Jornada, La, 156, 184

Juana Inés de la Cruz, Sor, 30–31
Juárez, Benito, 33–34

Kapuscinski, Ryszard, 139
Kelman, Herbert C., 68–69
kidnapping, 136, 221
Knight, Alan, 198, 199, 275
Krasner, Stephen, 314n32

La Garrucha, 208, 211, 219–21
La Ley, 288
labeling, 267–68
    by media, 325n72
    See also "free market";
        "Indian" (label)
land expropriation and redistrib-
        ution, 224
    governmental, 36, 39, 44, 49, 95
    Zapatistas and, 214–18 passim
land occupation, 4–5
land ownership, 36, 204
land reform, 40
language rights, 291–92
Las Casas, Bartolomeo de, 11–12
Las Guacamayas, Michoacán, 62–
        64 passim
Latin American "underdevelop-
        ment," 90
law, 56–60
Ledesma, Ernesto, 214–19 passim

Leguízano, Manuel, 4
León, Antonio de, 224
Leonel Solórzano, Carlos, 220
Lerdo de Tejada, Sebastián, 34
Ley de Herodes, La, 59
literacy, 102
Little Bit of So Much Truth, A, 157
López Bárcenas, Francisco, 200,
        203–04, 224–26 passim,
        283–84
López Bernal, Alberto, 173
López, Florentino, 186–87
López Mateos, Adolfo, 4
López Obrador, Andrés Manuel,
        15, 16, 152, 166
Los Angeles Times, 174

Madero, Francisco I., 37–40 pas-
        sim, 307n67
Madrazo, Roberto, 145, 148
Maldonado, Dominga, 105
malnutrition, 100
"manifest destiny," 33, 92, 121, 270
Mann, Charles, 196–97
Manuel, José, 130
maquiladoras, 81, 127
marches, 153–55 passim, 166–67,
        170, 174, 181–84 passim
    by police, 173
    Gloria Arenas Agis and, 241,
        246
    Guerrero, 250, 252

Marcos, Subcomandante, 74–75, 221, 260, 261, 293
  on capitalism and indigenous peoples, 283
  on "rule of law," 51
  on Salinas's offer of pardon, 194–95
  tours as "Delegate Zero," 208, 209
marijuana, 220
Marmolejo, Mauricio, 178
Martínez, Carmela, 60, 62
Martínez, Evencio, 228–29
Martínez, Pablo, 160
Martínez, Pedro, 160
Martínez Sánchez, Felícitas, 222–23, 228–30 passim
Martínez, Victor Raúl, 144
Marx, Karl, 1, 313n4
massacres, 45, 48, 278–79, 295
  Aguas Blancas, Guerrero, 252–54
  Chiapas, 221
  El Charco, Guerrero, 258–59
  Oaxaca, 224
  Mexico City, 45
Mateos, César, 167
Matías, Pedro, 226
Maximilian I, 33
Maxtla, 24
media, 15, 325n72
  fail to report mass kidnapping, 137
  Oaxaca, 150, 157

partisanship, 156–57
takeovers by APPO, 157–58
See also press; radio stations; television
Memmi, Albert, 279, 280
Méndez, Sara, 60–62
Mendoza Nube, German, 160
mestizaje, 198, 199, 281–89 passim
Metlatónoc, 7–8, 100
Mexican-American War, 33, 121, 274
Mexican Army, 192
  Chiapas, 206, 216–20 passim
  Guerrero, 254, 256
  drug trafficking and, 54–64 passim
Mexican Liberal Party. See PLM
Mexican Revolution, 1, 29, 37–42 passim, 307n61
Mexico City
  APPO march, 2006, 166–67
  earthquake (September 19, 1985), 47
  Zapatista visit, 207
migration, 105–138 passim
  statistics, 119
Milenio, 157, 162, 181
military bases, 216–17, 255, 256
millionaires, 8, 95, 99, 131, 275
milpas, 107
Mixteca, 223
Mixtla de Altamirano, Veracruz, 102
Moctezuma II, 26, 305n25

Mondragón, Pedro, 63
Montalvo, Pedro, 102
Montemayor, Carlos, 325n69
Morales, Ignacio, 242
Morales, José, 213
Morelos Agrarian Workers Party.
    See PAOM
Morelos, José María, 32
Morín, Manuel Gómez, 44
MULT (Movement for Triqui Uni-
    fication and Struggle), 225–26
MULTI (Independent United
    Triqui Movement for Strug-
    gle), 226
murals, 211
murder, 57, 136, 160, 168
    of women, 80–83, 223
    See also assassinations; execu-
        tions; state killings

Nadler, Richard, 125
NAFTA, 49, 96, 120–23 passim,
    127, 272–75 passim
Nahuatl, 102
naming, 267–68
    Doni Zänä, 291–92
    See also "Indian" (label)
Ñañú, 291–92
National Action Party. *See* PAN
National Autonomous University
    of Mexico. *See* UNAM

National Coordination of Educa-
    tion Workers. *See* CNTE
National Democratic Front, 48
National Human Rights Com-
    mission, 61, 70
National Journalism Award, 229
National Peasant Confederation.
    See CNC
National Population Council. *See*
    CONAPO
National Revolutionary Party. *See*
    PNR
National Union of Education
    Workers. *See* SNTE
nationalism, 37–38
    indigenous peoples and, 201
native peoples. *See* indigenous
    peoples
Negri, Antonio, 322n20
neoliberalism, 127
New Imperialism, The (Harvey),
    273
New Laws (Spain), 27
New Spain, 22, 29–32 passim
newspapers, 145, 156–57
Nomads of the Longbow (Holm-
    berg), 196
Noriega, Pilar, 264
North American Free Trade
    Movement. *See* NAFTA
Noticias, 145, 157, 160
Ñu Savi, 223
Núñez Magaña, Mario, 52

Oaxaca, 28–29
  uprising of 2006, 139–87
Oaxaca Peoples' Popular Assembly. *See* APPO
Obregón, Álvaro, 41, 277
obsidian, 23
Ochoa, Digna, 264, 320n14
oil field nationalization, 44
Olvera Ruiz, Francisco, 292
Opportunities (health assistance program), 101
oppression
  definition of, 10
  Gloria Arenas on, 244
  Paulo Freire on, 290
  See also massacres; police, torture
Organization for the Defense of Indigenous and Peasant Peoples' Rights (OPDDIC), 215
organized crime, 53. *See also* drug cartels
Orizaba,Veracruz, 238–41 passim
Osorno, Diego, 157, 173, 181
Other Campaign, 78, 79, 171, 208–10, 218, 286–87
Oventik, Chiapas, 205, 210

PAOM, 3
PDLP, 46, 247, 260. *See also* PROCUP-PDLP
PFP, 173, 174, 310n28

PGR, 179
PLM, 36–37
PRD, 49, 108, 128, 251
  San Andrés Accords and, 207
PRI, 3, 4, 13, 37–38, 42–49 passim, 306n46
  economic growth and, 95
  election of 1988 and, 48, 49, 96, 250
  fraud and, 250
  in films, 59–60
  legacy of, 108, 128
  Oaxaca, 142, 144–48 passim, 152, 156
  PAN and, 44–45
  presidency and, 278
  San Andrés Accords and, 207
  Triquis and, 225
  Veracruz, 243
  Zapatistas and, 217–21 passim
Pacheco, Arnulfo, 79
Padilla, Felícitas, 234
PAN, 13, 37–38, 44–45, 108, 128
  in films, 59
  San Andrés Accords and, 207
paramilitary groups, 207, 214–18 passim, 221
pardon (proposed), 194–95
París, María Dolores, 229–30
PARM, 48
Partido Acción Nacional. *See* PAN
Partido Agrario Obrero Morelense. *See* PAOM

Partido Auténtico de la Revolución. *See* PARM
Partido de la Revolución Democrática. *See* PRD
Partido de los Pobres. *See* PDLP
Partido Liberal Mexicano. *See* PLM
Partido Revolucionario Institucional. *See* PRI
Partido Revolucionario Obrero Clandestino Unión del Pueblo. *See* PROCUP-PDLP
Party of the Authentic Mexican Revolution. *See* PARM
Party of the Democratic Revolution. *See* PRD
Party of the Poor. *See* PDLP
Pasos, Heriberto, 225, 228
passwords, 247–48
peaches, 131
People's Front in Defense of Land, 73–74, 79
Pereda Fernández, Benito, 178
Pérez Hernández, Isaíah, 158–59
Pérez, Juan, 167
Peters, Edward, 68
photographs , 102–103, 186
    of Brad Will shooting and aftermath, 172, 181
    of drug violence, 51–53 passim
physicians. *See* doctors
Plan of San Luis Potosí, 38, 40

plantónes, 139–40, 145, 146, 167, 174
Policía Federal Preventiva. *See* PFP
police, 14
    attack flower vendors, 73–80 passim
    attack marchers in Veracruz, 243
    attack media, 161–62
    attack strikers and protesters in Oaxaca, 140–43, 150, 158–62 passim, 168–77 passim, 182, 184
    aid soldiers in Chiapas, 219–20
    beat and disappear teacher, 161
    break arms of elderly protesters, 250
    deport kidnappers and kidnapped, 136
    disappear human rights activist, 183
    drug traffickers and, 51–57 passim
    human rights organizations on, 65–67 passim
    kill copra workers, 45–46
    are killed and beheaded, 51–52
    shoot Indymedia reporter, 171
    shoot protesters in Guerrero, 252–53

shoot teachers and parents, 46
take bribes at the U.S. border,
    133–35 passim
use torture and rape women,
    71
See also Policía Federal Pre-
    ventiva; *rurales*
political ads, 15–17 passim
political corruption
    drug trafficking and, 53–71
        passim
political prisoners, 241, 252
polleros (smugglers), 109, 132–37
Popular Revolutionary Army. *See*
    EPR
Popular Revolutionary Front. *See*
    FPR
pots and pans as noisemakers,
    154, 156
poverty, 9, 18, 85–103, 240
    Ciudad Juárez, 81
    indigenous peoples and, 203,
        318n24
    revolt and, 186–87
presidency, 277–78
press, 145, 165
    drug-related violence and, 52
    partisanship, 156–57
press conferences, 148–49
prisoners, 231–265 passim. *See
    also* political prisoners
prisons, 234–38
privatization, 96, 274
Proceso, 156

PROCUP-PDLP, 247, 260
Procuraduría General de la
    República. See PGR
protests and demonstrations, 14,
    16, 37, 49, 241
    Guerrero, 250, 252
    Oaxaca City, 139–87 passim
    San Salvador Atenco, 73–74,
        78–79
    See also marches

racism, 30, 35, 123, 197–99 passim
radio stations, 150–58 passim,
    227, 288
    Radio Cacerola, 155, 160, 161
    Radio Copala, 222, 226–30
        passim
    Radio Plantón, 150
    Radio Universidad, 150–54
        passim, 158, 160, 172,
        175–79 passim
Rahnema, Majid, 85
railroads, 35
rape, 14, 46, 80, 212, 254, 256
Raramuri, 102
rebellion and rebellions. *See*
    revolt and revolts
Reforma, 156
Regeneración, 37
remittances, 120, 127
repression. *See* oppression

revolt and revolts, 36, 139, 269, 280, 288–96 passim
  Chiapas, 189–230 passim
  Gloria Arenas on, 264–265
  indigenous peoples, 28–29
  Oaxaca, 139–187 passim
rich people. *See* billionaires; millionaires
Riding, Alan, 22
Rivas, Marisela, 291, 292
Rivera Cortés, Antonio, 133
Robledo, Fernando, 128–29
Robles Catalán, José Rubén, 253
Rocha, Ricardo, 253
Rodríguez Mendoza, Alejandra, 73
Rojas Saldaña, Mercedes, 155
Román Ruiz, Feliciano, 220
Ross, John, 319n41
Rueda, Enrique, 146–47, 170–71
Ruiz Ortiz, Ulises, 14, 140–52 passim, 167–68, 173–75, 184–85
  advertorials and, 157
  Flavio Sosa on, 161
  releases assassin, 226
  Triquis and, 224
rurales, 36

SNTE, 145
Sabines, Juan, 220
Sachs, Jeffrey, 87–90

Said, Edward, 13, 21, 313n10
Salgado Vicario, Isabel. *See* Arenas Agis, Gloria
Salinas de Gortari, Carlos, 48–49, 96
  EZLN and, 190–94 passim
  privatization and, 7, 96, 98, 121, 274
Salinas Jardón, Jorge, 79
Salomón, José Antonio, 291, 292
San Andrés Accords, 206, 319n41
San Cristóbal de las Casas, Chiapas, 191, 193
San Juan Copala, Oaxaca, 222, 226–28
San Luis Potosí, 263–64
San Pablo Cervantes, Lorenzo, 162
San Piedro El Viejo, 99–100
San Salvador Atenco, 14, 72–80 passim
Sánchez García, Fidel, 173
Sandoval, Juan Manuel, 122, 275
Santa Anna, Antonio López de, 33
Santiago Cruz, Andres, 160
Santiago El Pinar, Chiapas, 101
Santiago Zarate, Avel, 172
Saucepan Radio, 155
Scarry, Elaine, 69–70
schools, 113–16
Semo, Enrique, 31, 91, 197
senators, 167–68

sexual harassment of women, 245–47 passim
Silva Nogales, Jacobo, 232–34 passim, 247–48, 263–64
silver mining, 29–30
Sindicato Nacional de Trabajadores de la Enseñanza. *See* SNTE
Sirionó, 196
ski masks, 205
skin color, 30
slaves and slavery, 27–28, 30, 90–93 passim
Slim Helu, Carlos, 7, 98, 274
Smith, Adam, 313n8
Soberanes, Fernando, 184
social class, 6–11 passim, 286–87
    elections and, 16–17
    law and, 57
    See also *castas*
solidarity, 186–87, 285–89 passim
Soriano Velasco, Juan Carlos, 172
Sosa, Flavio, 161, 174
Spain, 22–33 passim, 91–95 passim, 200, 269, 305n25
Special Forces, 54, 141, 174
    Chiapas, 216
squatters, 46
state power, 25
state killings, 25, 46, 251, 261
statues, 145, 306n47
Stephen, Lynn, 158
strikes, 2, 14, 37, 42, 43
    Constitution of 1917 and, 41

Oaxaca, 139–43 passim, 168–71 passim
oil workers, 44
students
    battle police in Oaxaca, 174–77
    disappeared, 183–84
    offer opinions on migration, 113–15
Subcomandante Marcos. *See* Marcos, Subcomandante
sugar mills, 1–2
Supreme Court, 253

Taber, Robert, 257
Tarahumara, 28
Tarascans, 24, 25
Taylor, Zachary, 121
teachers, 14
    unions, 140–47 passim, 166–71 passim
tear gas, 140–43 passim, 173, 175, 182
television, 15, 150, 161, 162, 165
    on Massacre of Aguas Blancas, 253
TV station takeover by women, 155–56
Telmex, 98
tent cities. See *plantónes*
Teotihuacan, 23
Tepanecs, 23–24
TINAM, 242, 243

Tlatelolco Plaza massacre, 1968, 45
Tlaxcalans, 24, 25
Todorov, Tzvetan, 284–85
Tohono O'odham Nation, 137
Toledano, Lombardo, 43
Toltecs, 23
torture, 46, 52, 63–71 passim, 177–80 passim, 311n40, 312n48
    Guerrero, 256, 259
    of Gloria Arenas and Jacobo Silva, 233
tourists and tourism, 149–50, 169
Triple Alliance, 22, 24, 26
Triquis, 222–28 passim
Trujillo Martínez, René, 177–78
tumultos, 30
Turner, John Kenneth, 239

UNAM, 47
Union of Ejidos of the Selva, 217, 218
Union of the People, 247
unions, 1, 41–46 passim
    teachers, 140–47 passim, 166–71 passim
United States, 42, 48, 270, 274, '276
    attack on Veracruz, 41, 322n11
    drug trafficking and, 53

media coverage of Mexico, 325n72
    Mexican immigration, 105–38
    military imperialism of, 86
    See also maquiladoras; Mexican-American war
Universal, El, 156, 172
Universidad Nacional Autónoma de México (UNAM), 47
uprisings. *See* revolt and revolts
utopia, 324n67

Valadez López, Manuel, 124, 125
vanguard, 260, 264
Vásquez, Faustino, 222–23, 228–30 passim
Vásquez, Yanira, 228
Vázquez, Gerardo, 169
Vázquez Rojas, Genaro, 254
24 de Diciembre, Chiapas, 217
Veracruz
    U.S. attack on (1914), 41, 322n11
Villa, Francisco, 40, 43, 44
Villareal, José Manuel, 156
Villoro, Luis, 280
voting
    corrupt practices, 3, 16
    Zapatistas and, 210

Wallerstein, Immanuel, 272
Wangeman, Henry, 169–70
War of 1846–48, 33, 121, 274
War of the Flea (Taber), 257
Washington Office on Latin
   America, 82
wheat, 107
Will, Brad, 171–72, 180–81
Wixaritari, 293
Womack, John, Jr., 307n67
women, 30–31, 171
   as rearguard workers, 248
   convene in Chiapas, 211–13
   march and take over broadcast
      media in Oaxaca, 154–56
   murdered in Ciudad Juárez,
      80–83
   murdered in Oaxaca, 223,
      228–30 passim
   See also feminist movements;
      sexual harassment of
      women
women guerrillas, 231–265
women radio hosts, 222–23
World Bank, 86
Wright, Erik Olin, 9

Yaquis, 28, 29, 293

Zacatecas, 123–31 passim
Zamora, Erika, 259
Zapata, Emiliano, 1, 36–42 pas-
   sim, 276–77
Zapatista Army of National Lib-
   eration. *See* EZLN
Zapotecs, 22
Zarate Aquino, Manuel, 152
Zavala Tapia, Ricardo, 259
Zedillo, Ernesto, 217, 253
Zetas, Los, 54, 62
Žižek, Slavoj, 18, 287, 304n18,
   324n67, 325n69
Zongolica Mountains, 241–43
   passim

ABOUT THE AUTHORS

JOHN GIBLER has been covering national and regional politics from Mexico since January 1, 2006. He has reported on indigenous social movements, politics in Oaxaca, and the Mexican presidential elections, among other issues. His writing and photographs have appeared in many publications, including *New Politics*, *Yes! Magazine*, *Z Magazine*, *In These Times*, *Left Turn*, and elsewhere. He reports regularly for *Flashpoints* on Pacifica Radio's KPFA and has also reported for *Democracy Now!*, KPFK, and WBAI. Previously, Gibler worked for various human rights and social justice organizations in Mexico, Peru, and California. He has reported on environmental justice issues and water privatization for *Terrain Magazine*; *ColorLines*; *Race, Poverty, and the Environment*; and elsewhere.

GLORIA MUÑOZ RAMÍREZ was born in Mexico City. From 1994 to 1996, she worked for the Mexican newspaper *Punto*, for the German news agency DPA, for the U.S. newspaper *La Opinión*, and for the Mexican daily *La Jornada*. In 1997, she left her work, her family, and her friends to live in the Zapatista communities in Chiapas, Mexico, where she remained for seven years. Today she writes for *La Jornada* and is a member of the editorial board of its supplement on indigenous issues, *Ojarasca*. Gloria is author of *The Fire & The Word, A History of the Zapatista Movement*.